LEGENDARY LOCALS

OF

CULLMAN COUNTY

ALABAMA

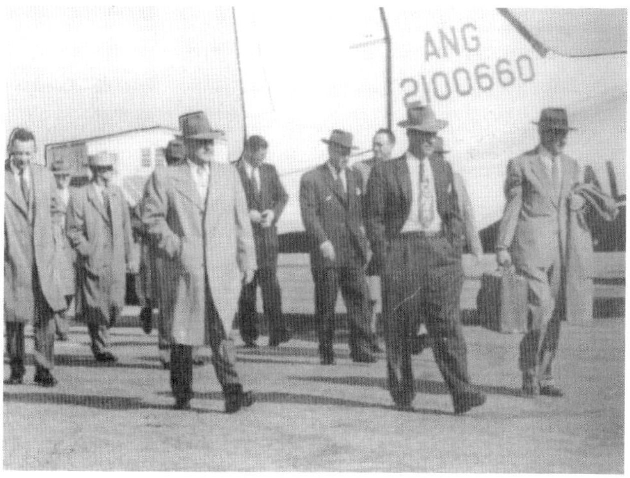

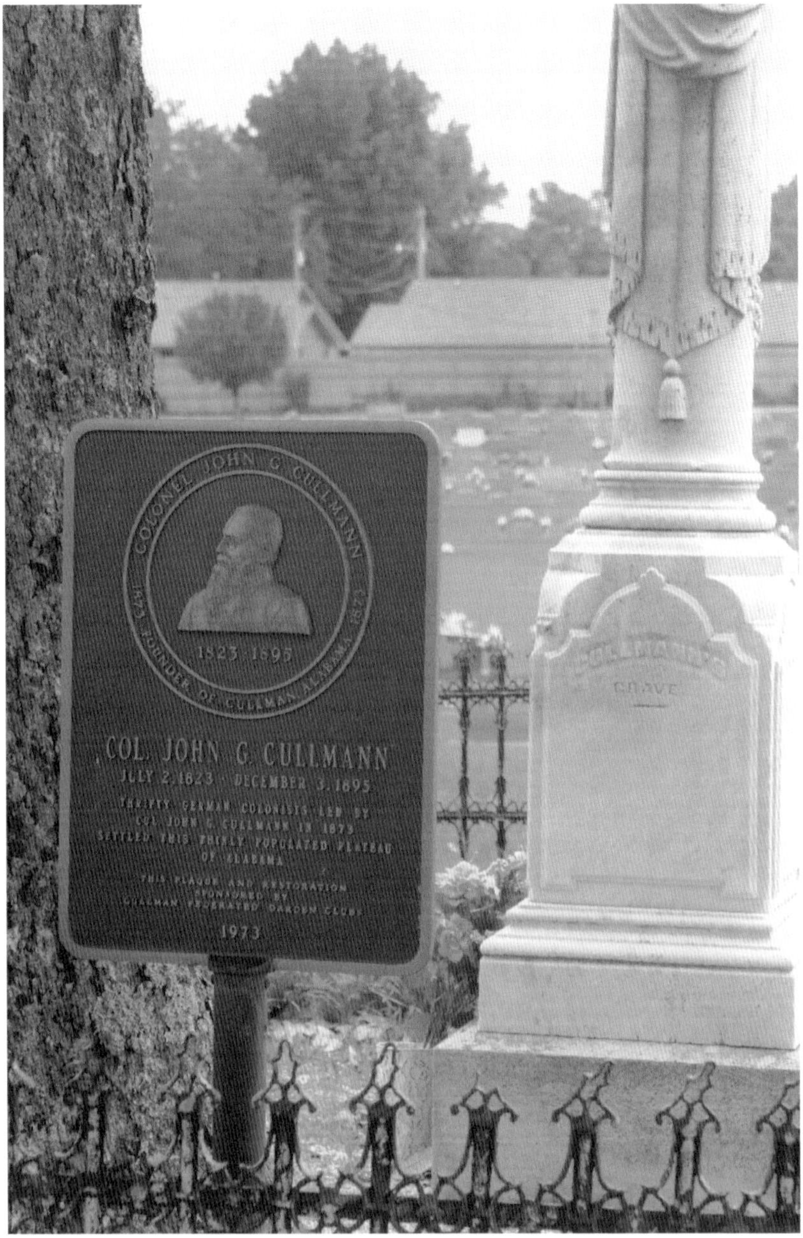

The Founder

Col. Johann G. Cullmann is buried in the middle of Cullman City Cemetery beside his son Otto. Otto was the only family member who joined the German native in the new town he had founded. Otto died at age 29 after one of his trips to Germany to bring back new settlers. (Courtesy Greg Richter.)

Page 1: The Flying Fifty

A volunteer group of businessmen, the Flying Fifty searched for new industry in the 1950s. For additional information, see page 15. (Courtesy Cullman County Chamber Commerce.)

LEGENDARY LOCALS

OF

CULLMAN COUNTY

ALABAMA

KAY CAGLE AND GREG RICHTER

LEGENDARY LOCALS

ISBN 978-1-4671-0162-2

Legendary Locals is an imprint of Arcadia Publishing
Charleston, South Carolina

Printed in the United States of America

Library of Congress Control Number: 2014932210

For all general information, please contact Arcadia Publishing:
Telephone 843-853-2070
Fax 843-853-0044
E-mail sales@arcadiapublishing.com
For customer service and orders:
Toll-Free 1-888-313-2665

Visit us on the Internet at www.arcadiapublishing.com

Dedication

To the people of Cullman County who generously and tirelessly contributed to the publication of this book. Their time, information and photographs made this effort possible.

On the Front Cover: Clockwise from top left:
Nelle Fuller St. John (Courtesy St. John family; see page 54), Pastor Bob Kurtz (Courtesy Baker Photography; see page 97), P.H. Kessler (Courtesy Karen Hassell; see page 68), Earlene Johnson (Courtesy Earlene Johnson; see page 93), Charles Kleibacker (Courtesy Columbus Museum of Art; see page 114), Mother Angelica (Courtesy EWTN; see page 51), Catherine Clark Voss (Courtesy Fr. Marcus Voss; see page 96).

On the Back Cover: From left to right:
Col. Johann Cullmann with ladies at coffee (Courtesy Cullman Museum), Bert McGriff (Courtesy Kay Cagle; see page 34).

CONTENTS

ACKNOWLEDGMENTS

The authors gratefully acknowledge the many individuals, families, and local entities who have willingly donated photographs and whose stories have contributed to the success of this publication. Many have shared photographs and stories. We thank Finis E. St. John IV, Steve Singleton, Julian McPhillips Jr., Candace Grissom, Larry Baker Photography, Fr. Marcus Voss, Steve Griffith, Wade and Wes Warren, Dr. John Morris, Dan Keel, Barry Willoughby, Virgil Fowler Jr., Betty Leeth Haynes, Brian Lacey, Grady Smith, Gail Neal, Linda Johnson, Asa Lee Brandon, Kay Powell, Barbara Yost, Billy Faulk, Frances Cooper, Bob Palys, and Michael Sullins.

We gratefully and deeply appreciate Drew Green, Julie Burks, and Elaine Fuller at the Cullman County Museum, the Columbus Museum of Art, Shrine of the Most Blessed Sacrament, Cullman County Historical Society, Holly Pond Historical Society, Cullman Area Chamber of Commerce and the *Cullman Times*.

Greg wishes to thank his wife, Laura Axelrod, and his parents, Louie Richter and Jean Moore, for their understanding of the time needed in this undertaking.

INTRODUCTION

The area now known as Cullman County was first inhabited by native peoples. Cherokee and Choctaw were living in the area when white settlers first showed up. Both groups were forced to move west in the 1830s under the Indian Removal Act. Some Native people reportedly hid and remained behind while most were forced to take the Trail of Tears. Many Cullman County residents claim Indian ancestry.

Blount, Walker, Winston, and Morgan Counties were all a part of what now is Cullman County. During the Civil War it was a haven for some Confederate deserters, since some residents were Union sympathizers. Walker County seceded from the state of Alabama during the war, which included what is now the northwestern portion of Cullman County.

A minor battle occurred in the county when Union colonel Abel Streight faced Confederate general Nathan Bedford Forrest in the Battle of Day's Gap and other skirmishes. After the war, a group of freed slaves gathered in what is now the southern part of the county, naming their settlement Colony. Meanwhile, a civil war had been raging across the Atlantic in the Germanic states.

Col. Johann G. Cullmann, born in Frankweiler, Bavaria, on July 2, 1823, was a merchant who fought on the side of democracy during the revolution. His side was defeated when the Prussian army joined the Bavarian monarchy, and the financially broken Cullmann fled the country, leaving his wife at home with their children to care for her ailing mother.

Cullmann first moved to London and stayed there while he awaited the end of the American Civil War. Once in America, he settled in Philadelphia, then in Cincinnati, where he worked as a clerk in a bookstore. Cincinnati had a large German population, but Cullmann was looking to establish a settlement for immigrants and began looking south.

He met Alabama governor Robert Miller Patton and was pointed to the Florence area. But many residents there were still wary of foreigners after recently losing the war, so Cullmann continued his search.

Inspecting the area that would come to be named for him, Cullmann purchased an option as land agent for the South and North Alabama Railroad. Cullmann had found the home for his dream colony, so he returned north to find settlers. He moved the first five families from Cincinnati in April 1873. Each was given a plot of land where they built log homes and tended their gardens. Included were the Schueing, Betz, Strahl, Reed, and Alberding families along with one bachelor, Rene von Lobstein. Fred Betz became Cullman's first mayor.

The City of Cullman was incorporated in 1874, and by 1877 Cullman County had been formed. It was decided to drop the second "n" in the city's and county's names. Cullmann continued traveling the north and Europe to bring in more residents.

But some of the settlers who had arrived long before the Germans were not always happy with those they considered European interlopers.

One of those settlers gave Cullmann a gash that forced him to show only the left side of his face in photographs. Not all accounts of the confrontation agree. The often-told story appeared in a book on the city's centennial in 1973.

According to that account, Cullmann was attempting to incorporate the town in 1874. Several squatters had been given allotments of land along with the German settlers, but they wanted more. An argument lasted several days, and as Cullmann left Prinz's Store one night he was struck with a knife thrown by one of the squatters. The man escaped but was arrested years later on another charge. Cullmann refused to press charges.

But descendants of the man who reportedly left that scar say that is not the true version.

"The Colonel wanted to make some extra money by making a railroad spur from Cullman to Jasper," Delton Blalock, publisher of the *Cullman Tribune*, told *Cullman Oktoberfest Magazine*. When Cullmann told David Speegle that the project would require using his land an argument ensued, and Speegle cut Cullmann in the face.

Blalock backs up family member accounts that Speegle owned a proper title to the land, granted by the State of Alabama, and was not a squatter. He and his family had been residents of the state since its founding in 1819.

"Ironically, they became good friends later," Blalock said.

When Cullmann, trained as a civil engineer, laid out the town, he made sure the streets were wide enough for four wagons to pass, 100 feet wide to be exact. The city blocks were one acre each and divided into fourths.

Several fires during the city's early years brought about two changes: building codes that required businesses not to be built of wood and a lowering of the railroad tracks in the 1910s, which allowed fire trucks to cross without waiting for a train.

Those who moved into the newly formed Cullman County did not always settle in the City of Cullman. Some moved to Garden City, some to Vinemont, where grapes were grown for wine. Hanceville was a larger city than Cullman when the county was first formed, but it failed to be named the county seat because the county line at the time split the town, with part of it sitting in Blount County.

With its German roots, Cullman managed to become one of only two counties in Alabama—the other being Baldwin—that were allowed to sell draft beer. This made Cullman a popular weekend destination for people who wanted beer on tap. A number of bars and hotels sprang up near the depot, and each became popular with people from certain areas. For instance, one hotel would be frequented by people from Birmingham while another would be filled with visitors from Decatur.

These visitors would spend the whole weekend in Cullman, so various forms of entertainment sprang up to keep them occupied when they did not have a glass in their hand. Bowling, music, and more was available, and after a while some of the raucous activity got to be too much for some residents. In the early 1940s, Cullman outlawed alcohol sales. Beginning in the 1980s, multiple attempts were made to bring back alcohol sales, but vote after vote failed until 2010. Cullman Oktoberfest, which had been celebrating the area's German heritage since the early 1980s, finally was able to offer beer.

In the 1940s, Cullman became famous for its strawberries and would ship them north by train. The wild parties of the now-closed bars were replaced by an annual Strawberry Festival that began in the early 1940s and continued into the 1950s. The Strawberry Festival has been revived in recent years.

No stranger to storms, Cullman has seen tornadoes change its landscape multiple times.

A tornado in the 1930s caught residents by surprise and left many dead. Tornadoes during the 1972 outbreak did severe damage, and the April 27, 2011, storms wiped out a large portion of Cullman's downtown historic district. Tornadoes also did major damage in Hanceville the same day.

Sitting just off Interstate 65, Cullman today pushes forward with industrial growth and various forms of entertainment that draw visitors from throughout the United States.

CHAPTER ONE

Community Defined by Growth

Cullman County's success was built by those who saw a need and were willing to fill it. Col. Johann G. Cullmann founded the colony for German immigrants in 1873, and started the work of recruiting settlers. Cullman's first mayor, Fred Betz, was among the first five families recruited by Cullmann. Betz, like other Cullman residents, wore many hats, acting as tax collector, tax assessor, and coroner. Another of the original settlers, Christopher Scheuing, donated land for the county's first courthouse and served as undertaker and coroner in addition to running a livery stable. Rene von Lobstein, a French bachelor who also came with the first five families, was the area's first tanner.

It was not always easy. Some people considered leaving, and a few actually did. Von Lobstein is said to have walked back to Cincinnati, only to return. Businesses sprang up to supply needs. Stiefelmeyer's was a popular store that sold a variety of goods, and on the opposite side of the same block, Dreher's built furniture. Hauk's Ice House kept iceboxes cool and provided rental space for storing meat. Saloons provided a respite after a weary day, and Klein's provided dairy products as well as being the popular hangout for those looking for a malt or sundae.

Newspapers kept people up date, but so did plain old gossip. By the turn of the 20th century the corner of First Avenue and Second Street Southeast, where Stiefelmeyer's store sat, was the busiest place in town on Saturdays. That is when folks from the county came into town to buy supplies. They also could get printed death notices from just down the block.

Over time, institutions such as Kiwanis, Elks, Lions, Boy Scouts, and Girl Scouts were formed. As technology progressed, gas and electric lines were installed. The Cullman-Jefferson Counties Gas District and the Cullman Electric Cooperative helped get utilities to people.

As of 2011, more than 80,000 people made their homes in Cullman County. Those first five families who came in 1873, which had grown to 123 a year later, formed the backbone of a community continuing to grow.

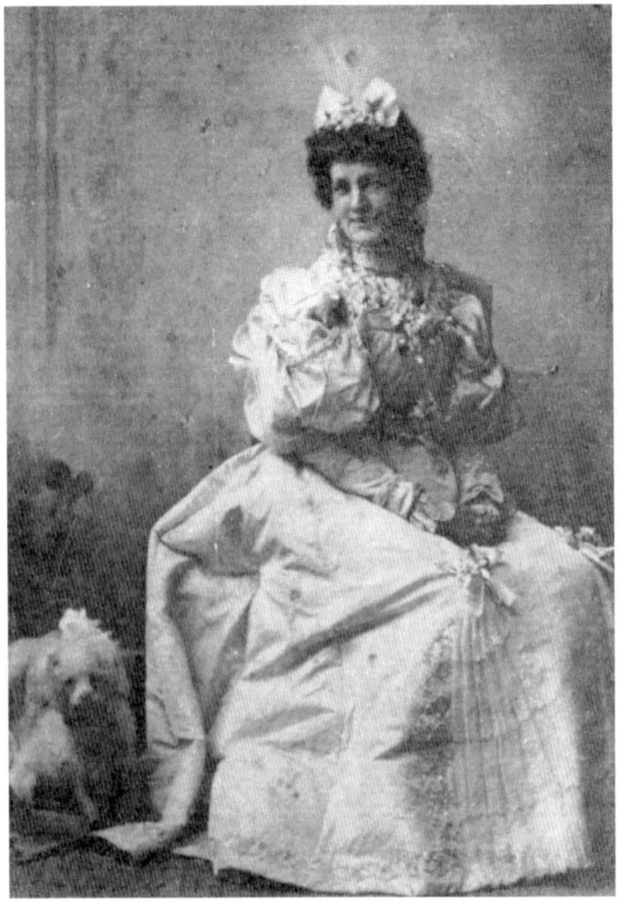

Amalia Dinckelberg

Santa Claus came to town, and Amalia Dinckelberg kept him 365 days a year. Best known for her Santa Claus Store with Jolly Old Saint Nick sitting on the front porch year-round, her business actually sold a variety of items from ribbons, overalls and food. She also operated a delicatessen and biergarten. The store sat on the northwest corner of the block occupied by St. John's Evangelical Church, of which Dinckelberg was a member. She planted a magnolia tree in the biergarten, which stood until the early 2000s. Born in northern Germany in 1849, Dinckelberg was taught early by her mother the importance of an education. So she learned reading, writing, and "numbers," but also was taught to sew, cook, and make hats and wigs. She also learned to make beer and wine. Her mother stressed the importance of marrying well, and when she brought G.O. Dinckelberg home to meet her parents, they were impressed; he knew about business. After the couple moved to America, they also came to know Col. Johann Cullmann, who was seeking residents for his fledgling colony in Alabama. The Dinckelbergs took a chance and moved south from Cincinnati. While Amalia operated the Santa Claus store, her husband helped found Cullman Building & Loan, becoming its first president. He also was member of the volunteer fire department and was killed battling a large fire that burned down the first courthouse in the mid 1890s. Dinckelberg was always accompanied by a small white dog and was known for providing bargains in her store. Women came from as far away as Birmingham and Decatur to buy her dresses, and she rented out costumes for balls. The child of any customer who bought a pound of coffee would get a peppermint stick. If someone bought a pair of overalls, he would get a free plug of tobacco. Prohibition in Cullman in 1918 meant the end of her biergarten, and Dinckelberg's Christmas Store is now a distant memory. Amalia Dinckelberg died at the age of 81. (Courtesy Cullman County Museum.)

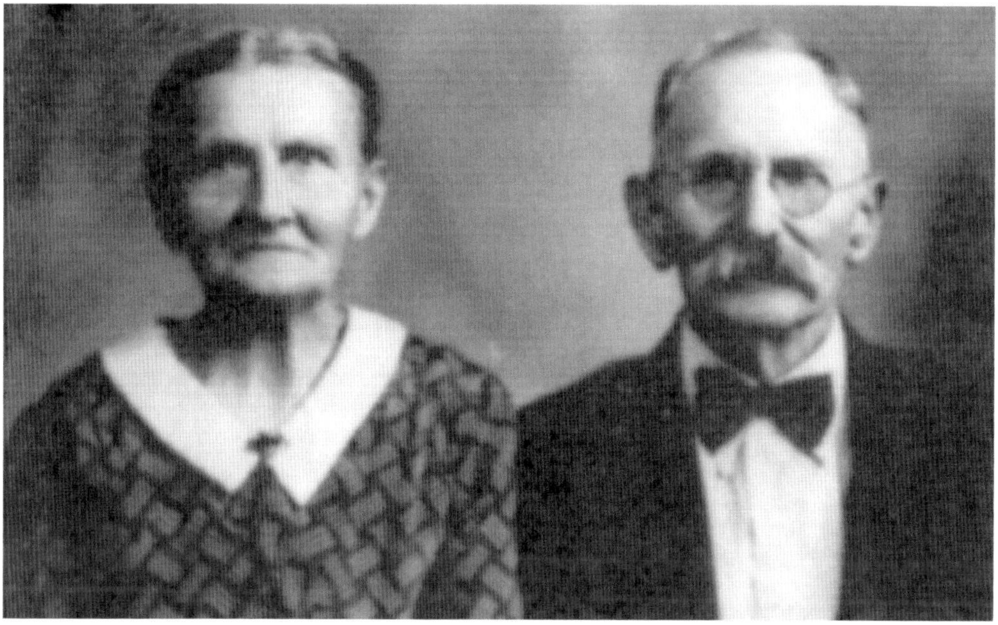

Nick and Kate Ruehl
Col. Johann Cullmann recruited Nick Ruehl from Cincinnati. Nick built a modest house, then sent for his wife, Kate, and their infant son. There was little in the German community, so when Kate, raised in the city, arrived, she saw only wilderness. They were a day early. No one was there to pick them up. Kate said if there had been a train going north at the time, and if she had the money, Cullman and Nick Ruehl would have been minus a citizen, wife, and son. Kate adapted to the new lifestyle and was a midwife. Nick was Cullman's first coffin-maker and made barrels, was a blacksmith, and a conservation farmer. He built many of Cullman's earliest homes and was an organizer of St. John's Evangelical Protestant Church. (Above image courtesy Michael Sullins; below image courtesy Peinhardt Living History Farm.)

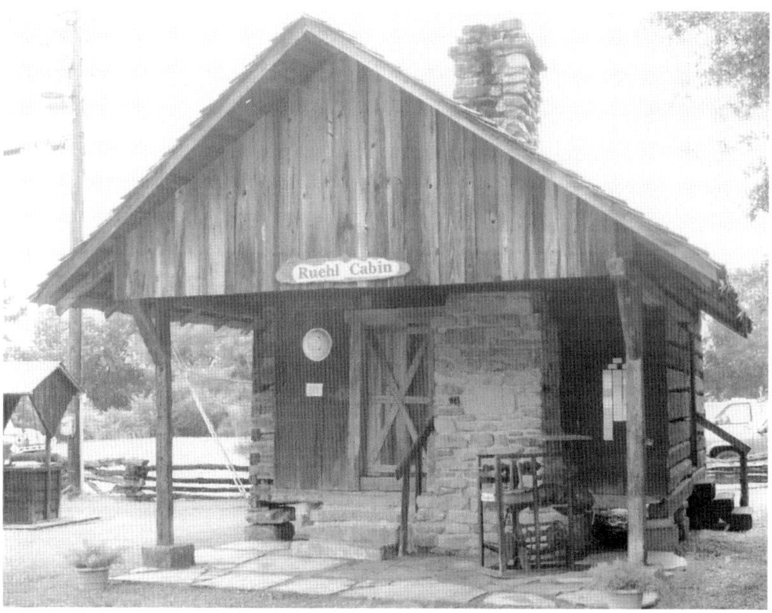

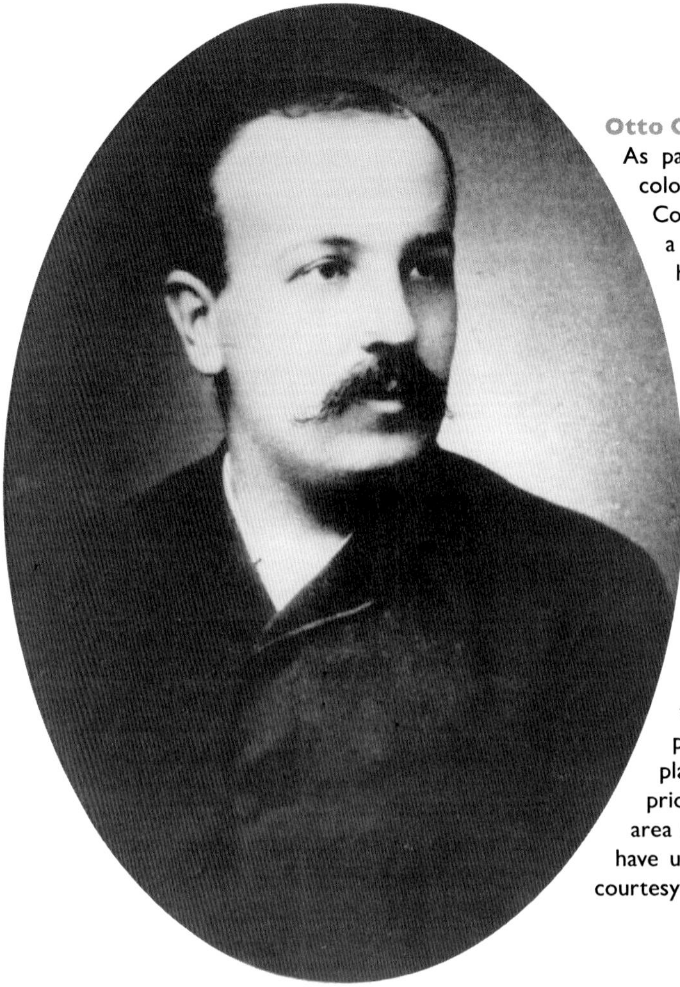

Otto Cullmann

As part of his effort to bring new colonists to his fledgling community, Col. Johann G. Cullmann founded a German newspaper, edited by his son, Otto. *Der Nord Alabama Colonist* told Germans in cities throughout Europe about his new settlement. According to some estimates, Cullmann's efforts brought up to 100,000 European settlers to the South. Previously, they had sought lands in the West, as the late 1800s were a time of westward expansion in America. But Cullmann knew many of them feared attacks by Indians, and he played up the fact that Alabama was free of such worries. His paper also stressed that no slave plantations had existed in the area prior to the Civil War since the area had previously been thought to have unproductive land. (Both images courtesy Cullman County Museum.)

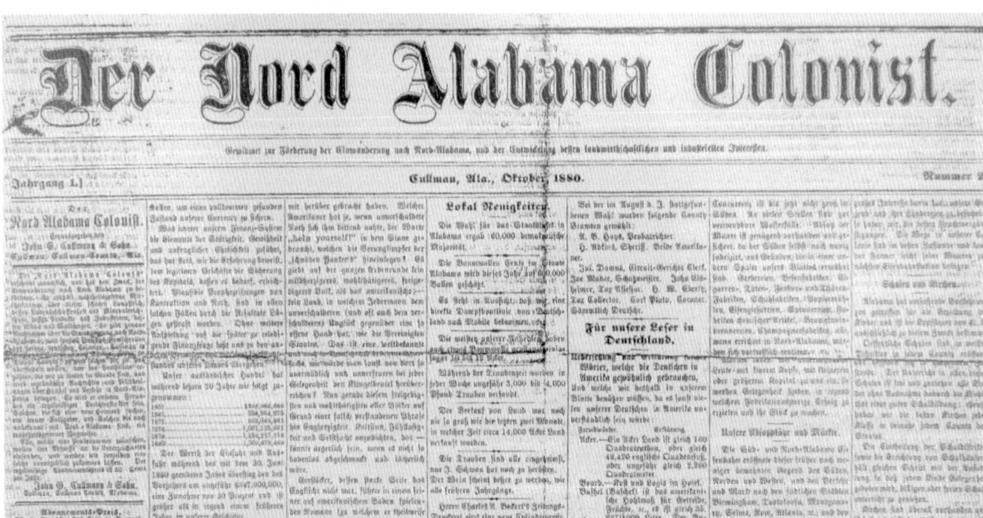

Der Nord Alabama Colonist.

Gewidmet zur Förderung der Einwanderung nach Nord-Alabama, und der Entwickelung dessen landwirthschaftlichen und industriellen Interessen.

Jahrgang I.] Cullman, Ala., Oktober, 1880. Nummer 2.

Der Nord Alabama Colonist. Herausgegeben von John G. Cullmann & Sohn. Cullman, Cullman-County, Ala.

Lokal Neuigkeiten.

Für unsere Leser in Deutschland.

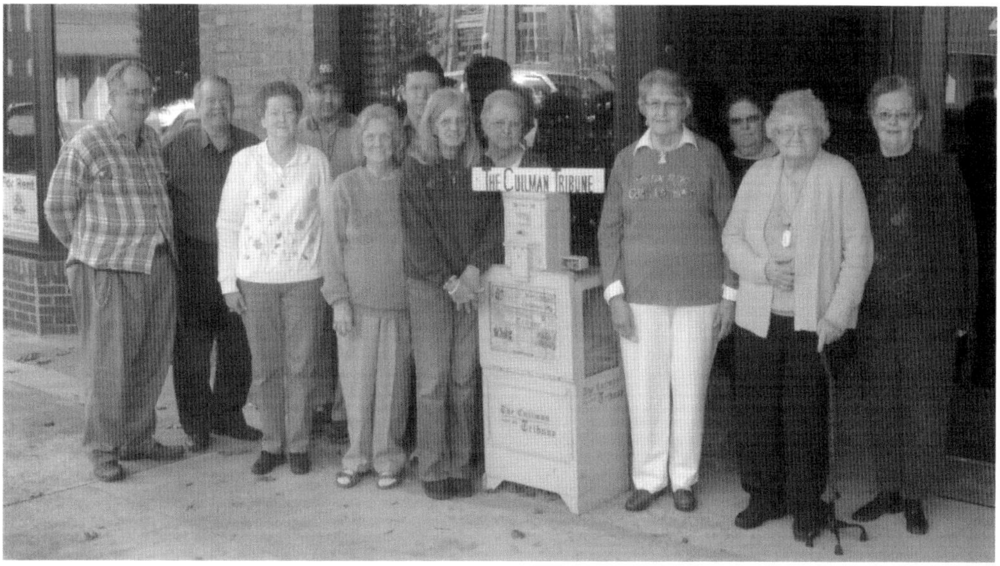

Delton and Barbara Blalock

Delton Blalock and his wife, Barbara, bought the *Cullman Tribune* in 1990. Barbara died in 2000, and Delton still holds the title of publisher. The *Tribune* is Cullman's oldest newspaper, and also Cullman's oldest continuous business. It was founded in 1874. There are other news outlets in town, but Blalock has found a niche by keeping a focus the history of the area alive and publishing stories of with a hometown flavor. In 2013, Barbara was inducted into the Alabama Newspaper Hall of Honor. As business manager, she began a drive to help Cold Springs School when it burned in the 1980s, and she and Delton helped raise money to fund Heritage Park soon after buying the paper. Pictured here are Delton Blaylock, second from left, and his staff members. (Both images courtesy *Cullman Tribune*.)

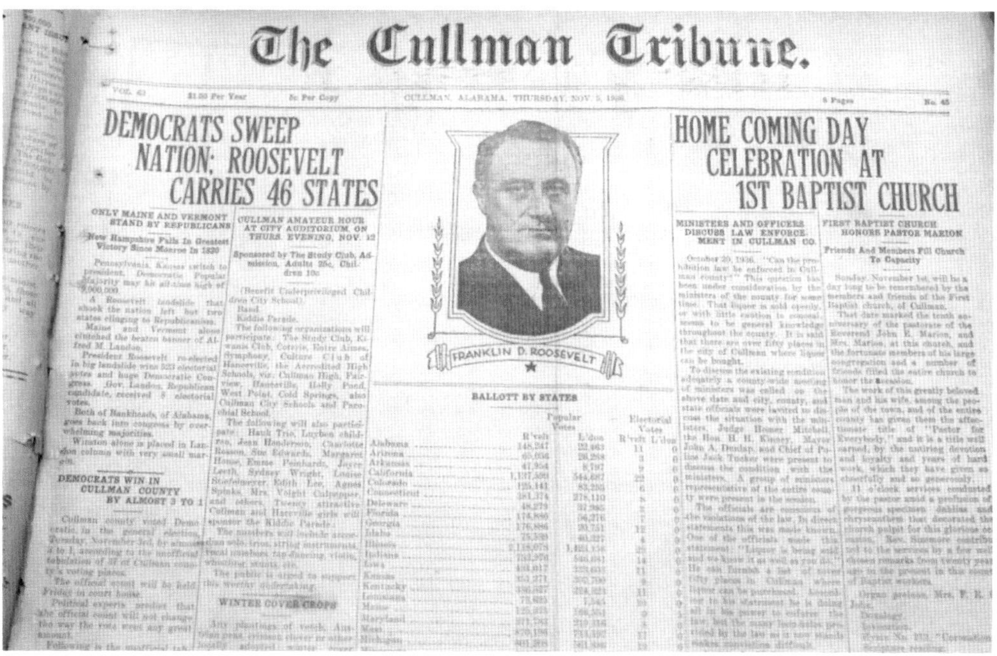

The Cullman Tribune.

$1.00 Per Year — 5c Per Copy — CULLMAN, ALABAMA

DEMOCRATS SWEEP NATION: ROOSEVELT CARRIES 46 STATES

ONLY MAINE AND VERMONT STAND BY REPUBLICANS

New Hampshire Falls In Greatest Victory Since Monroe In 1820

CULLMAN AMATEUR HOUR AT CITY AUDITORIUM ON THURS. EVENING, NOV. 12

Sponsored by The Study Club, Admission, Adults 25c, Children 10c

DEMOCRATS WIN IN CULLMAN COUNTY BY ALMOST 3 TO 1

WINTER COVER CROPS

FRANKLIN D. ROOSEVELT

BALLOTT BY STATES

HOME COMING DAY CELEBRATION AT 1ST BAPTIST CHURCH

MINISTERS AND OFFICERS DISCUSS LAW ENFORCEMENT IN CULLMAN CO.

FIRST BAPTIST CHURCH HONORS PASTOR MARION

Friends And Members Fill Church To Capacity

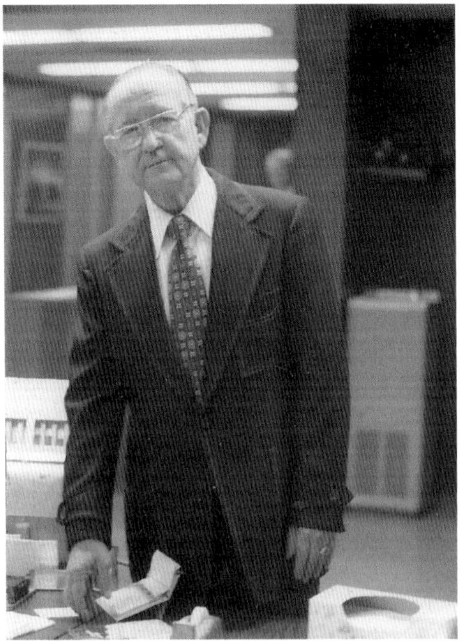

Claude Wood

Claude Wood was the longest-serving manager of the Cullman Electric Cooperative. When Alabama Power refused to run power lines into Cullman County in the 1930s, a group of 14 farmers formed the Cullman Electric Cooperative. Cullman Power Board provided electricity to city residents, but was unable to service the county. Wood was hired 1941 as an engineer and manager and served 40 years. (Courtesy Cullman Electric Cooperative.)

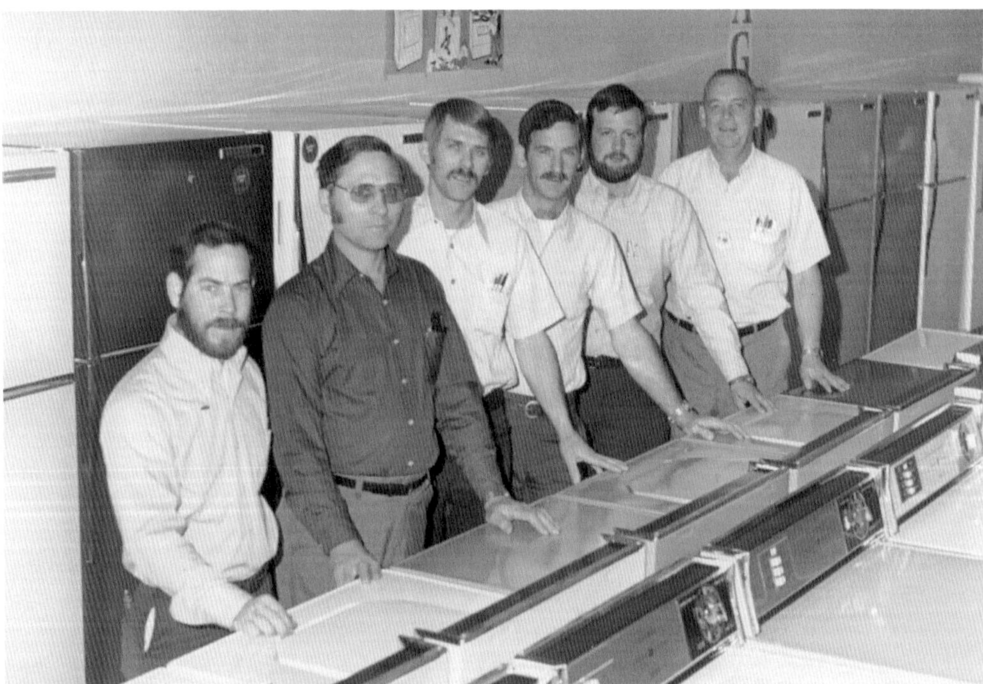

Luyben and Boike

Ross Luyben and Julius Boike emigrated from Germany in the late 1800s and their sons, John Luyben and George Boike established an appliance business. George Boike purchased Luyben's portion, but the prominent name, Luyben and Boike was retained, owed by Doug Boike. From left in the mid-1950s: Mike Linker, the late George Boike, Doug Boike, Dennis Spradlin, Donald Hunter, and Dick Fink. (Courtesy Boike family.)

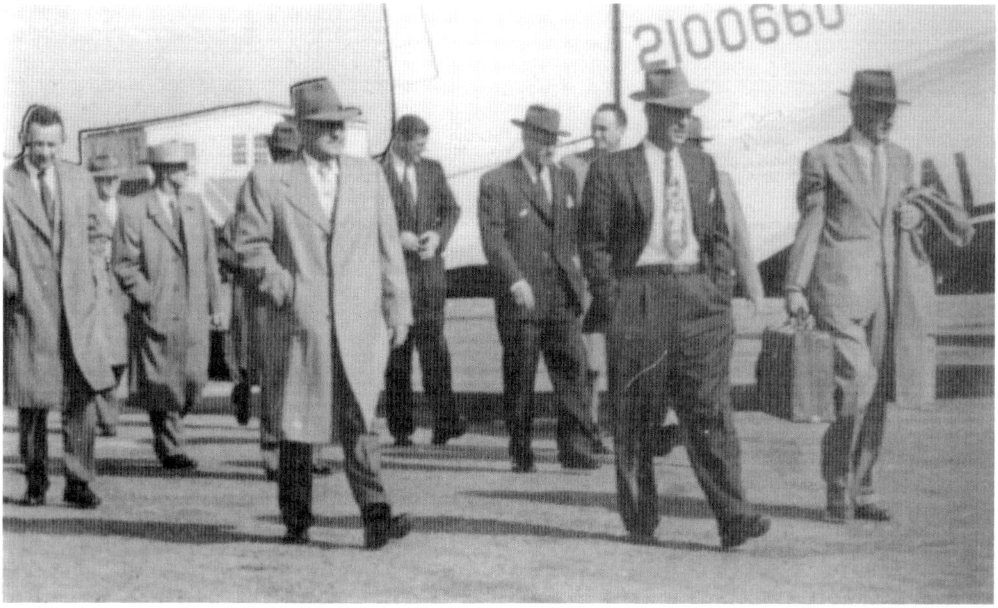

Flying Fifty

The Flying Fifty was a volunteer group of businessmen who searched for new industry in the 1950s. With no appointment, they climbed aboard a National Guard plane, then flew commercial to Jacksonville, Florida. They rented a hotel ballroom to meet with tobacco magnate Carl Swisher, which brought King Edward Cigar to Cullman. Other industries followed. Some members of the group were Roy Drinkard, Dr. R.F. Williford, Joe Sapp, Ottis Burrow, Mickey Clem, Crant Waldrop, Dr. Dwight Fuller, Fred Hale, Luther Hinds, Grady Moss, Elbert Ponder, Bill Wachter, Robert Schaefer, Kermit Gorham, Larkin Yates, and Hudson Millar. Ernie Reddick, below, was the first managerial staff member for King Edward. Ernie Reddick has made the area his home and is a volunteer, along with his wife, for the Meals on Wheels Program. (Both images courtesy Cullman County Chamber Commerce.)

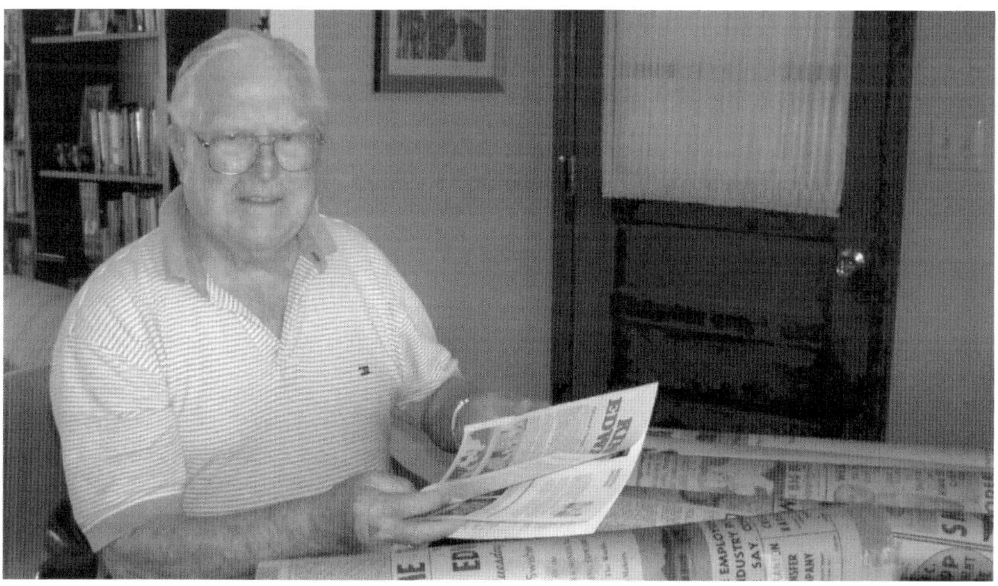

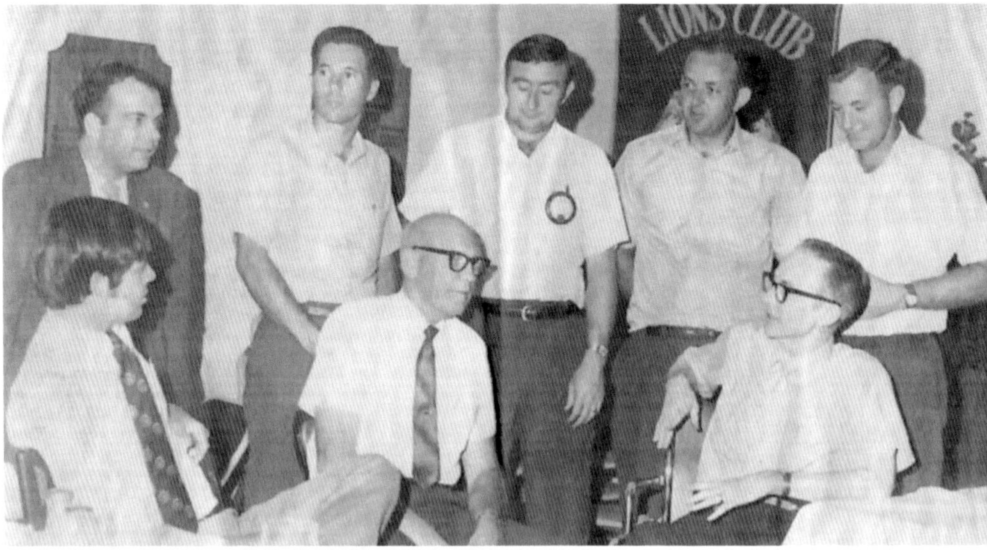

Dillard Johnson, Lions Club

Shortly after the Cullman Lions Club was founded 1954 it was looking for a way to raise funds. Lion Dillard Johnson, seated center, suggested starting a county fair. The Lions agreed, and Johnson was named Cullman County Fair manager, a position he held until 1995. He also served as president and vice president of the club many times over the years. (Courtesy Cullman Lions.)

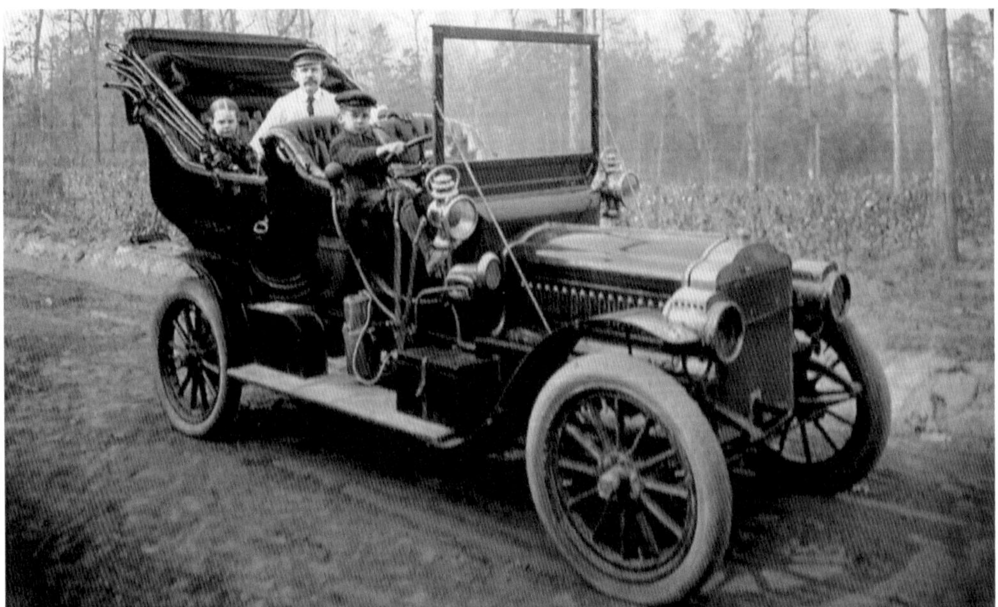

M.L. Robertson, Kiwanis Club

M.L. Robertson was first president of the Cullman Kiwanis Club at its founding in 1921. He had already established himself in town, having been elected mayor of Cullman in 1910, a position he held for 22 years. In 1895, he bought the *Cullman Tribune*. He married Mary Alice Parker, daughter of banker George H. Parker, in 1897. (Courtesy Cullman Kiwanis Club.)

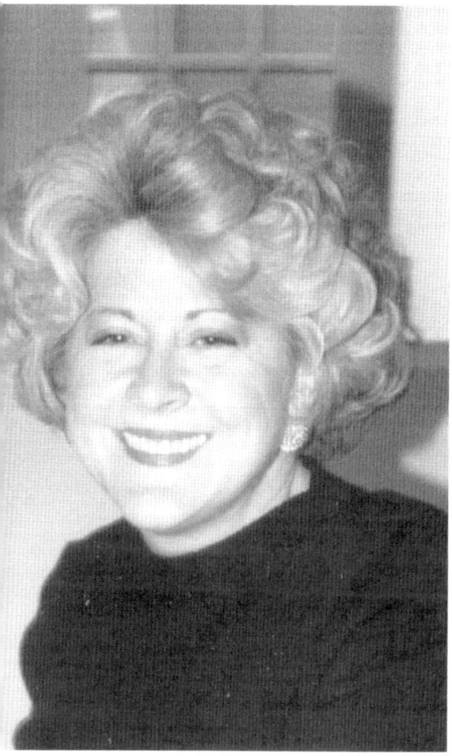

Debra Buettner, Rotary Club

Debra Buettner was Cullman Rotary's first female member and elected president in the 1990s. She paved the way for women to be members of what had been an all-male service club. She died in 1995 at age 40. A scholarship in her memory was established at Wallace State Community College for female business majors. (Courtesy Buettner family.)

Freddy Day, Elks Lodge

Freddy Day, kitchen-catering manager, and volunteers from the Elks Lodge cook and serve their way to fund the club's charitable projects. Over a year, the Elks cook hundreds of Boston butts, racks of ribs, hams, turkeys, and catered events serving 10,000 or more people. This project has funded drug awareness, provided dictionaries for all third graders in the county, scholarships, and Christmas for children and families. (Courtesy Kay Cagle.)

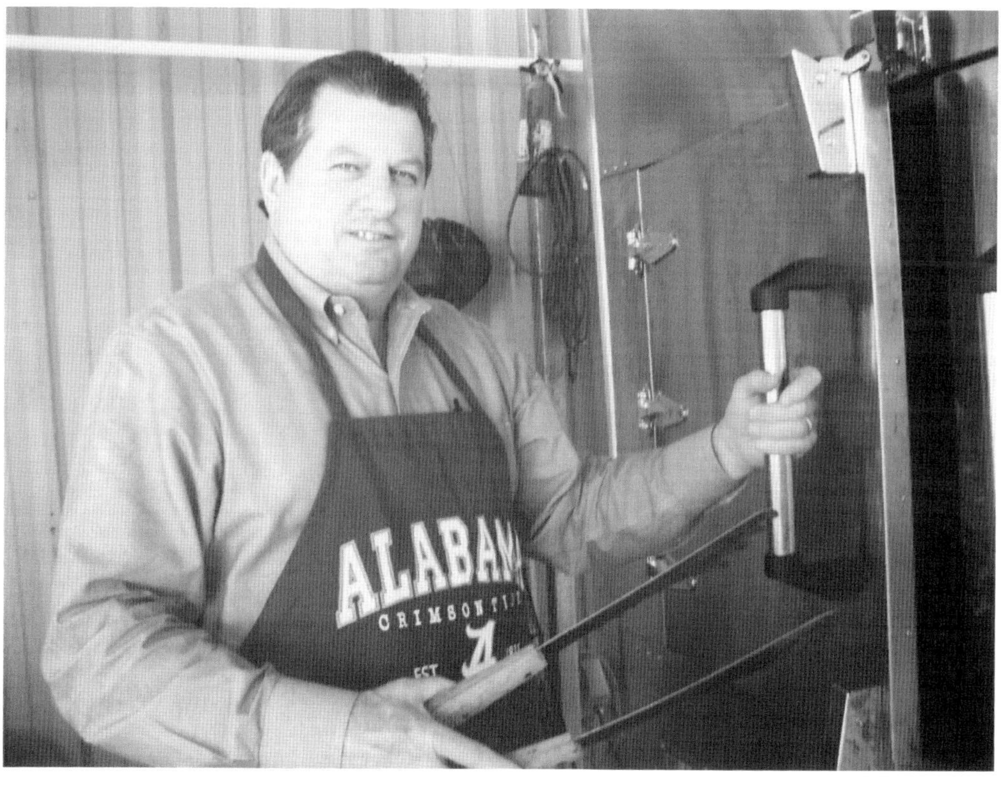

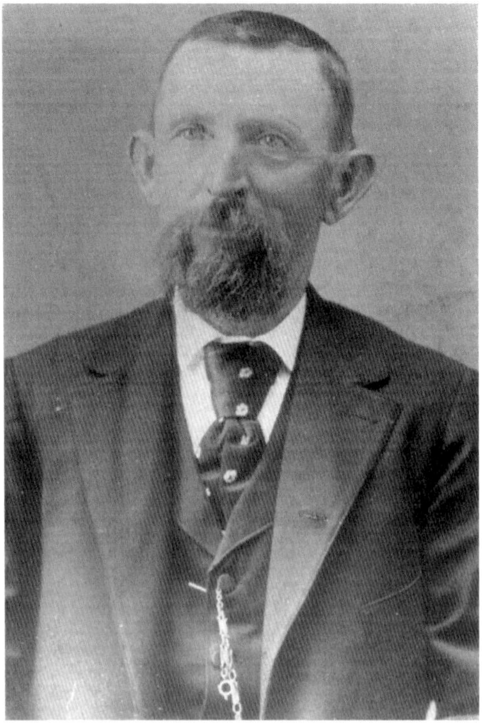

Adam Dreher Sr.

Adam Dreher Sr. moved to Cullman in 1877. He purchased Southern Novelty Works, which became Dreher Furniture Factory, the only such factory at that time south of the Mason-Dixon Line. Dreher's occupied several locations in Cullman, one of which caught fire and burned almost the entire block in 1892, taking Stiefelmeyer's store with it. An entire suite could be bought for $6.50. (Courtesy Cullman County Museum.)

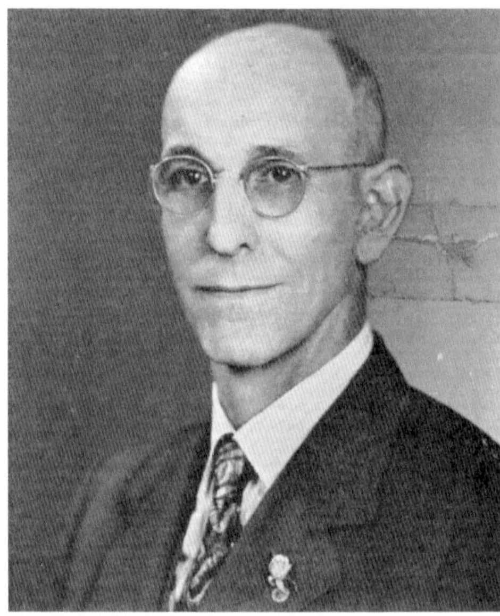

Charles Klein

Charles Henry Ernest Klein founded Klein's Creamery in 1924, which included a popular soda shop that lasted through the 1950s. Klein grew up on a farm and served in World War I. Klein studied agriculture at Mississippi State, then founded a large dairy business in Cullman County. By 1950, Klein's business distributed 500 gallons a day with routes in Garden City, Warrior, and Hanceville. (Courtesy Cullman County Museum.)

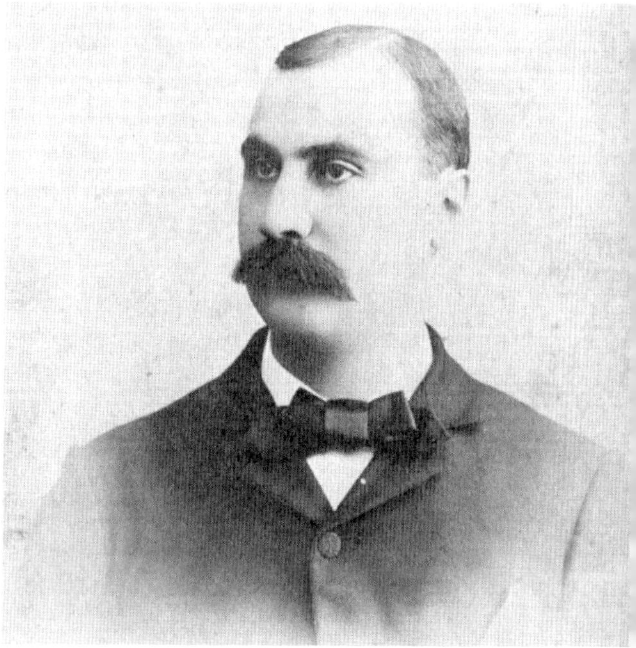

C.A. Stiefelmeyer

C.A. Stiefelmeyer established his store in 1888. The original building was lost to a fire in 1892. Stiefelmeyer rebuilt, and over the years added onto his store. Stiefelmeyer's remained open until the 1980s, run by family members. The building still stands and has been divided into offices, shops, and restaurants in historic downtown Cullman. (Courtesy Cullman County Museum.)

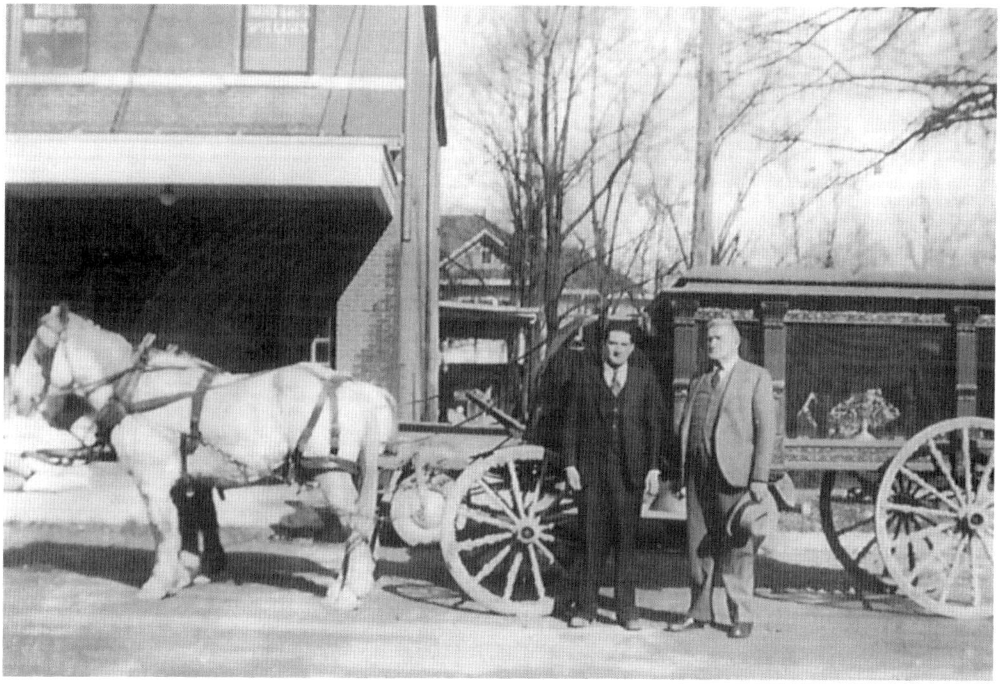

Oscar Fischer

Oscar Fischer operated an undertaking business in the mid-1900s. Sheriff C.B. Graves was convicted of murder in 1920, so Coroner Oscar Fischer served as acting sheriff one month. In 1940, a death occurred in Holly Pond, and heavy rains made roads impassable by car. Fischer pulled out a 35-year-old horse-drawn funeral coach and put it in service as a solution to the problem. (Courtesy Cullman County Museum.)

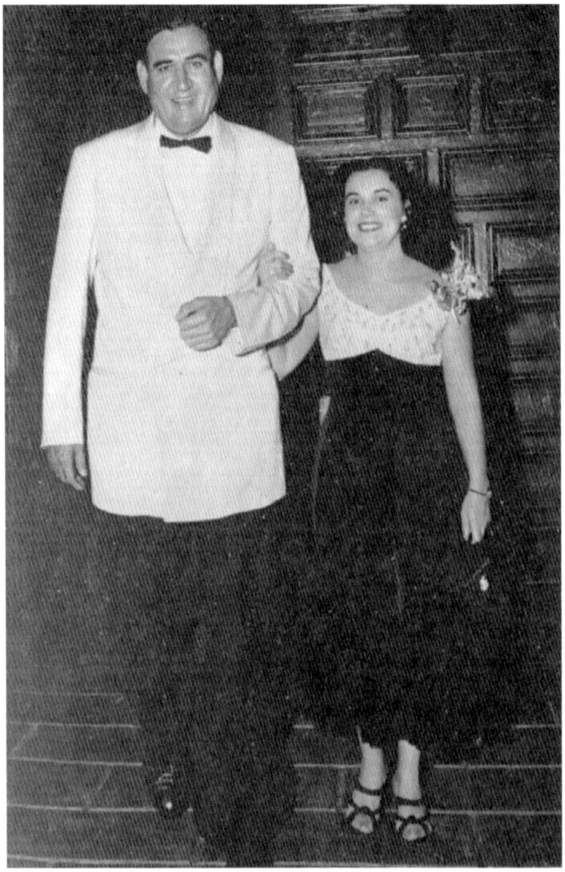

Gov. James E. "Big Jim" Folsom

Born in 1908 in the Coffee County town of Elba, James E. "Big Jim" Folsom served as a deputy sheriff, tax collector, and as a member of the Coffee County Commission. He also served in the Merchant Marines and held jobs in the Civil Works Administration and the Works Progress Administration. He moved to Cullman in the late 1930s with his family after unsuccessful runs for Congress and governor. A populist who championed equal rights for blacks and women among other progressive causes, Folsom was the first person to serve two terms as governor of Alabama. He fought the Big Mules, based in Birmingham, who favored segregation and opposed education reforms. Essentially, everything Folsom believed in was at odds with the Big Mules. Still, he won two terms, 1947–1951 and 1955–1959. Running as "the little man's big friend," the six-foot-eight-inch Folsom campaigned with a hillbilly band and a mop and bucket he said he would use to clean out corruption at the state capitol. Threatened with scandal himself, Folsom said on the campaign trail, "I plead guilty to stealing. That crowd I got it from, you had to steal it to get it . . . I stole for you, and you, and you." During his second term, compromise in the legislature on some issues was prevented by white reaction to the *Brown v. Board of Education* decision, the Montgomery bus boycott, and the controversy around Autherine Lucy trying to attend the University of Alabama. Folsom favored equal rights for blacks and refused to exploit race while trying to pass his agenda. Still, he succeeded in expanding state services and getting reapportionment of the legislature. Folsom ran again for governor in 1962 against his former protégé, George C. Wallace. A television appearance in which Folsom appeared drunk, along with the renewed scandal stories, handed the election to the segregationist Wallace. Folsom's associates later said his drink had been drugged. He made one more attempt at the state's top office in 1966, but lost to Wallace's first wife, Lurleen. (Courtesy Cullman County Museum.)

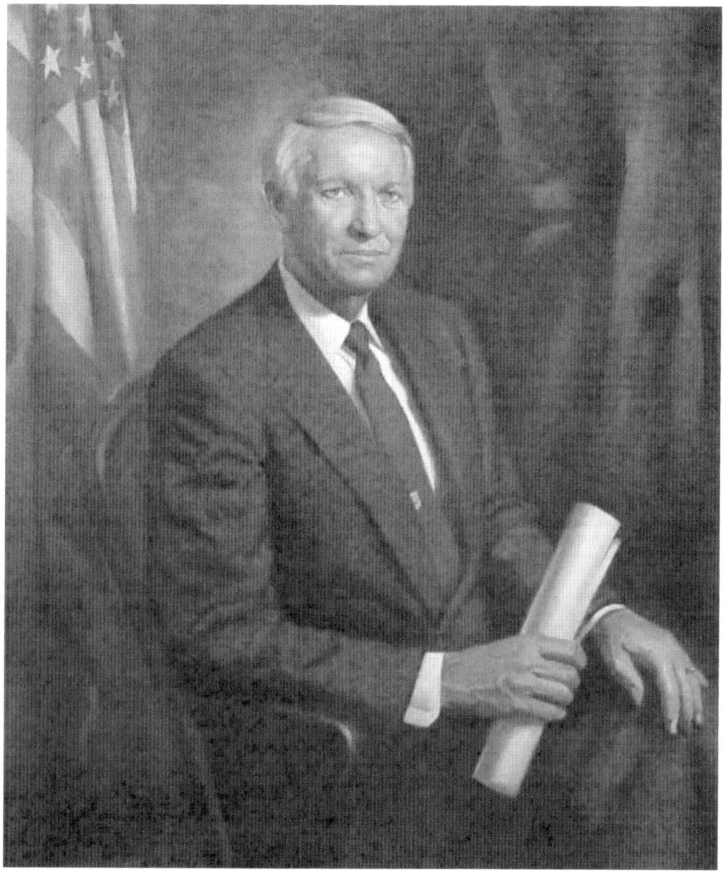

Gov. Guy Hunt

Born in Holly Pond in 1933, Guy Hunt was a proud Republican in a then-solidly Democratic state and county. Hunt was a farmer and Primitive Baptist minister long before he got into politics. He ran unsuccessfully for state senate in 1962 but was elected Cullman County probate judge in 1964 on the coattails of Barry Goldwater's presidential campaign. He was reelected in 1970. Hunt led the Alabama delegation to the Republican National Convention in 1976, supporting former California governor Ronald Reagan. In 1978, he made his first run for governor, but was defeated by Democrat Fob James. In 1980, he again served as chairman of the Alabama GOP delegation, this time seeing his candidate, Reagan, elected president. Reagan appointed Hunt state executive director of the Agricultural Stabilization and Conservation Service, a position he held until 1985, when he resigned to run again for governor. Hunt won his party's nomination, but again was not expected to defeat the Democratic nominee, whoever it ended up being. But when Attorney General Charlie Graddick defeated Lt. Gov. Bill Baxley in a runoff, some charged that Graddick had encouraged "crossover" votes from the Republican primary, which did not have a runoff. The Justice Department said this diluted the black vote, and they ordered the Democrats to either certify Baxley as its candidate or hold a new runoff. They chose to certify Baxley, angering many voters, who ended up handing Hunt an unexpected victory. Hunt was the first Republican governor of the state since Reconstruction and, in his first year in office, was named one of America's best governor's by *U.S. News and World Report*. He was reelected in 1990 but was ousted from office in 1993 on a felony conviction for misusing campaign funds. Hunt maintained his innocence and was pardoned by the State Board of Pardons and Paroles in 1998. He ran again for governor that year but was defeated in the GOP primary by the incumbent, and now Republican, Fob James. Hunt died in 2009 after a long battle with lung cancer. (Courtesy Cullman County Museum.)

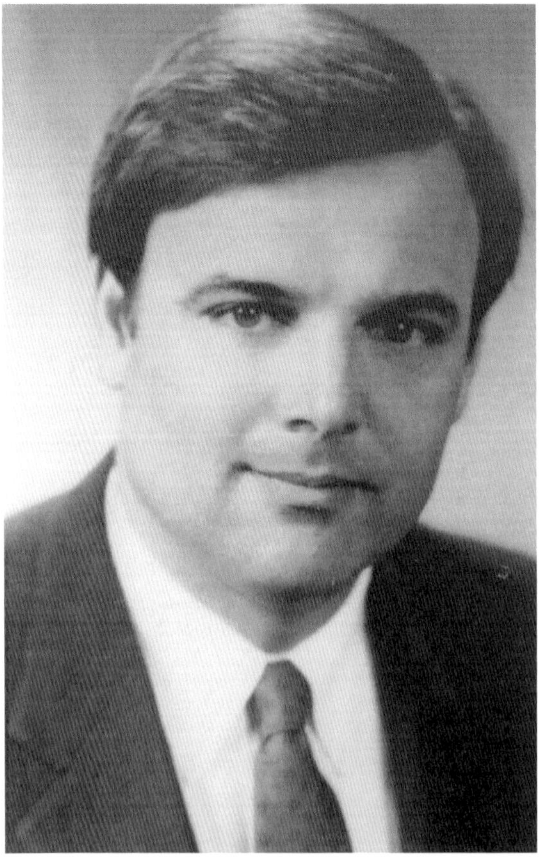

Gov. Jim Folsom Jr.
Jim Folsom Jr. was governor from 1993 to 1995. Son of Gov. James E. "Big Jim" Folsom, he continued many of his father's policies, appointing several blacks and women to his cabinet. He ordered that the Confederate battle flag stop being flown over the Capitol. He recruited Mercedes Benz to Alabama, leading to industrial expansion. Folsom is the longest-serving lieutenant governor in state history. (Courtesy Cullman County Museum.)

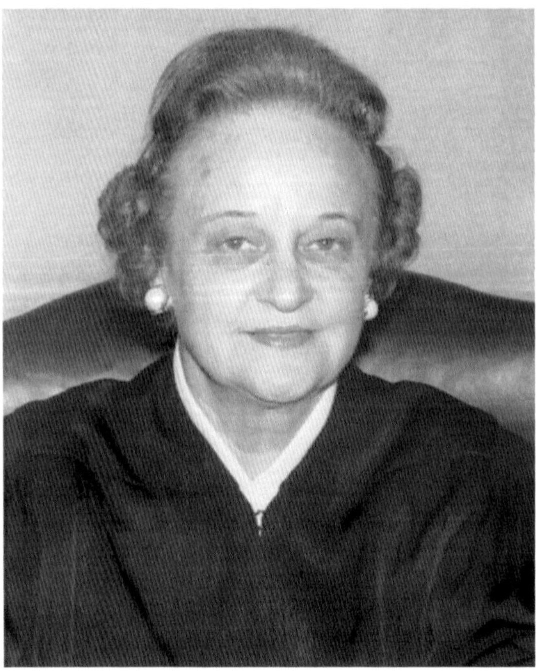

Justice Annie Lola Price
Annie Lola Price, born in Cullman in 1903, was the first woman on an appellate court in Alabama. In 1947, she became assistant legal adviser to Gov. James E. "Big Jim" Folsom, who appointed her legal adviser in 1950 and to the Alabama Court of Appeals in 1951. She was presiding judge until the Alabama Court of Criminal Appeals was created in 1969. (Courtesy Alabama Women's Hall of Fame.)

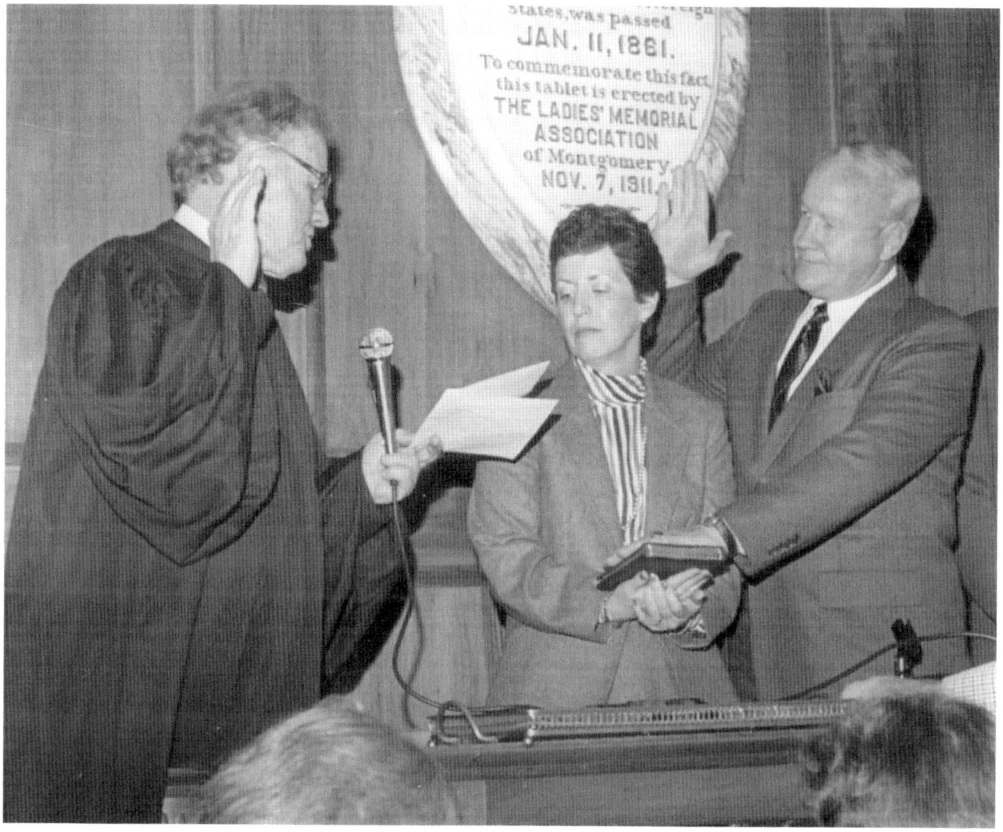

Rep. Tom Drake

Tom Drake, elected for two consecutive terms as Speaker of the Alabama House of Representatives, was called, "Alabama's Fighting Legislator." It is not because of squaring off on the legislative floor, but for making a name in professional wrestling and athletics before his stint as an elected official. He played football for the Cullman High School Bearcats and received a scholarship at the University of Chattanooga. Playing in the Blue-Gray game, he crossed paths with the Gray Coach, Paul "Bear" Bryant. He was the 15th draft choice of the Pittsburgh Steelers, but Uncle Sam got him first. He spent time at Fort Benning, Georgia, and it was there he saw his first live wrestling matches. With his college background in wrestling, Tom, with the aid of a promoter, was launched into wrestling. He was also known as the "Cullman Comet." In 1957, he married Chris McKoy, and in 1958 went back to school at the University of Alabama. That was the year he was hired by Bryant as wrestling coach. He entered law school at the university in 1960 and in 1962 dropped out of school to run for state representative of Cullman County and won without a runoff. He would serve in the State Legislature for 32 years, not only serving the two terms as speaker, but chairman of the Rules Committee and member of the powerful Ways and Means Committee. Tom would finish law school later and join his wife, Chris, in a business partnership in Cullman. He appeared on NBC's *What's My Line?* The panel was told he was a lawyer, state legislator, and farmer, but they had to guess his "side line." He was unable to stump the panel, who guessed he was also a wrestler. He was inducted into the International Wrestling Institute and Museum in Newton, Iowa; the Professional Wrestling Hall of Fame in Amsterdam, New York; and National Wrestling Hall of Fame, Stillwater, Oklahoma. Pictured are Christine McKoy Drake with her husband, Tom, who is being sworn in as Speaker of the House by Judge Newton Powel, his uncle, and then judge for the 8th Judicial Circuit. (Courtesy Tom Drake.)

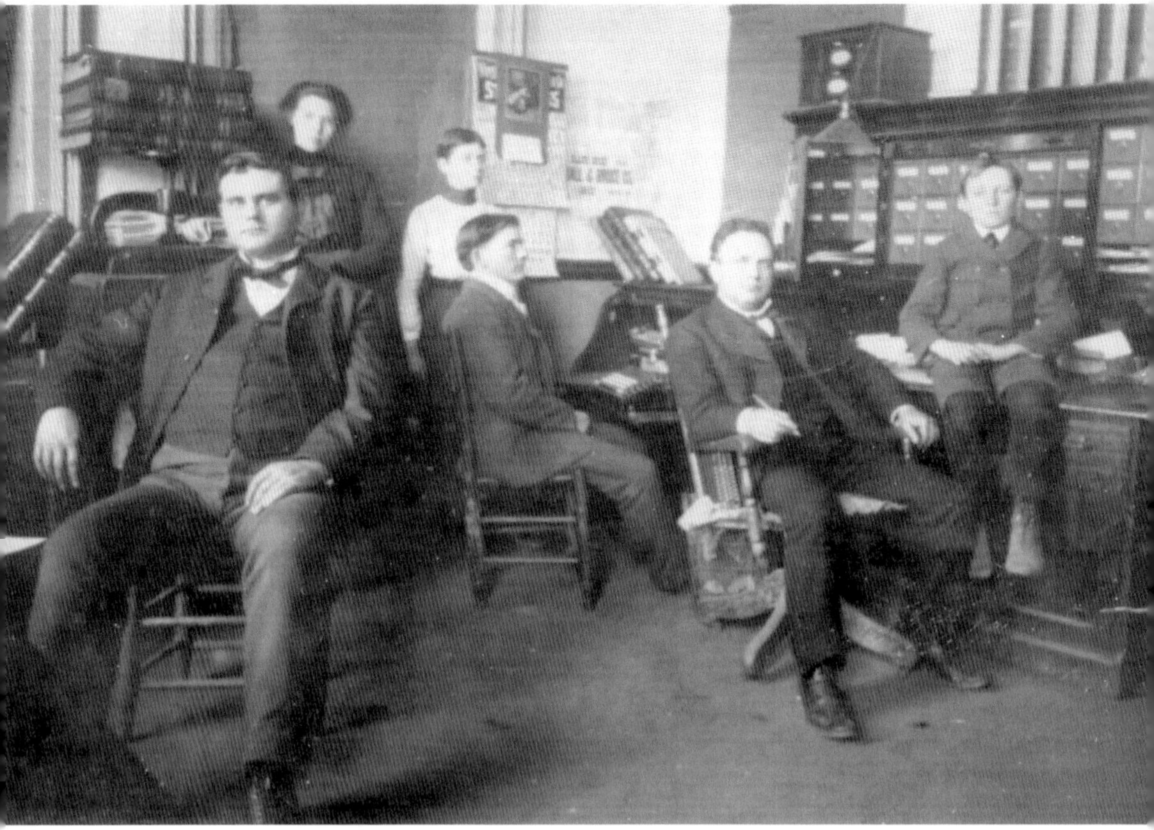

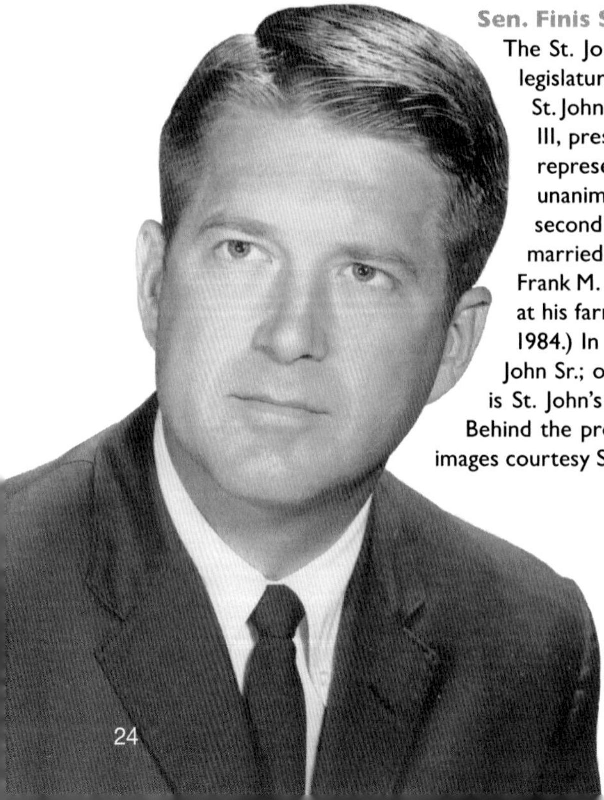

Sen. Finis St. John III

The St. John Family has four generations in the state legislature: William Powell St. John, 1853; Finis Ewing St. John, Finis Ewing St. John Jr., and Sen. Finis St. John III, president pro tem. Finis St. John III was elected representative and then senator in 1978. He was unanimously elected president pro tem, putting him second in the succession line to governor. He was married to Juliet Given, niece of former governor Frank M. Dixon. Pictured is Finis St. John III (who died at his farm on the outskirts of Cullman, October 25, 1984.) In the group picture, seated at left, is Finis St. John Sr.; on the right side, seated, with pencil in hand is St. John's father-in-law, Sutton Fuller, probate judge. Behind the probate judge is Wynelle, his daughter. (Both images courtesy St. John family.)

CHAPTER TWO

Then and Now

Cullman County in North Central Alabama—about 40 minutes from North Birmingham and Southern Huntsville—is an important geographical location for business and industry. Generations have planted roots in Cullman County, and businesses are still operated by the same families. These individuals are role models for their business acumen and commitment to community. In the late 1800s, business-minded individuals with a hearty pioneer spirit stepped forward and established their own niche, contributing to a burgeoning economy. Their spirit of commitment was founded on a willingness to work long, hard hours, with determination to be a pulsating, thriving force in the community. Pioneer families aspired to take the images in their dreams and turn them into stone and mortar, establishing businesses that have survived for generations. There are also notable individuals who began as employees for a company, rose through the ranks and purchased the business, distinguishing its niche in the economy.

Families and individuals have continued offering the necessities of life from building and office supplies to food and medicine. From the first store that opened in 1873, forests were cut down and lumber hauled to sawmills. Settlers started to build, and wagon factories, furniture stores, dairies, clothing stores, and ironworks emerged. A forward path was set. *Businesses Then and Now* is a review of historic and current individuals who have impacted the local economy.

The city of Cullman and county seat is within 600 miles from half of the United States. Industries and commercial developers choose the area because of its central location and easy access to interstates, railways, rivers, and airports. Located in the southwest portion of the county is Smith Lake, which boasts of 21,000 acres of boating, fishing, and waterfront living.

Since 2002, thirty-nine new industries have located in Cullman and commercial growth has skyrocketed. In 2011, forty-eight new and expanding businesses created 693 jobs. The top employment industry is Walmart Distribution Center, employing 1,400 people. The Cullman Economic Development Agency was named one of 10 economic development groups in the nation by *Site Selection* magazine for attracting new industries.

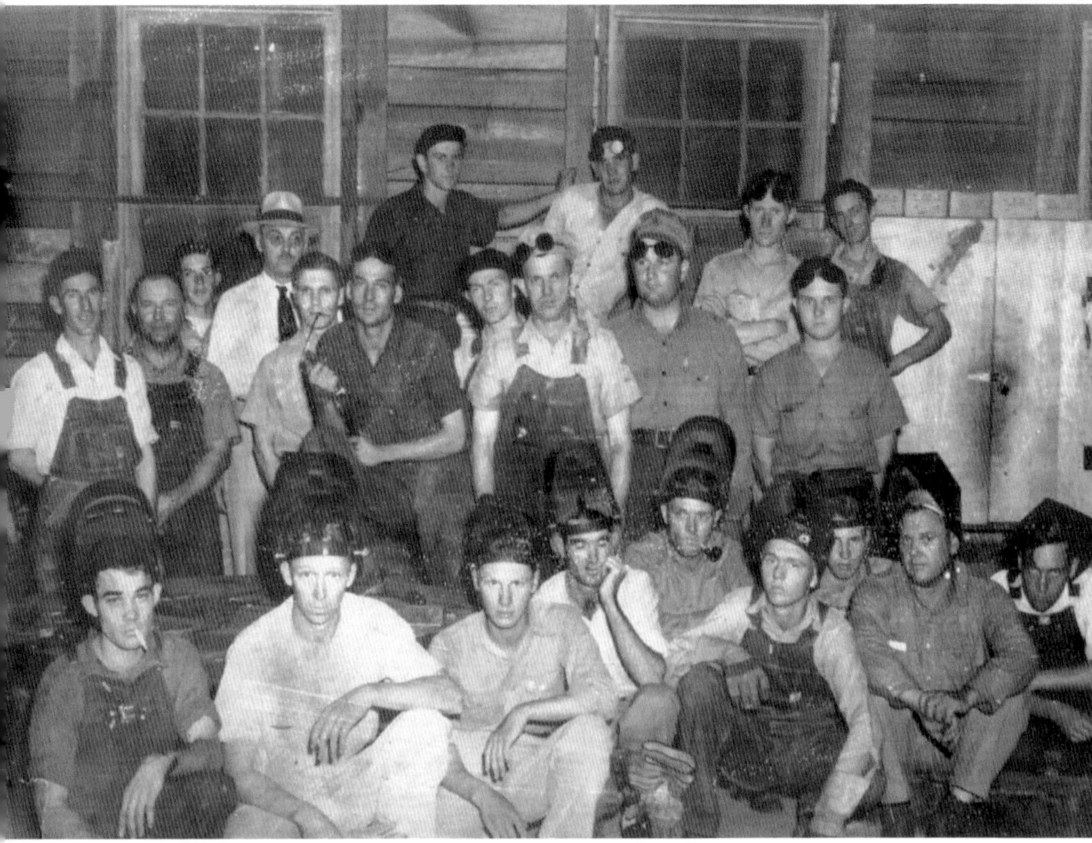

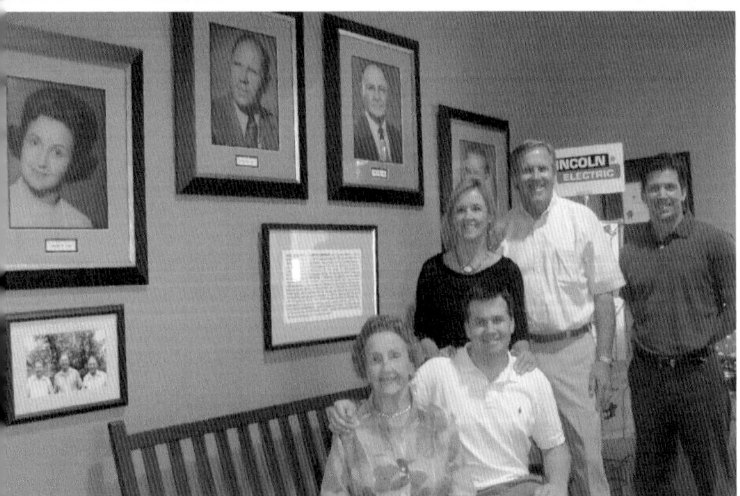

Ehrensperger-Apel Era

When the Ehrensperger and Apel families combined their ideas, it boosted the local economy, providing employment that spans over a century. Henry Ehrensperger founded Cullman Iron Works in 1897. It burned but rose from the ashes, passing to son, Al Ehrensperger. Fritz Apel, working in the foundry at the age of 16, joined Ehrensperger, and with his brothers Edward, Arthur, and Ervin purchased the industry. It was renamed Apel Machine and Supply. Arthur and Edward became sole owners. With foundry industries declining after World War II, an enterprising Edward Apel learned and incorporated electronic welding. An influencing economic factor within the community, the family operation drilled water wells, plumbed chicken houses, ran water lines, and provided mill supplies. Pictured, from left are Mrs. Arthur "Maebell" Apel, Nicholas Apel, Cheri Apel Dalgleish, John Apel (president), and Chad and Nicholas John's sons. (Both images courtesy Apel family.)

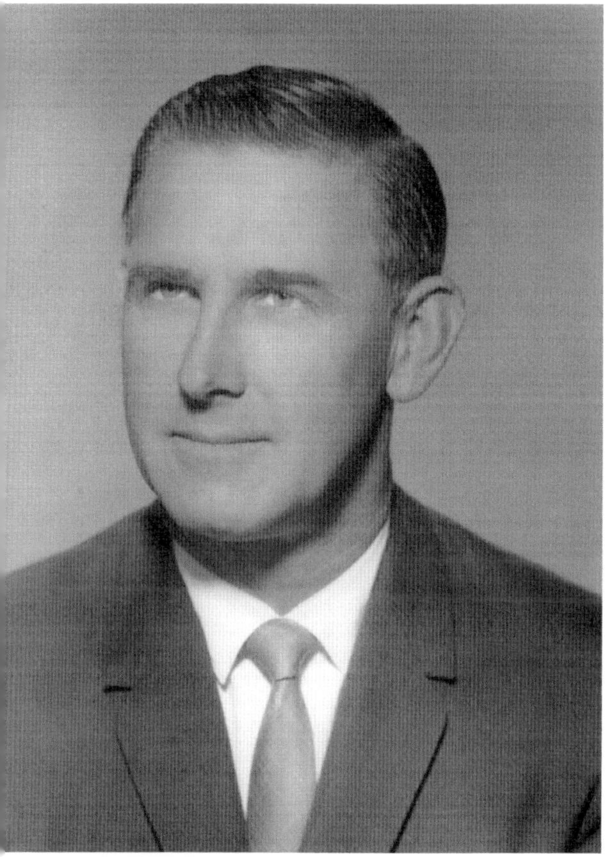

Men of Steel

An entrepreneurial spirit thrived in the Apel family. Edward Apel retired and sold his business portion to nephew Ronny Apel. Apel Steel Corporation was the outgrowth of that decision. Raw materials rolled in, and out the finished door, fabricated for commercial building construction. These local products reach markets across the United States and Puerto Rico. In the photograph below, from left to right are Ronny Apel (president), his cousin Catherine Apel Haggard, and Ronny's sons Hank Apel and Kurt Apel, all company employees. In a mid-1940s welding class, Edward Apel, back row, is fifth from the left; Fritz "Pop" Apel is in overalls beside Mr. Ehrensperger in the white shirt. The picture was taken in the original shop on First Avenue Southeast in downtown Cullman. Cullman Iron Works was established in the Old Bucket Factory. (Both images courtesy Apel family.)

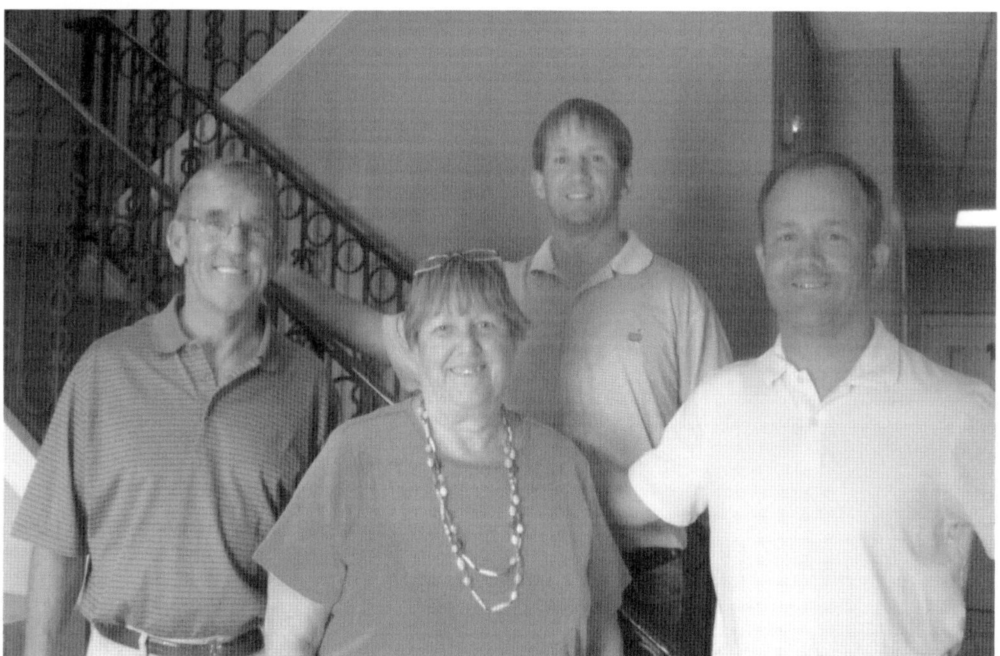

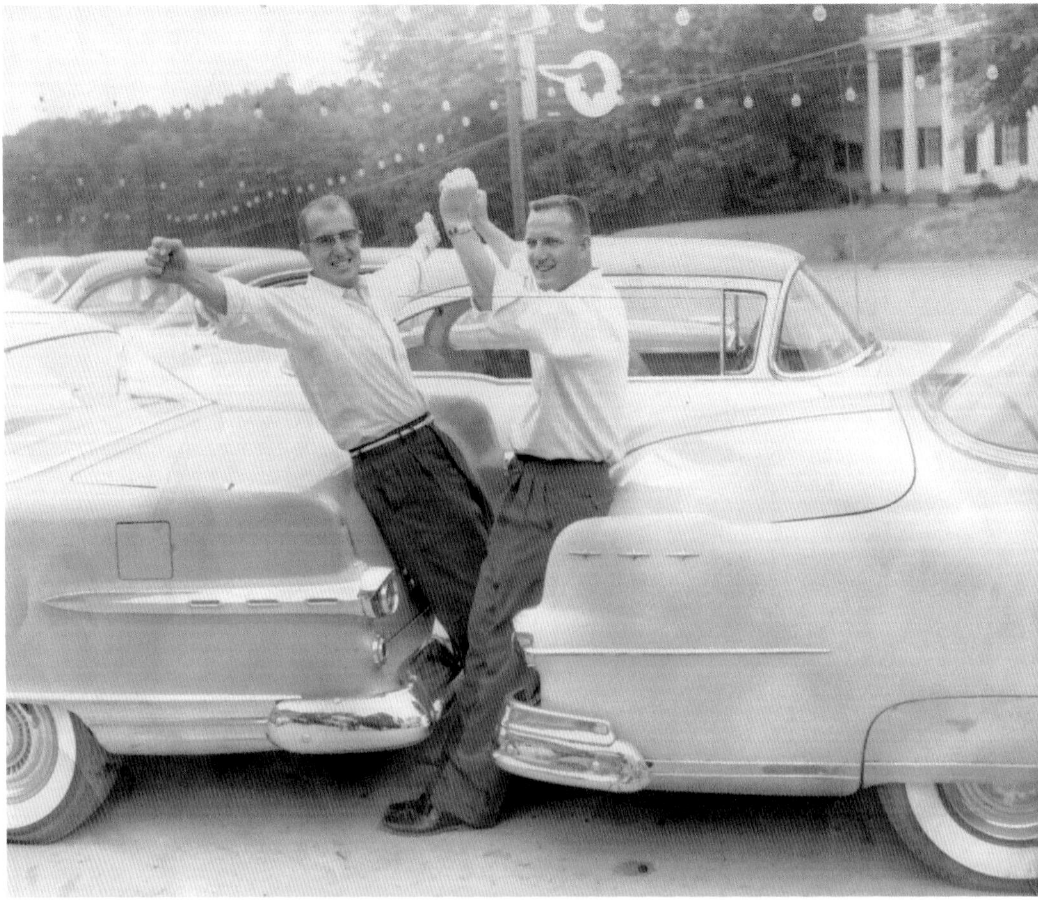

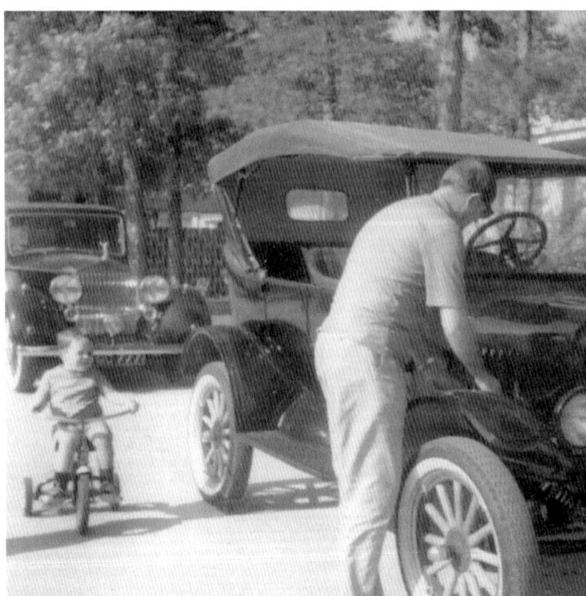

Bill Smith and Jimmy Waldrop

In 1949, brothers-in-law Bill Smith and Jimmy Waldrop, working at Sapp brothers' stores, were occasionally allowed to sell a car from the adjacent parking lot. A blaze of success established Smith and Waldrop car lot, capped by acquiring the only area Pontiac franchise for $700. Pontiac was the belle that brought them to the ball with the 1956 models. For 26 years, a tall, wooden Chief Pontiac stood vigilantly over the showroom floor, becoming a landmark site to Cullman County and visitors throughout North Alabama. Pictured, Bill Waldrop and Jimmy Smith celebrate, acquiring the Pontiac franchise. The two year old playing in his own vehicle is Bill Smith Jr., son of the cofounder who runs the dealership, covering several acres, in Cullman. (Both images courtesy Bill Smith Jr.)

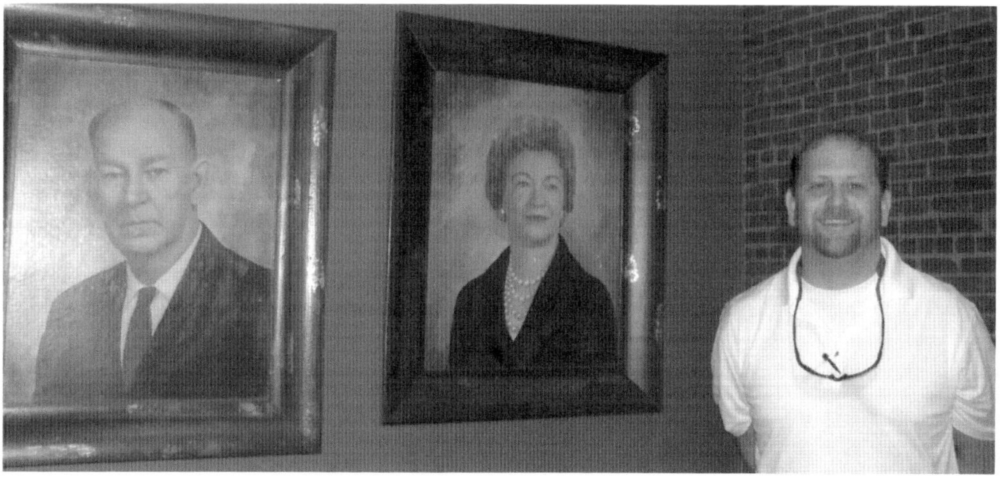

Lucille Wallace

Matt Heim carries on the tradition established by Mrs. Ewing (Lucille Speegle) Wallace. The Wallaces purchased the All Steak Restaurant in 1946, originating in Pulaski, Tennessee, with the Millard Buchmanns, Mrs. Wallace searched for the right customer-appreciation gesture. Two warm orange rolls were added to the meal breadbasket and a tasty tradition exploded. Orders poured in, and a trip through Cullman calls for a stop, indulging the appetite with legendary, warm and buttery orange rolls. Disaster struck in the mid-1960s when the restaurant burned. It was rebuilt by the Wallaces. On a Bahamas trip, wearing an All Steak T-shirt, Matt heard another tourist calling, asking if he had any orange rolls. No one knows the recipe origin, but orders for Mrs. Wallace's orange rolls are shipped throughout the country. (Above image courtesy Kay Cagle; below image courtesy Steve Singleton.)

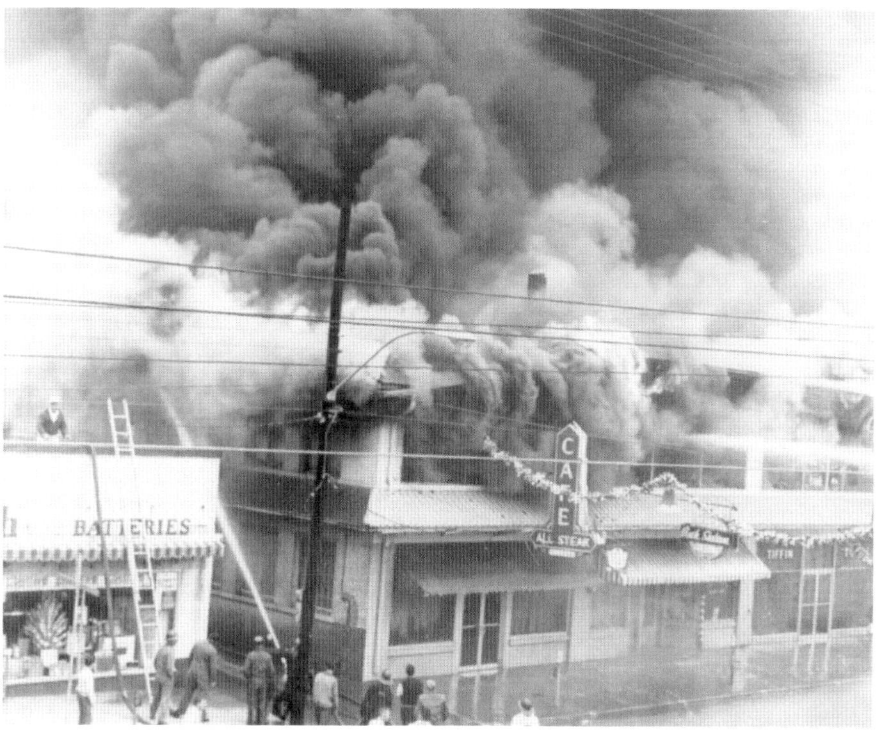

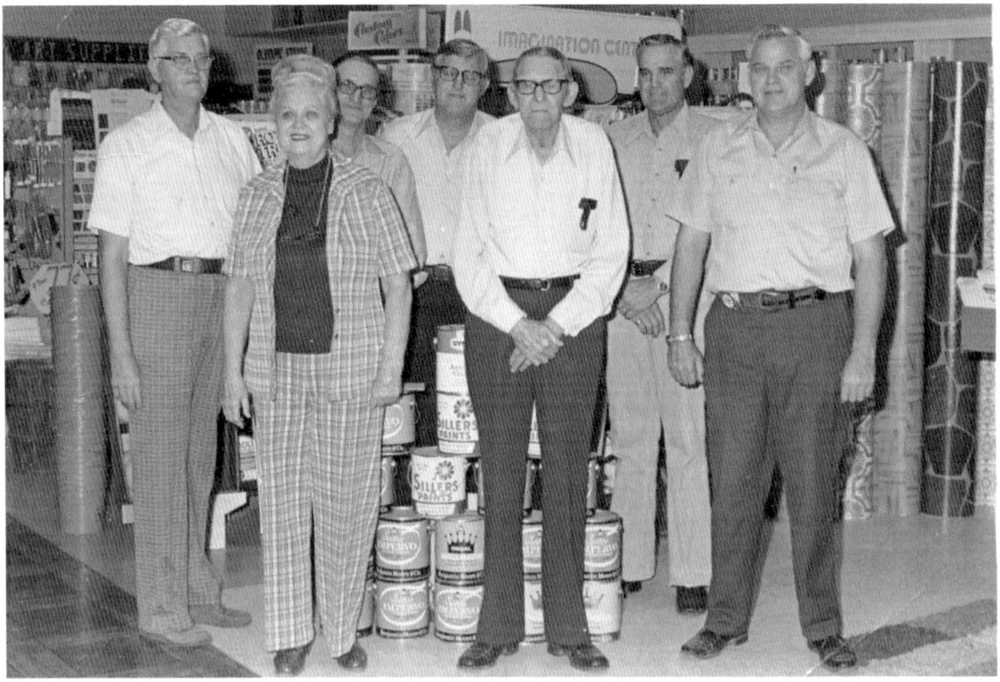

O.F. Richter

O.F. Richter established the paint and retail business in 1946 to provide employment for his five sons, returning from World War II. The Richter family arrived in Cullman in 1883. O.F. Richter worked in the Ruehl Wagon Factory, painting wagons, then houses. Over a century later, 12 family members work in the business and eight others are associated. Pictured above from left to right are Arthur, daughter Evelyn, Frank, Hubert, O.F. Richter, Clarence, and Roy Richter. Tim Richter, son of Evelyn, is president. Maria Richter Shultz, daughter of Roy, is corporate secretary. In the photograph below, around the table from the left are Brandi Richter, Marie Richter Shultz, and Ellen Richter Fulmer. Nathan Richter is in the back on the left. (Both images courtesy Richter family.)

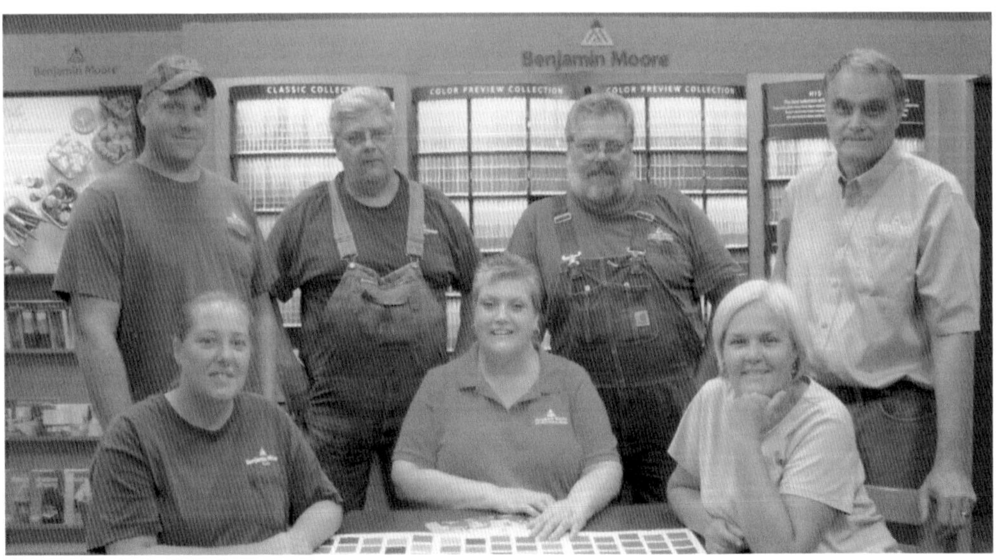

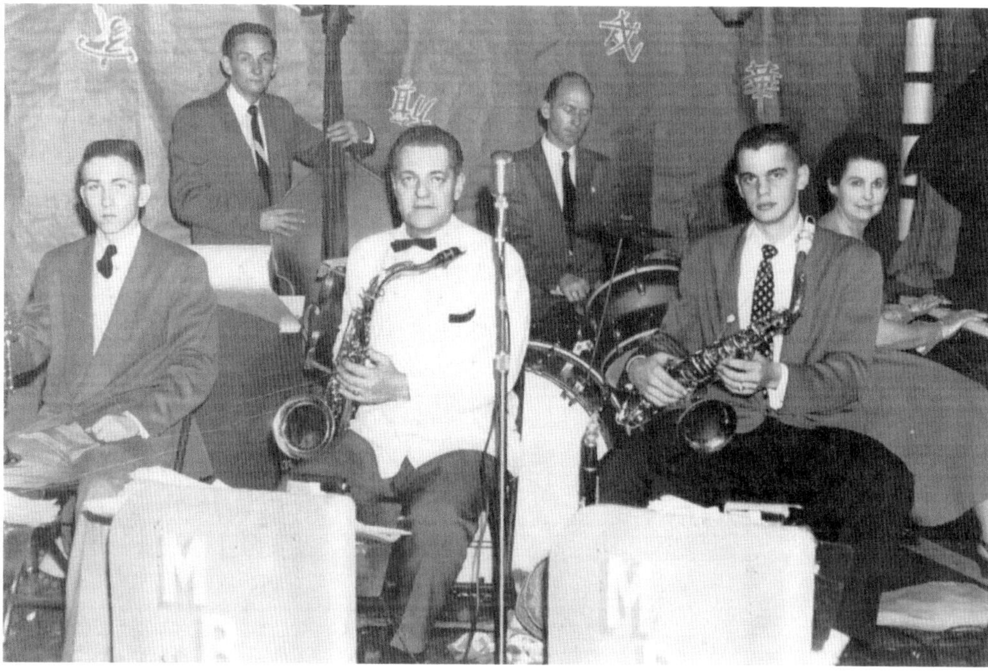

Millard Buchmann

Entrepreneur Millard Buchmann owned the original All Steak Café, in Pulaski, Tennessee, and Cullman's popular B&B Restaurant, with brother Herman. After World War II, new tires were rationed. He leased a Sinclair service station, learned to repair tires, then vulcanizing for recaps. Filling a need for vehicle owners, it led to Buchmann Tire and Recapping. As the name changed over the years from Big B, Big 10, then Peoples Tire, and he was joined by his son Ray, business sites were located throughout North Alabama and Southern Tennessee. A family's love for music never ended. The Millard Buchmann Orchestra and their Big Band music were founded in the early 1930s. Pictured from the left are Lane Parks, Lonnie McDaniel, Millard Buchmann, Jimmy Coward, Ray Buchmann, and Mrs. Millard (Nell) Buchmann. Ray and his wife, Benton, retired in October 2013. (Both images courtesy Ray Buchmann.)

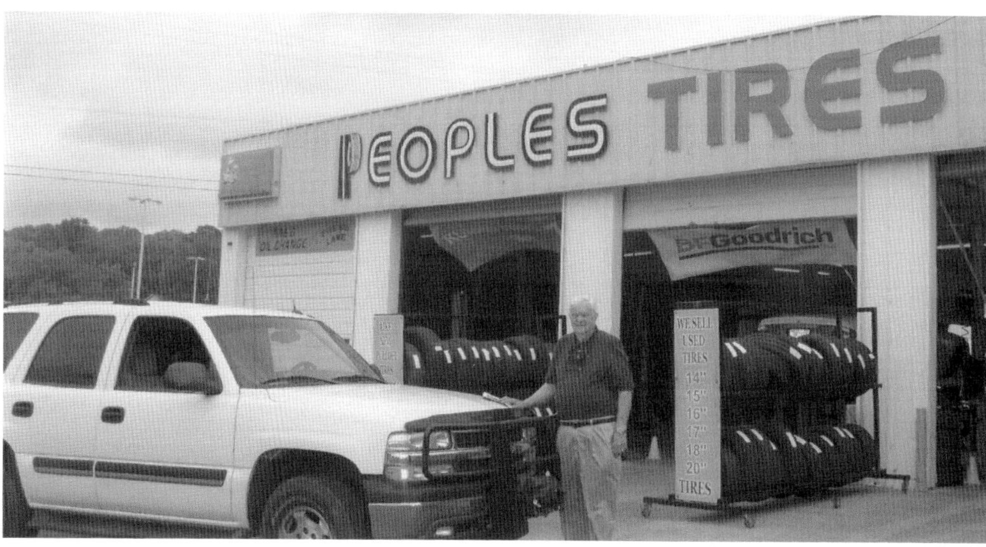

Powell Blair

When Powell Blair returned from World War II, he worked as a typesetter for Birmingham Printing. But, he had young-man aspirations to start a business in Cullman. With Joe Kreps as partner in 1946, Modernistic Printing was born in a garage. As the business grew, the partners split. Powell kept the printing division and Joe the office supply. Powell's son, the late Jim Blair, began working with his father in 1966. Modernistic Printing was relocated to its Third Avenue site in 1981. Powell was one of the Flying Fifty and Lions Club charter president. He and his son Jim hold the distinction of being father-son state presidents of the Elks Club. Today's Modernistic Printing family includes four working members: seated is Mrs. Jim (Betty) Blair, and standing from left are Jim's son Scott (president), Jan Blair Witte, and Mrs. Scott (Pam) Blair. (Both images courtesy Blair family.)

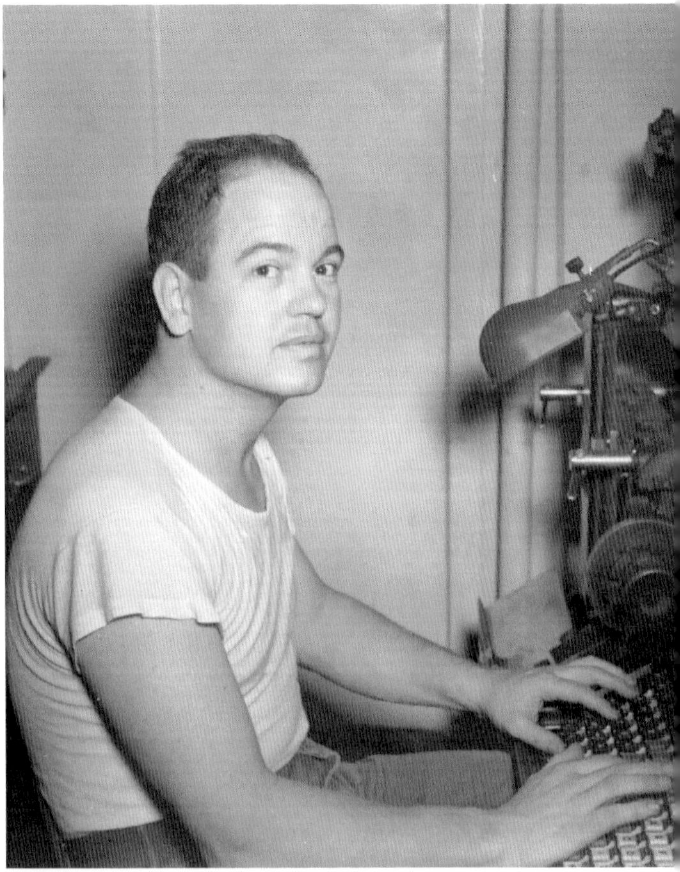

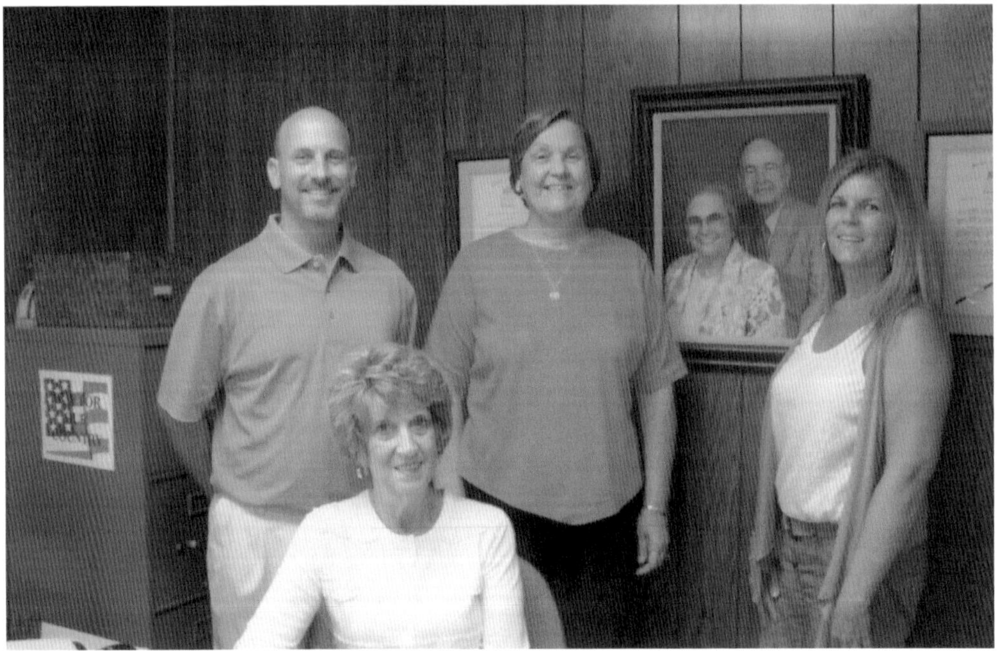

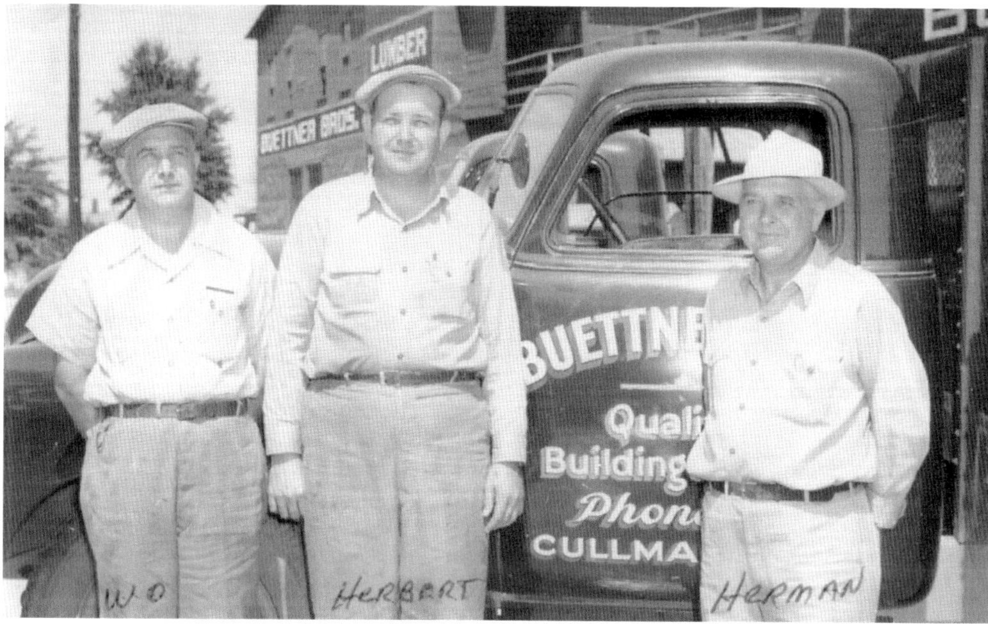

The Buettner Brothers

A visitor might be surprised at people relaxing on green, wooden benches advertising Buettner Brothers Lumber Company, but they have provided resting places for many years. Founded in 1892 by Hugo Buettner, a legacy continues. A modern sawmill was added in 1946, and the first pulp yard in the county established. Buettner brothers have been helping Cullman build for over a century. Herman and W.O. "Bill" Buettner purchased the business in 1924. Modern upgrades have cemented the legacy to provide materials from floor to roof. Bill and Herman Buettner retired. Pictured are W.O. "Bill" Buettner (left) and Herman (right), with brother Herbert. Buettner Brothers passed to its fourth generation in 1990, purchased by Charles Buettner, Jimmy Barnes, and John McPhillips. Pictured in front of a mill division are owners Jimmy Barnes, left, and John McPhillips. (Both images courtesy Buettner family.)

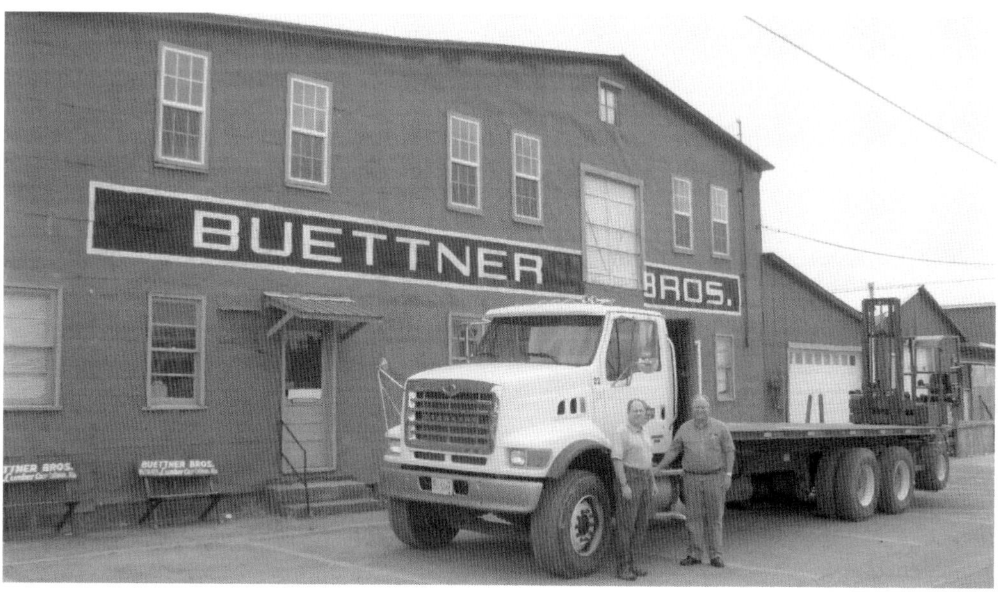

Bert McGriff

He was a sharecropper's son who became a self-made man. Bert McGriff is described as a visionary, entrepreneur and successful businessman. Returning home after World War II, he decided farming and trudging behind a mule was not for him. He headed into town to find a job. Like many soldiers, he sent money home while he was in service and this savings purchased a 1938 Chevy convertible. He landed a $35-a-week job as a gas jockey with a Standard Oil Station, mounting tires and washing windshields. His industrious nature did not go unnoticed by the Shell Oil Corporation, who watched him for three days. That led him to being a Shell station owner/operator. They offered him an owner-operator business deal. His cost would be a $1,000 investment, upfront. That $1,000 was a lot of money for a young man just out of the service. His father borrowed the money for his son from a friend. The loan helped turn the business into a full-service station, pumping 20¢-a-gallon gas. The Shell station was located in 1948 on Second Avenue and Arnold Street where McGriff Tire Retail store is today. He continued to live at home and build his business, but then met and married Berta Mae Holmes of the Providence Community. By 1954, his business included tires. He sold and repaired tires, which led to the retreading phase of his business. In 1976, he bought a building on Walnut Street, and made it the location of McGriff Industries. Bert McGriff still goes to work each day and remains CEO, but his son, Barry, is president of McGriff Industries which has evolved to include the retail McGriff Tire store, 11 commercial centers, two Bandag retread tire plants, and Southern Pines Development and Terri Pines Country Club and Golf Course (named after his youngest, Terri). His four children, Barry, Jeff, Cherri, and Terri still seek their father's wisdom and advice as the McGriff family moves into its third generation. (Courtesy Kay Cagle.)

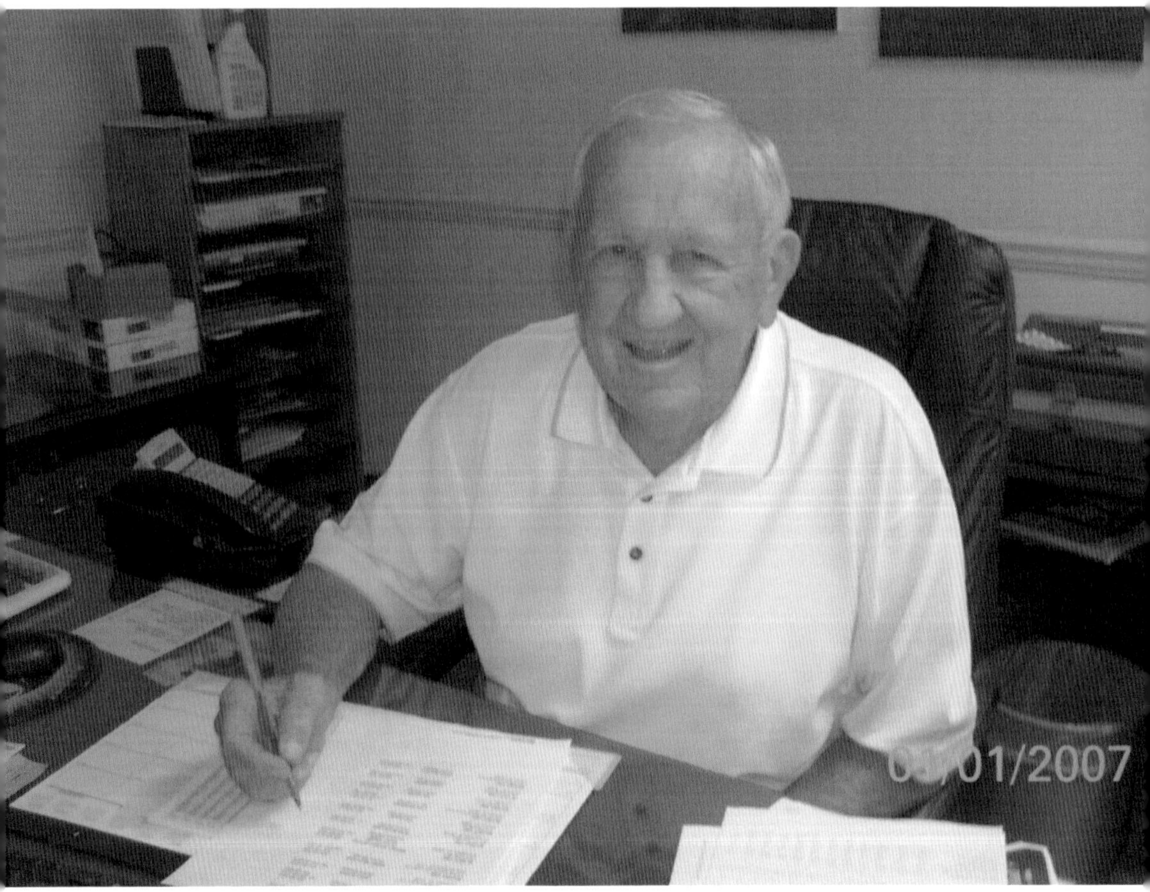

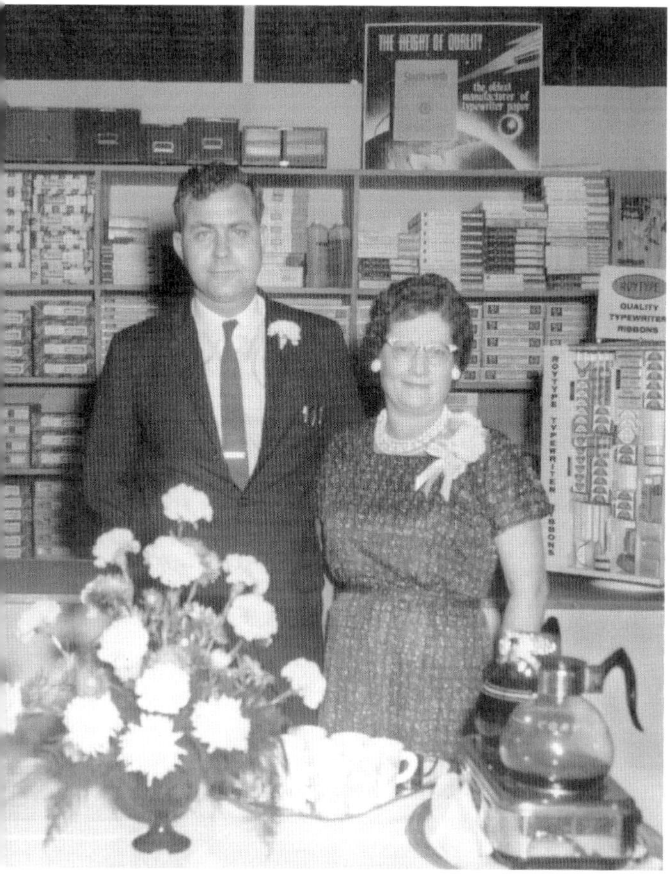

Joe Kreps

Pursuing the American dream of owning a business was Joe Kreps's goal. A linotype operator, the mission was accomplished with Powell Blair, partner. Years of hard work later, they added the *Cullman Banner* newspaper and partner Bob Bryan. By 1958, a community icon, three businesses under one roof called for decisions. Joe took the office supply business, Powell Blair took printing, and Bob Bryan got the newspaper, which became Cullman's daily publication. Joe's sons, Rickey and Rodney, worked for their dad in 1967 as teenagers picking up and cleaning manual typewriters in area schools. They were paid 25¢ per machine. After Joe's death, they purchased brothers Jimmy and Jerry's stock. Pictured are Joe Kreps, his wife Mary, and Ricky Kreps, celebrating the grand opening of Office Equipment Company at its present location. (Both images courtesy Kreps family.)

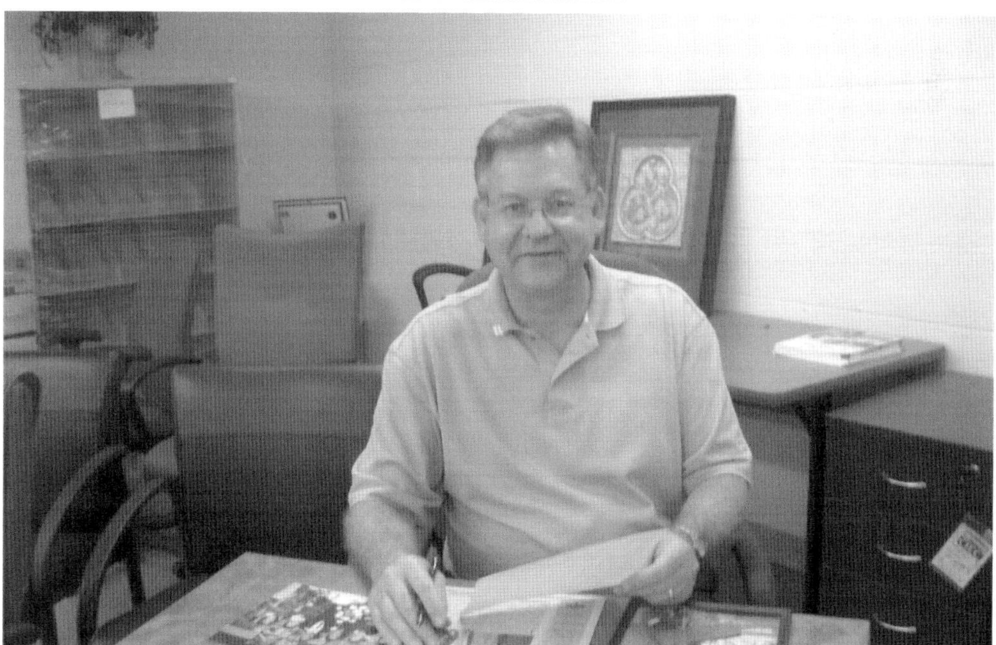

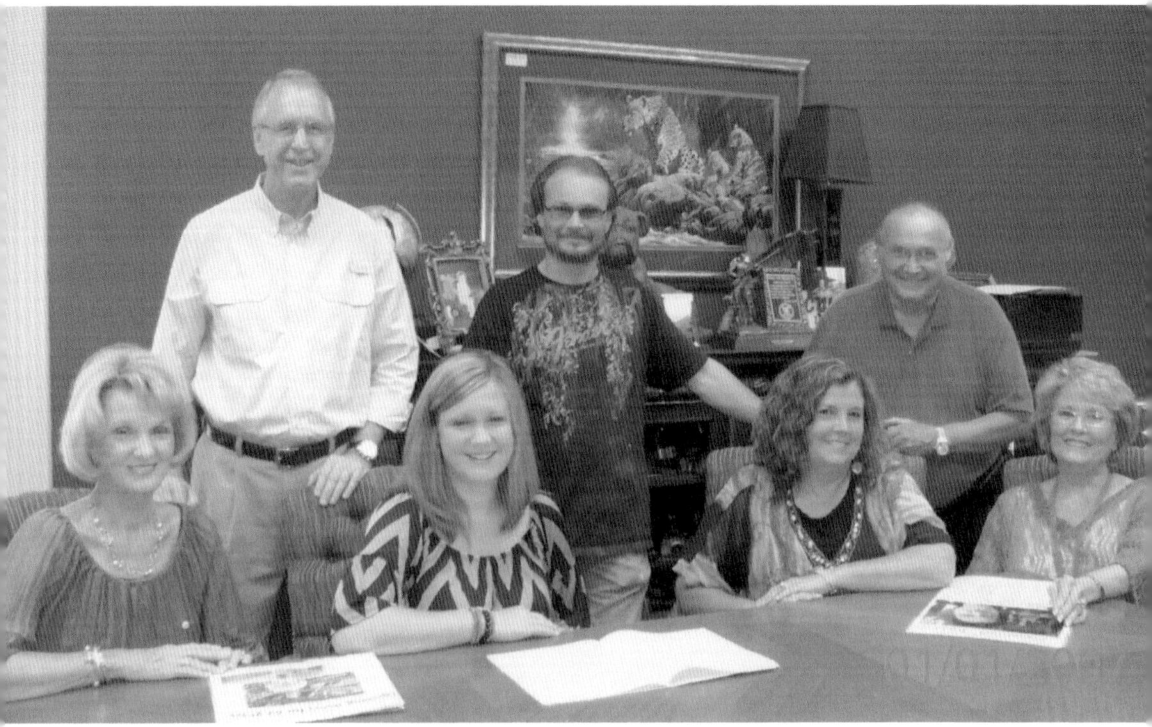

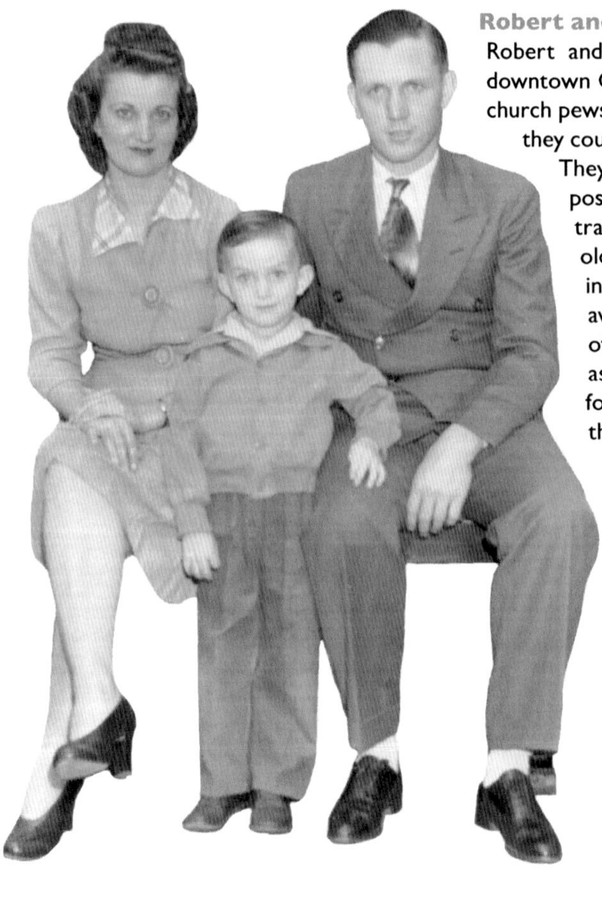

Robert and Edna Edge

Robert and Edna Edge opened Cullman Cabinet in downtown Cullman in 1947. They hung doors and built church pews and cabinets on site. He sold the idea that they could be built better off site and then installed. They purchased equipment to make laminated post-formed countertops and patented the trade name "Contour-top," making them the oldest post-form counter top manufacturer in the southeast. While Robert Edge was away, pricing a job, his son James learned of a building in Mississippi cut and ready for assembly. He bought the building and what followed was a land search, which took them to the present location on Childhaven Road. Pictured above, from left to right are (sitting) Deborah Edge McAfee, Amy McAfee Wood, Jamie Edge, and Nelson and Sandra Ratliff Edge; (standing) Danny McAfee, Robert Edge (grandson of the founding owner) and James Edge, owners. (Both images courtesy Edge family.)

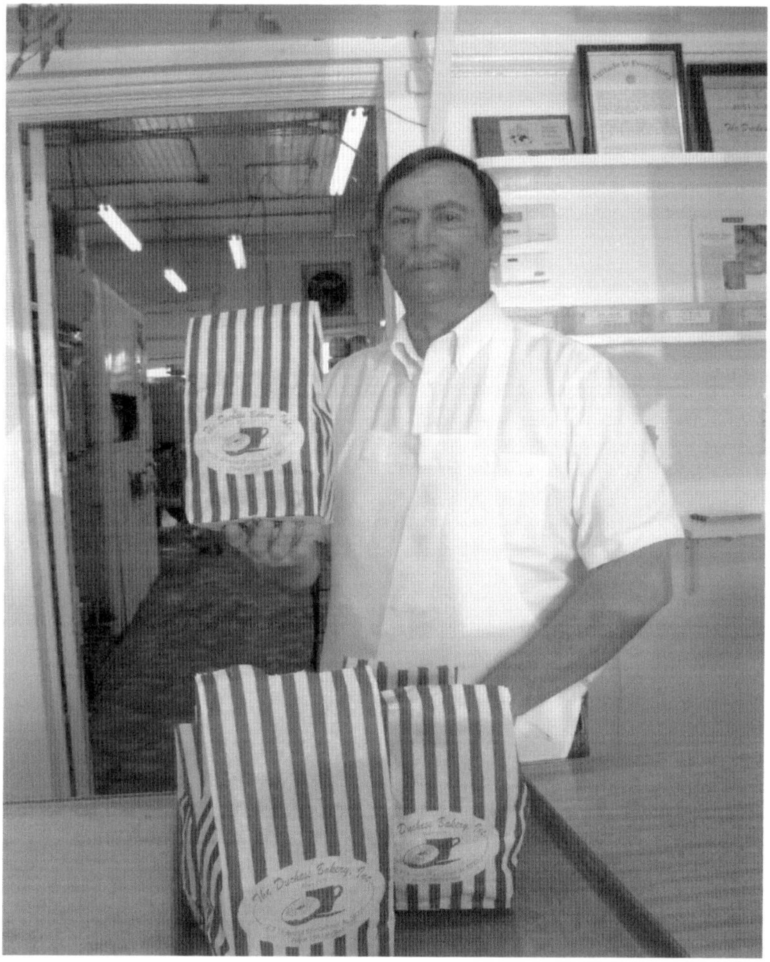

Larry Bontrager

Larry Bontrager's day starts early. The donuts must be made, gotten out of the kitchen, and ready for customers by seven o'clock. Early morning quiet on the Cullman city street is interrupted by the sound of a screen door slamming at the Duchess Bakery entrance. Customers rush to the downtown historic district area to purchase warm, melt-in-your-mouth donuts, straight from Larry's kitchen. He is the only remaining family to continue the bakery landmark, opened by Al Gasser in 1938. It was Larry's father who was to make a lasting impact on the county's baking industry. He went to work the second year the business was in operation and would be the third and final owner of Duchess Bakery after Gasser and a flour company rep named Tex. After the 1960 purchase, Troy developed a donut recipe that put Duchess Bakery on the map. He made them, and the customers came, traveling from around North Alabama to try the donuts. Tourists have the bakery on their itinerary when they come to Cullman. Larry partnered with his father in 1980. His father died in 1989. The employee-run business was incorporated in 2000. Employees can buy stock in the company. They are in the kitchen, however, at four o'clock in the morning to get ready for the seven o'clock rush. A bold, blue sign on the front window welcomes customers entering the ageless screen door. Their eyes are greeted to rows of warm donuts, bagged and waiting for take out. While donuts, still made from Troy Bontrager's recipe, are the biggest seller, there is also an array of bakery delicacies displayed in the store's glass counters. But it is the donuts that keep customers coming because when it comes to donuts, it is the duchess who wears the reigning crown. (Courtesy Kay Cagle.)

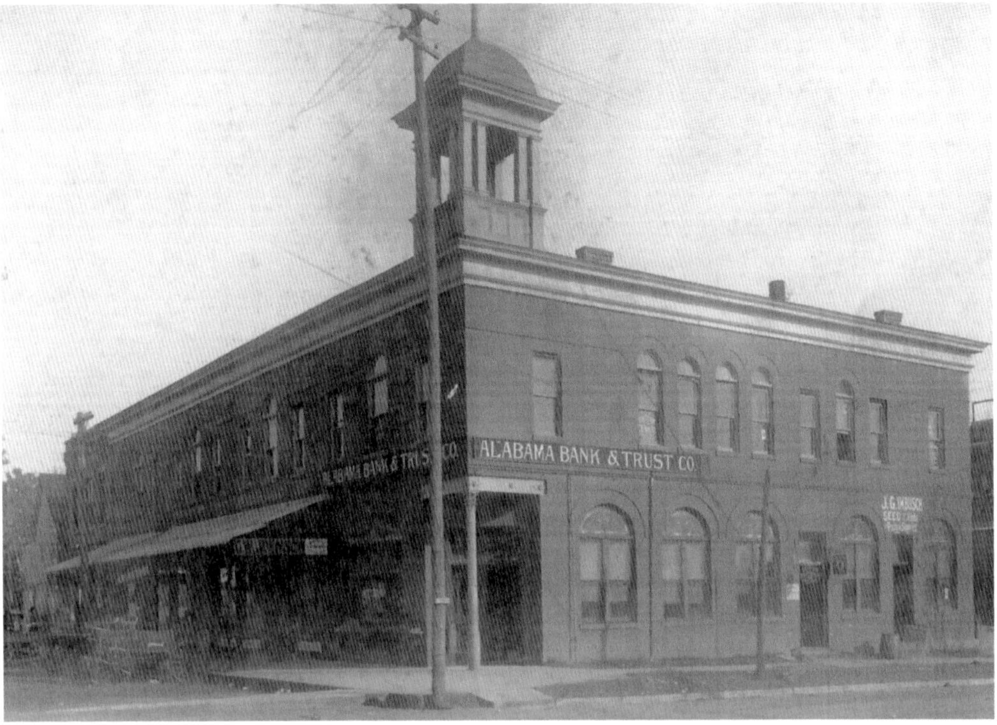

Raymond Young

Raymond Young and his family make additional efforts to keep the reputation of Mary Carter legend. It is a true hardware store with small, southern-town atmosphere. Walking down the aisles and seeing the shelf displays is a look into the past: case knives, clothespins, pots, pans, and clay churns are all visible. And, it is the only place that does free annual safety checks on pressure canners for home gardeners' food preservation. There's no charge for neighborly advice, either. Raymond put a halt to the buildings' business merry-go-round 49 years ago when Mary Carter opened. The building was constructed in 1894 and has been the site for many businesses, including its first occupant, the German Bank, then for a telephone company, and also a newspaper office. From left, the Young family visible here are sons Jeremy and Jeffrey, owner Raymond, and Raymond's wife, Brenda. (Above image courtesy Cullman County Museum; below image courtesy Kay Cagle.)

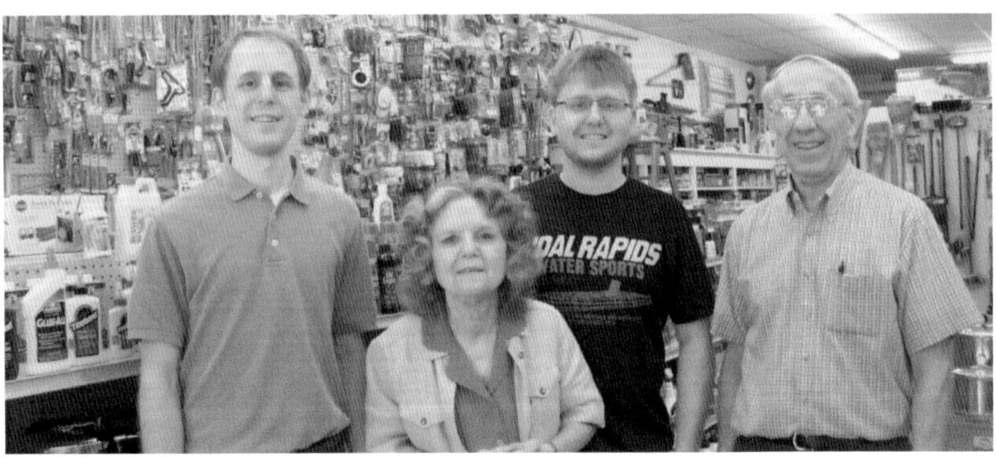

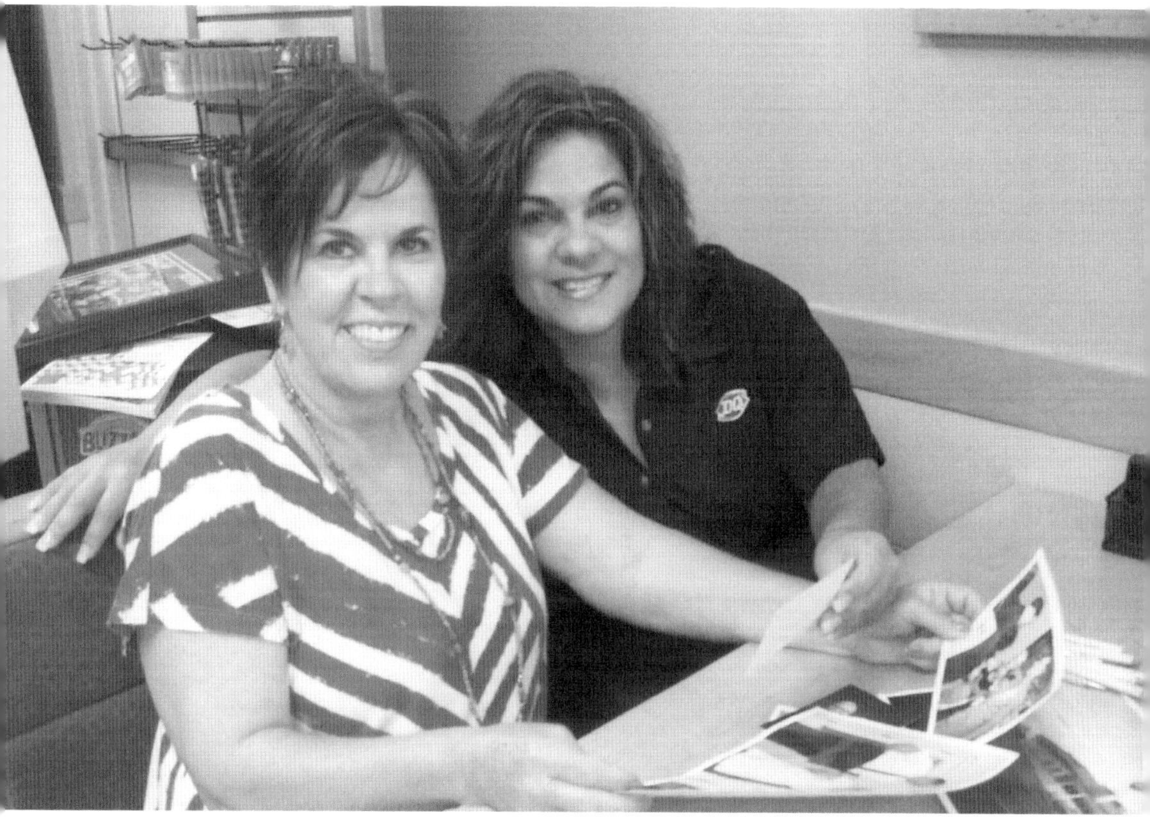

Carolyn Shadden

Carolyn Shadden emphasizes she started "just as an employee" at a Dairy Queen in Decatur, Alabama. But as her career unfolded, she not only purchased the Dairy Queen in Cullman, but took it to the No. 1-ranked business and was on the corporate board of directors for years. The original owners of the Cullman Dairy Queen, Mr. and Mrs. C.C. Adams opened the business in 1954. Carolyn purchased it from Mrs. Jo Adams, their daughter-in-law. A previous lease–real estate location, Carolyn purchased the building and land. The building has been rebuilt once and remodeled twice since she purchased it in 1982. A divorced mother, "it was a struggle at first with two children, Samantha and Joey, to educate. It was hard, but I was very determined to make a success of the business." That frame of mind has made the Cullman Dairy Queen location ranked the top store in Alabama and North Florida since the early 1990s. She listened and learned from other Dairy Queen owners, soaking up information and ideas like a sponge. "I was glued to hear successful DQ operators and how they achieved success. They taught me three basic rules of running a good business; clean store, great staff of friendly employees and the best quality of food, making sure it's hot and fresh." Carolyn emphasizes they're all about community. "We grow with the community. We've given to the community and the community as given back to us." They are big supporters and workers in the original DQ corporate sponsorship of the Children's Miracle Network, with the proceeds they collect at Cullman Dairy Queen donated to the Children's Hospital of Birmingham. As the business grew, Samantha and Joey worked with their mom when they were not in school, wiping off tables, carrying out trash, and making sure the containers were clean. "If they weren't, mom would make me redo them," Samantha says. Carolyn has retired from the Dairy Queen to open an antique store. Her daughter Samantha now owns the business, and Carolyn's grandchildren Emily and Kyle have shared the responsibilities working after school to keep the family business moving forward. (Courtesy Kay Cagle.)

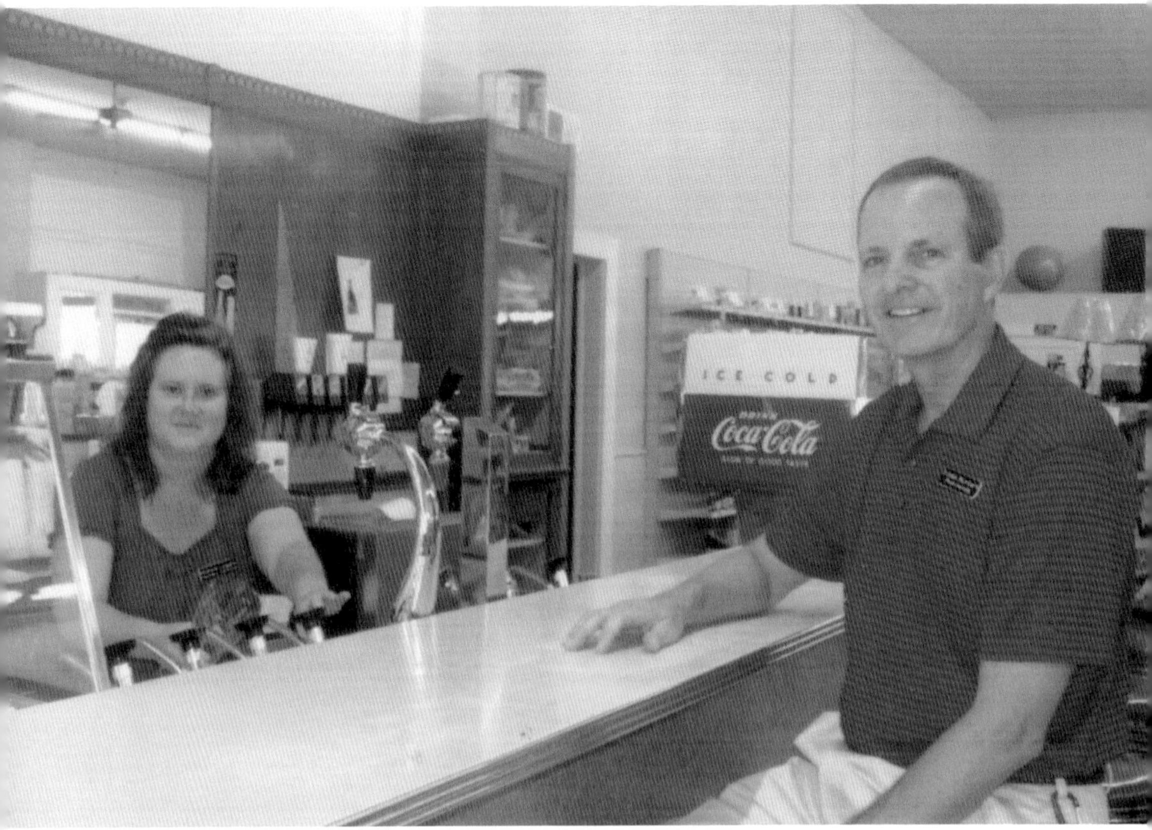

Eddie Burkart

When Eddie Burkart steps from behind the counter to take a break, he walks into the past. Not only is he the owner of Cullman County's oldest drug store, it boasts an old fashioned soda fountain that continues to draw folks who like to reminisce about the past and enjoy an ice cream treat. Hanceville Drug Store was established in 1916, and today, the Burkart's are instrumental in its preservation; their ultimate goal is keeping its small-town, personal atmosphere. Originally started by Ernest C. Veal and his brother Dr. David H. Veal, a dentist, C.T. Burkart and his brother-in-law Roy South purchased the drugstore. Mr. Burkart played football for the Crimson Tide before transferring to Alabama Polytechnic, which became Auburn University, to study pharmacy. In 1926, C.T. purchased his brother-in-law's interest. He retired after 50 years and sold the business to his son Eddie Burkart. His son continues the line of family pharmacists, still serving the local community from Hanceville Drug Store. Any day, one can find Eddie Burkart standing behind the counter, just inside the main street entrance, filling prescriptions, but it is a different scene when you look out into the soda fountain area with its 1950s décor of stools at the counter and cozy booths on the side. Hanceville Drug Store is a popular setting for early-morning coffee drinkers who meet to discuss local events. In the past, students from Hanceville High School met at Hanceville Drug Store to imbibe the popular drink of the time, a Cherry-Coke. It was also considered a proper place for young courting couples to meet with friends. Although there may have been soda drink changes through the years, the overall look and feel of Hanceville Drug Store has been preserved during improvements over the years by the Burkhart family. (Courtesy Kay Cagle.)

CHAPTER THREE

Spiritual Roots Run Deep

From the beginning, religion played a major role in the lives of settlers. Forging a new life in virgin territory was racked with daily hardships, but their faith never wavered. There were two theological concepts revealed in the opening of Alabama territories: the Virginia plantation owners who brought with them slaves and genteel Charleston mannerisms and the dirt farmers who brought a stern, fundamental faith, deeply rooted in the doctrine of universal atonement and free grace. The early churches were crudely built and poorly heated, but structures were secondary. Immigrants only wanted a place to worship according to their beliefs. On most occasions, the building also served as the community's school, becoming the civic, educational and cultural center of the community.

St. John's Evangelical Protestant Church was the first church established. The patriarch's name, Col. Johann G. Cullmann, heads the constitution of St. John's Church, formally established on May 1, 1874, exactly one year after the arrival of the first German colonists. Others in a vital role of founding St. John's were Andrew and Henry Kessler, Adam Dreher, Nick Ruehl, Jacob Kullmann, Jacob von Gerichten, Charles Hoffmyer, and Gottfried Prinz.

Southern Benedictine and St. Bernard Abbey were established in the early years to educate German children. Most recently the Shrine of the Blessed Sacrament was located in Cullman County. It is also the home of Mother Angelica, founder of Eternal Word Television Network. There were special individuals who did not seek praise for themselves, but served in positions to benefit their fellow man. Cullman has as many as 24 churches representing 14 denominations, and countywide, almost 300 rural churches, representing 23 denominations. In the beginning, Cullman offered to donate two acres of property to any religious denomination wanting to establish a church.

Spiritual roots may have trembled on occasion. Fire and storms have changed the physical appearance of worship centers but could not quell the spirit of rebuilding. The spirit was bent, but not broken. Evidence of this abounds in the rebuilding of churches heavily damaged and destroyed in the April 27, 2011, tornado.

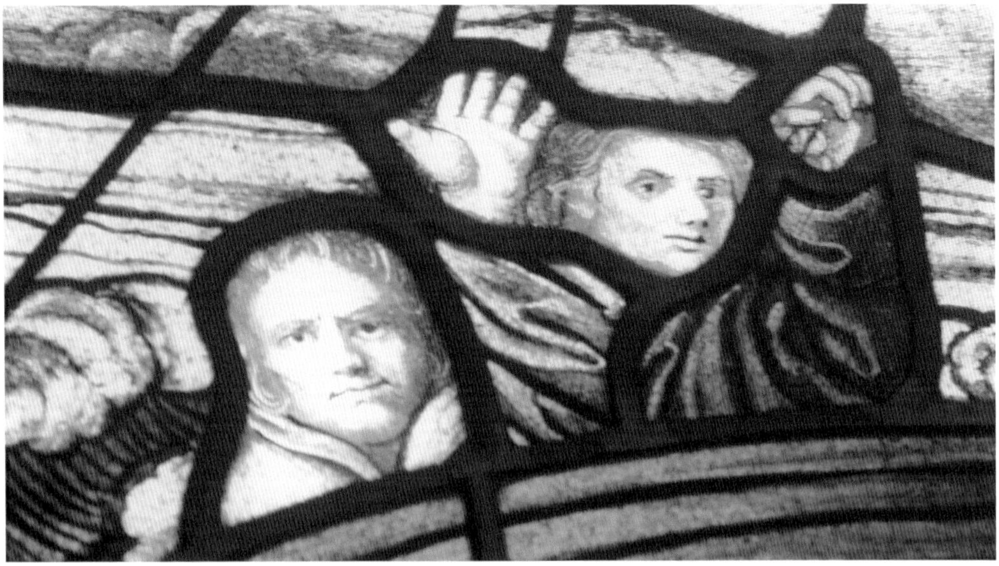

Theodore Von Gerichten

The stained-glass windows in St. John's Evangelical Protestant Church were made by the famed Von Gerichten Art Glass Company, headed by brothers Theodore and Ludwig Von Gerichten. They were nephews of Col. Johann G. Cullmann and started their business in Cullman. They then moved to Cincinnati, Ohio, and Munich, Germany. Theodore ran the Cincinnati operation, and when St. John's turned to him to help decorate their new sanctuary in 1922, he returned while the work was installed. The windows depict the life of Christ. Two of Von Gerichten's artists immortalized themselves in the window depicting Peter walking on water to meet Jesus. The faces of the two disciples still inside the boat are those of the artists themselves. On December 31, 1922, St. John's laid the cornerstone for the current building. (Both images courtesy St. John's Church.)

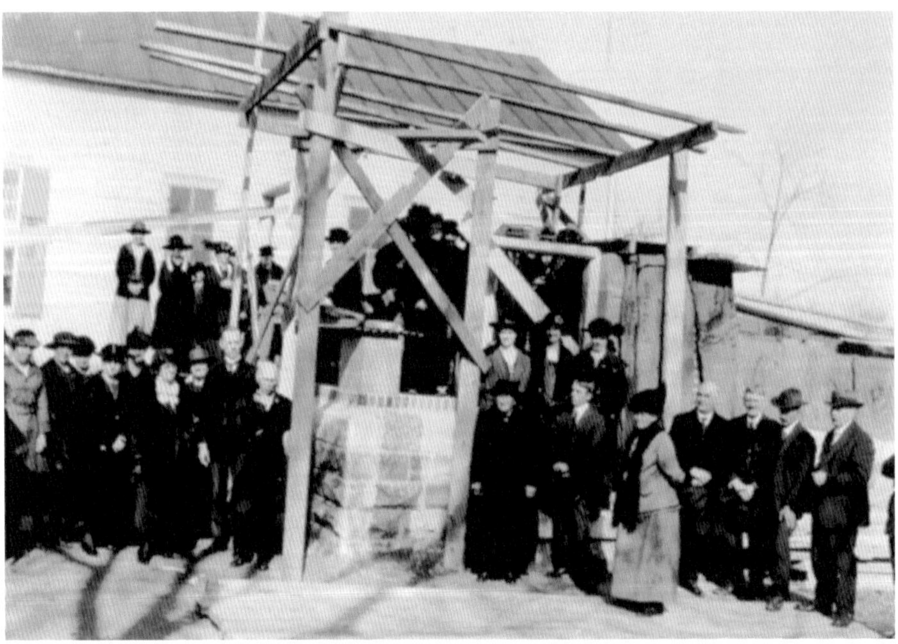

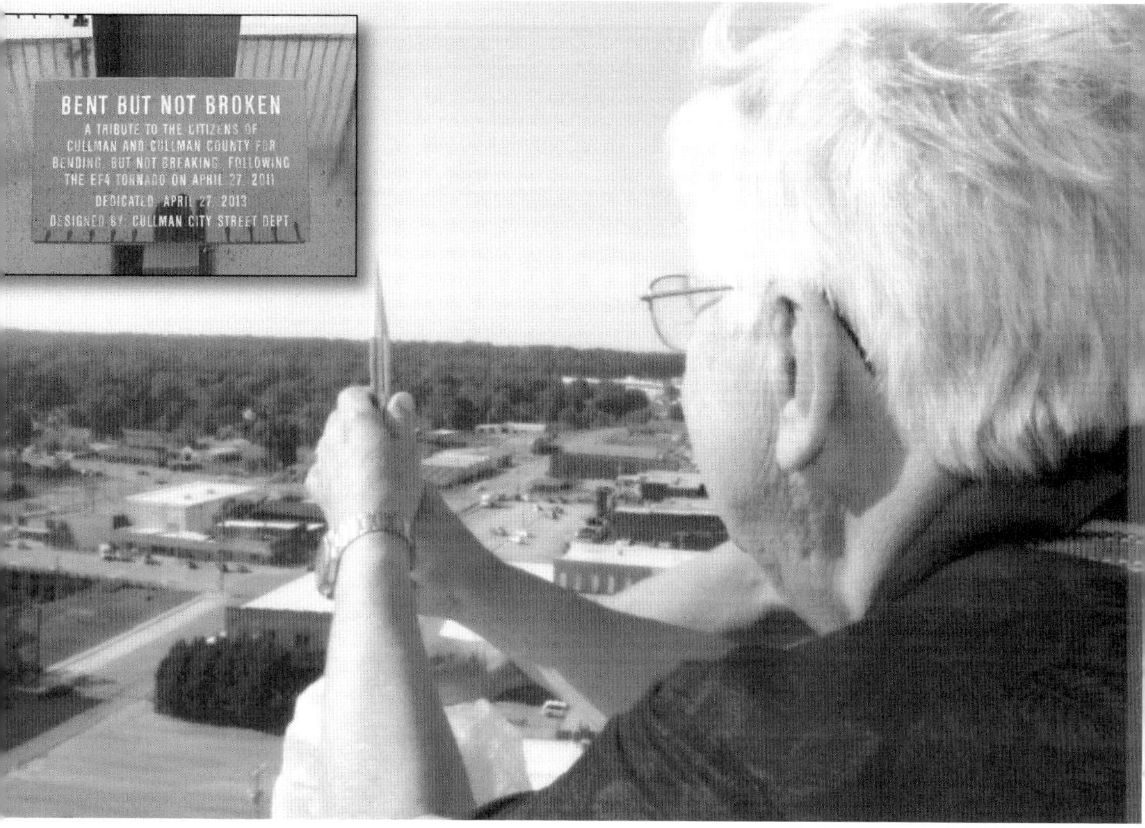

Dr. Edwin Hayes

On April 27, 2011, an EF-4 tornado destroyed or badly damaged approximately 63 businesses and 200 homes in Cullman. Approximately 300 homes were damaged or destroyed, along with multiple county businesses. A unified spirit was born to overcome nature's fury: "Bent But Not Broken." A memorial was placed in Heritage Park as a reminder, commemorating a spirit to rise from the rubble. Councilman Johnny Cook coined the phrase "Bent But Not Broken." When the steeple was replaced at First Baptist Church, Dr. Edwin Hayes, a retired minister, dedicated the newly placed cross by reading John 12:32. He prayed that all whose eyes were raised to view it would be drawn to Jesus, as the Lord had promised they would be. (Courtesy Jennifer Tanner.)

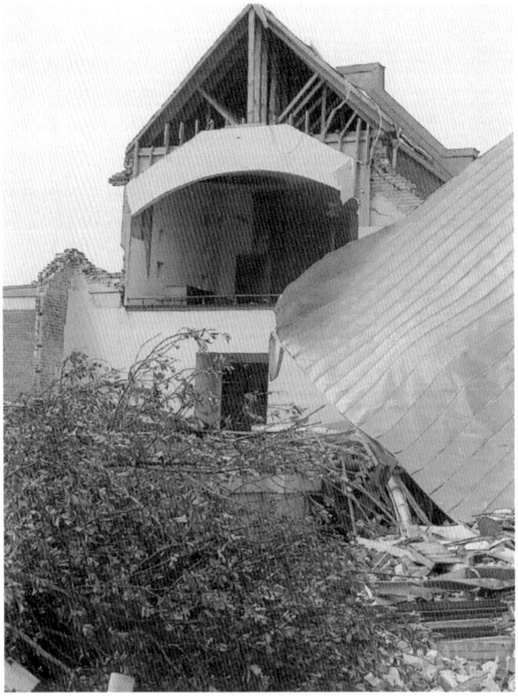

Zinsmeister and Posey Families

Buddy Zinsmeister, daughter Melody, and family pet Bear sought shelter in their home church, Christ Lutheran, when imminent tornado warnings sounded. They stood in the basement doorway hearing the destruction overhead. Randy Posey, his family, and 10 other people hovered in the stairwell basement at their church, First United Methodist Church. His family was headed to Hanceville, south of Cullman, but an earlier tornado in that city prevented them from going and he urged them to come to the church. Another woman was outside taking pictures. He got her inside and pushed the door shut when they began to hear the noise. The above destruction photographs of Christ Lutheran and First United Methodist are what the residents saw when they walked outside the church. (Both images courtesy First United Methodist Church and Johnny Fricke.)

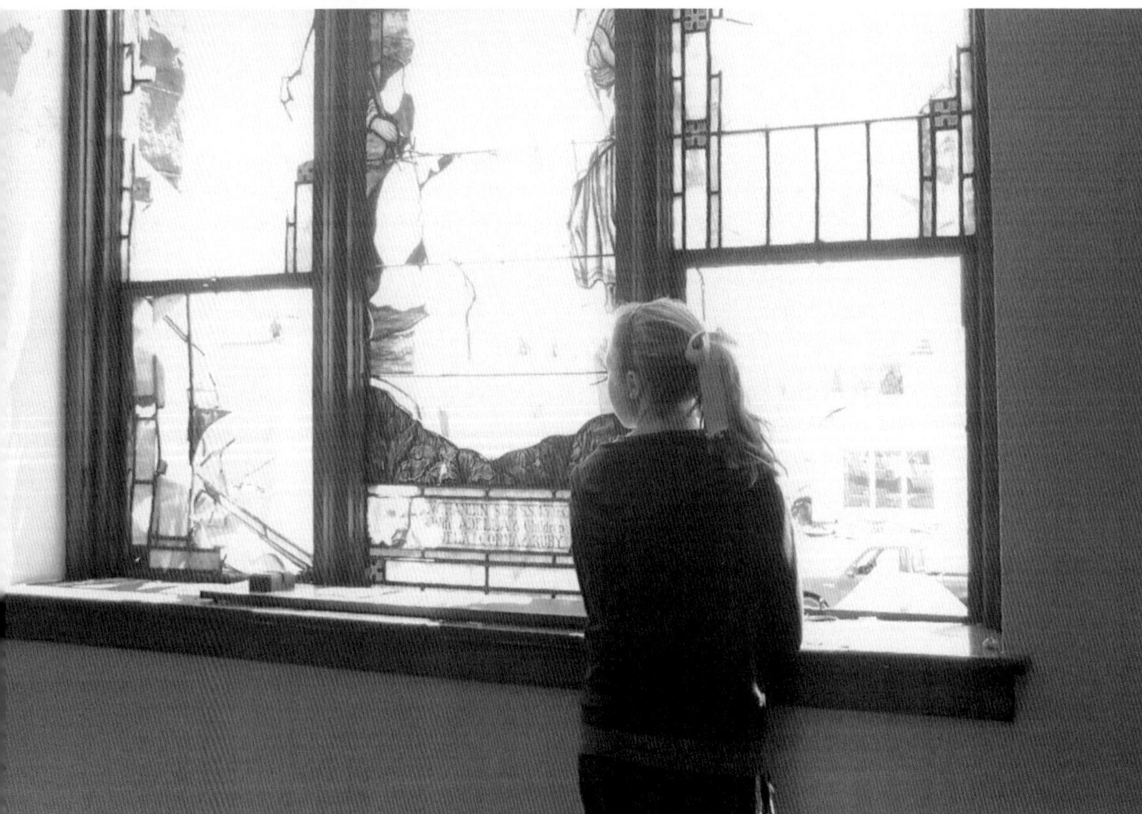

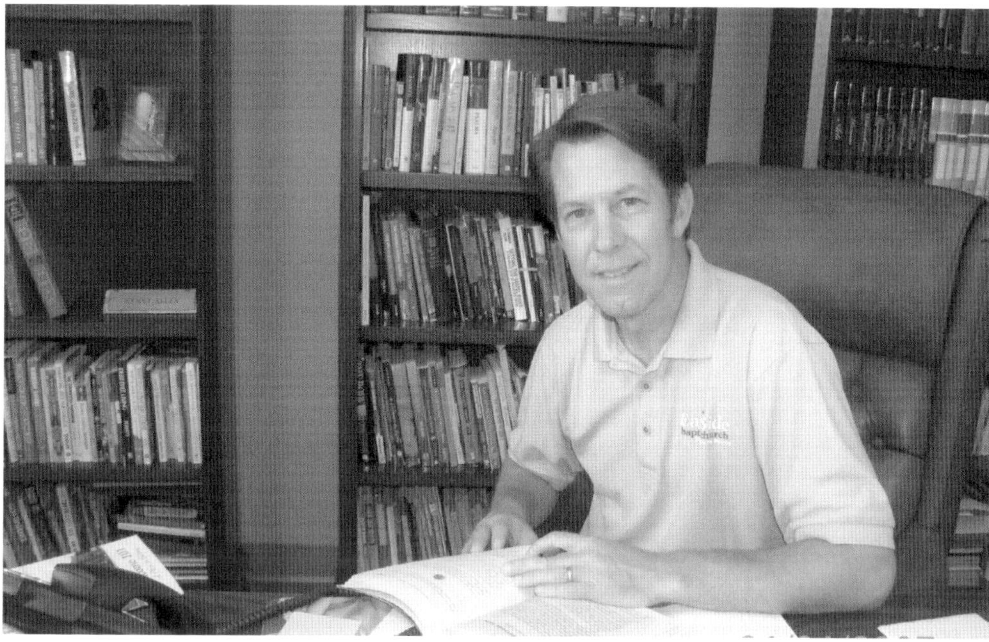

Pastor Ken Allen

The church was their shelter during a storm. Pastor Ken Allen, his family, church secretary and neighbors were at East Side Baptist Church, in the basement under the stairwell. Pastor Allen had his family close, watching the storms' progress on the Internet. "We kept looking toward downtown and asking where is it? We saw debris, but not the funnel. But then it was on us in seconds. My daughter recorded the noise, the sound and screams. When we walked outside, it was so surreal, like a bomb had gone off. It was a terrible sight." (Above image courtesy Kay Cagle; below image courtesy Ken Allen.)

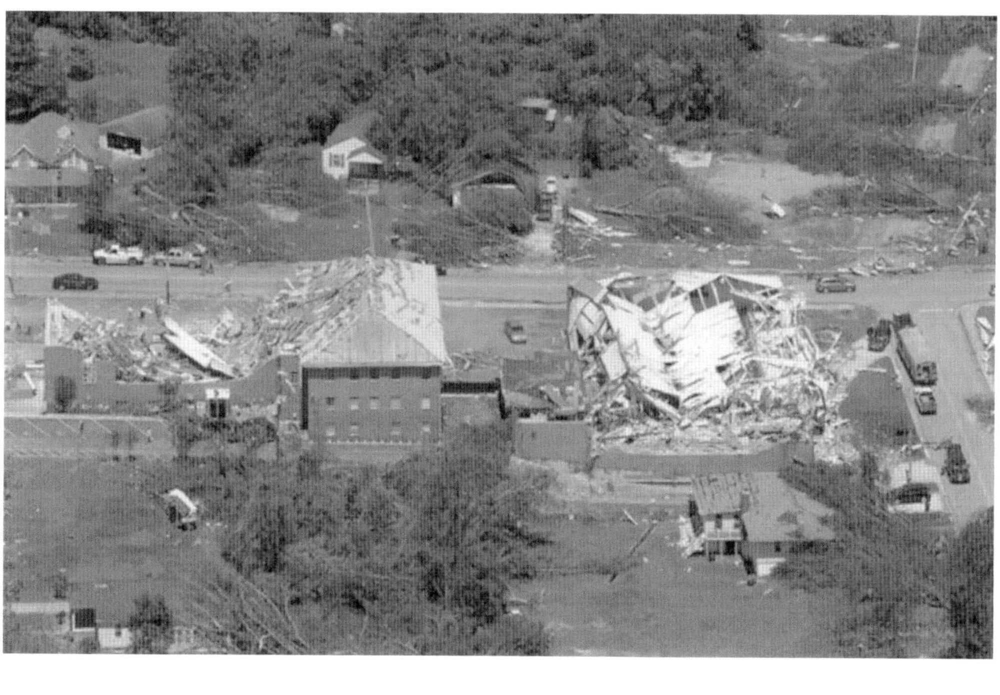

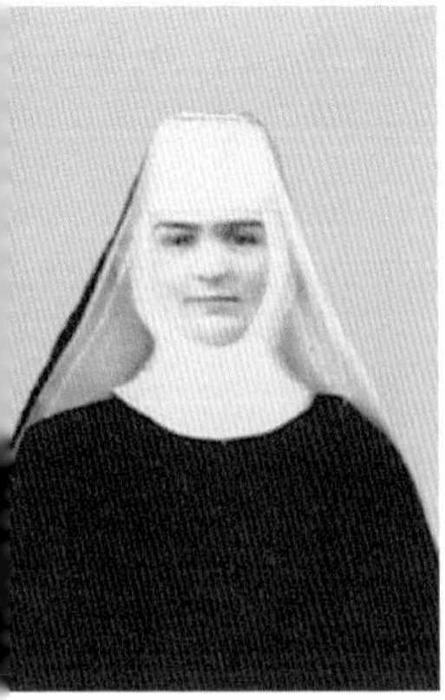
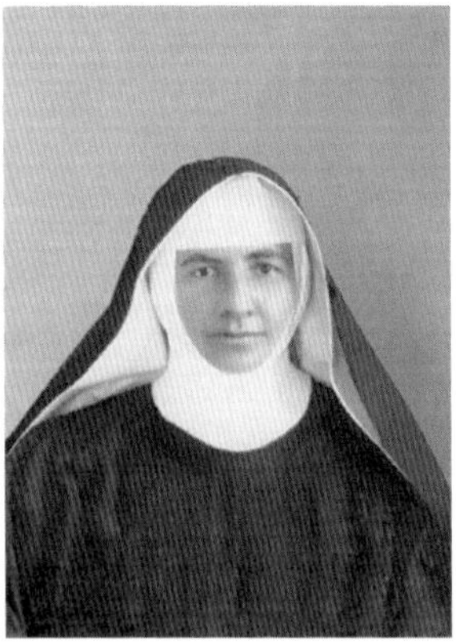
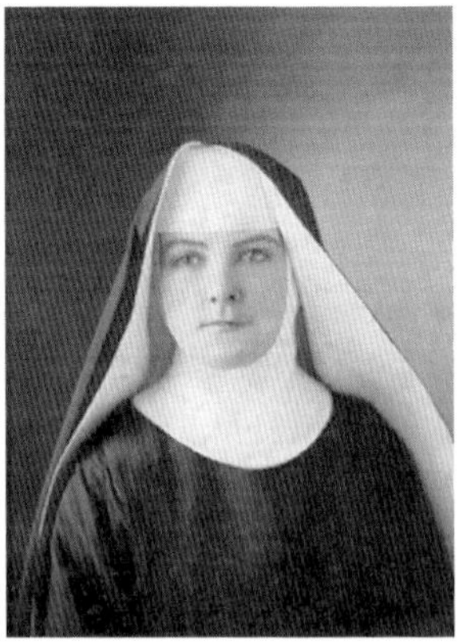
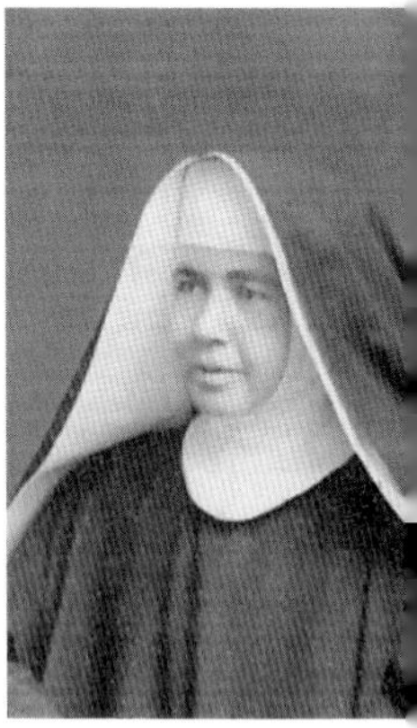

Sacred Heart Monastery

"We've been teachers from day one," says Sister Janet Marie Flemming, prioress of the Benedictine Sisters of Cullman, Sacred Heart Monastery. "We were needed to teach children of German immigrants answering Colonel Cullman's invitation to settle here and other sites in north Alabama. Today, we are still sisters teaching at high school and college levels." In addition, there are two ministries on the monastery grounds; Benedictine Manor, an independent living facility for senior adults, and the Benedictine Sisters' retreat center. The sister's professional involvement in the community and state includes a physician, lawyer, and nurses, as well as pastoral ministers in several parishes. "Our sisters use whatever God's gifts they may have to serve God's people," Sister Janet added. Two orders of Benedictine Sisters merged to establish the Sacred Heart Monastery: St. Walburg Convent from Covington, Kentucky, and Holy Name Priory from San Antonio, Florida. "They came here because the Bishop in Alabama wanted the sisters to educate girls and pray for people in his diocese," Sister Janet Marie says. The decision led 16 hardy pioneering sisters, ages 18–61 to Cullman, first in 1881 and then 1898. Most of the pioneers had already experienced hardships, preparing them for this daunting task in the small town of Cullman. Of the pioneers, one was a German immigrant and 10 were first-generation German Americans. Their families left Germany during the political turmoil, either the Revolution of 1848 or Bismark's *Kulturkampf* (an 1870s culture struggle to reduce the Church's power). Their first major decision was to select a leader in their risk-taking. On July 7, 1902, they elected Sister M. Ottilia, Haas O.S.B. as prioress. She lost no time. In 1903, the community bought 123.5 acres of farmland outside the city limits for $2,000, almost exhausting their combined treasury. They began saving to build a structure large enough for the sisters and an academy for girls. Some sisters lived in a small house on the property during construction. They helped build, and they denied themselves extra food, new clothing, and everyday staples in order to save money, and cleaned and carried stones for the basement and interior walls. This structure

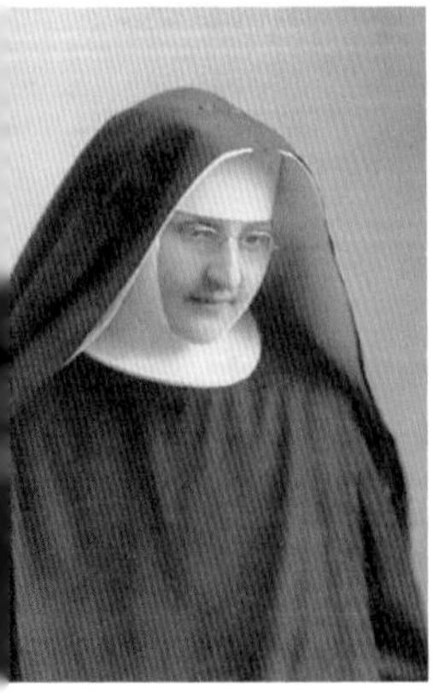
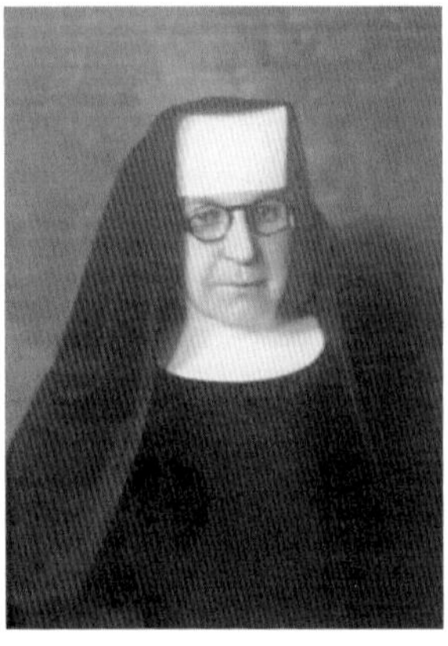
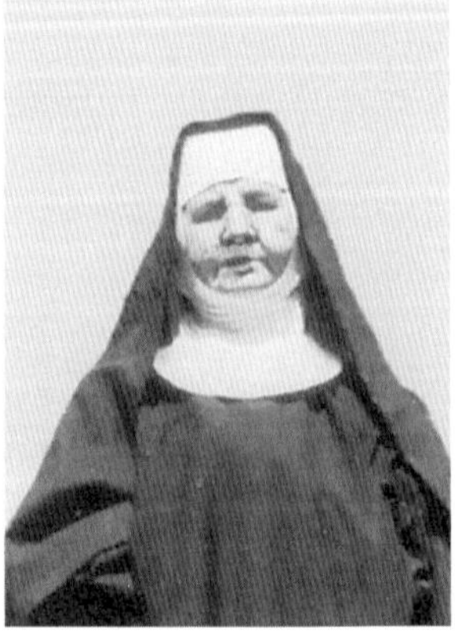
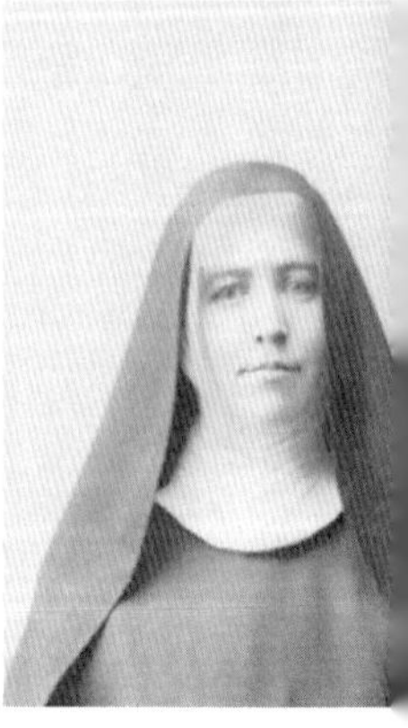

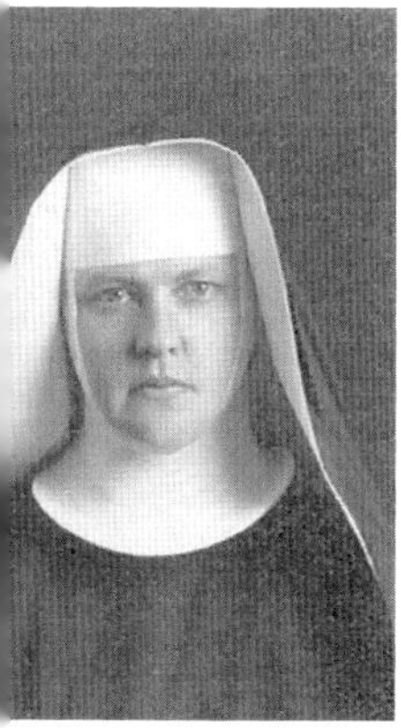
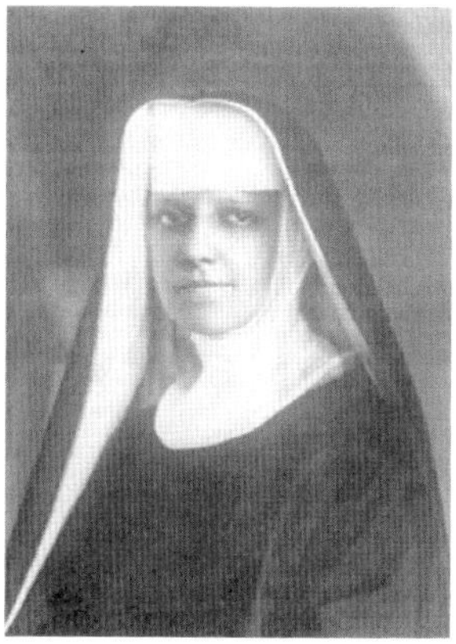
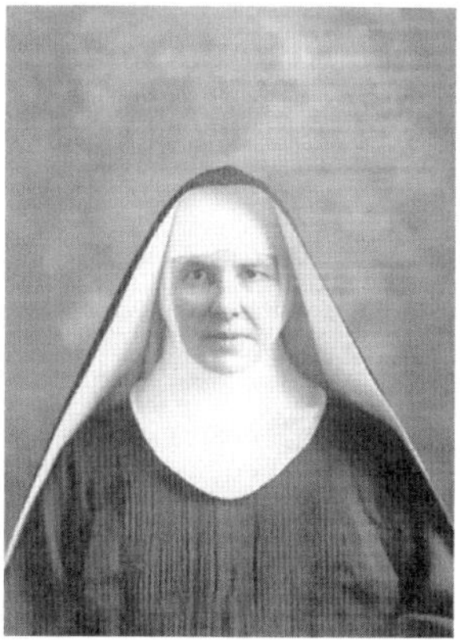
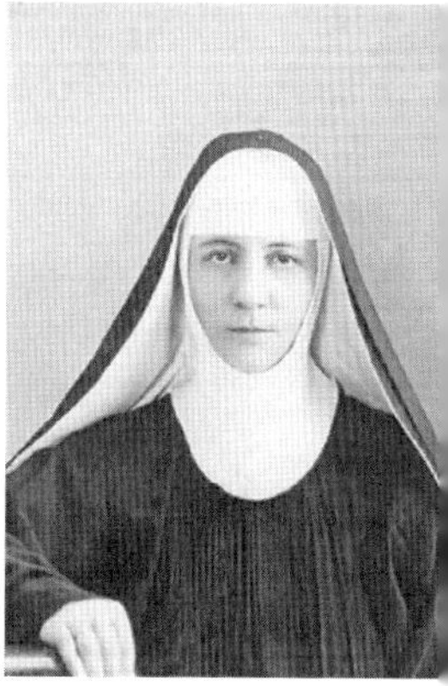

provided accommodations for classrooms, a library, small music practice rooms, parlors, office space, and a chaplain's room. The community's first educational ministry began September 14, 1904, when Sacred Heart Academy opened its doors to 29 girls for primary grades to high school. A standard curriculum was expanded to include an array music and art instruction. To pay off loans and support increasing numbers of students, Mother Ottilia borrowed from several banks. With good stewardship and efforts of all the building was debt-free by 1929. Then the sisters took on another project: building the beautiful Sacred Heart Chapel, providing much-needed work for Cullman artisans during the Great Depression. Both the community and academy grew rapidly; in 1940, Bishop Toolen asked the sisters to create a two-year school for women. In the early 1960s, the community built a large dormitory for college girls. When they wanted to name it Janeway Hall in honor of their second prioress, Mother Annunciata Janeway, she would not agree unless they named the original building Ottilia Hall in honor of the first prioress.

Another development has affected the current life of the sisters. They responded courageously to the mandates of the Second Vatican Council of the Roman Catholic Church by updating many of their customs and diversifying their ministries. They continued to move forward in serving God's people in Cullman and throughout the southeast. The sisters began in 1902 with a single hope; to serve wherever God led them. That same hope animates them today. They care carrying forward into a new millennium the ancient Benedictine life of prayer, community, and ministry. The founding sisters are, from left to right, (first row) Sister Adelaide Meyer, Sister Gertrude Nieman, Sister Boniface Jochum, Sister Benedicta McLaughlin, Sister Scholastica McLaughlin, Sister Perpetua Tape, Sister Ottilia Haas, and Sister Baptista Wagner; (second row) Sister Cecelia Oberfell, Sister Josephine Feldung, Sister Annunciata Janeway, Scholastica Feldung, Sister Mary Donahue, Sister Mary Grace Jankosky, Sister Agatha Geisler and Sister Boniface Feldman: (Images courtesy Benedictine Sisters, Sacred Heart Monastery.)

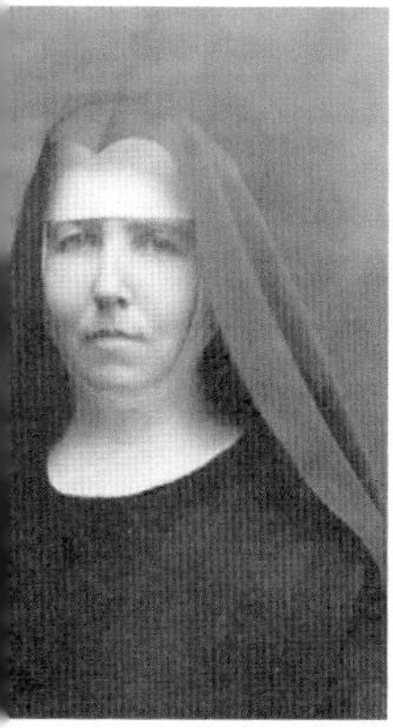
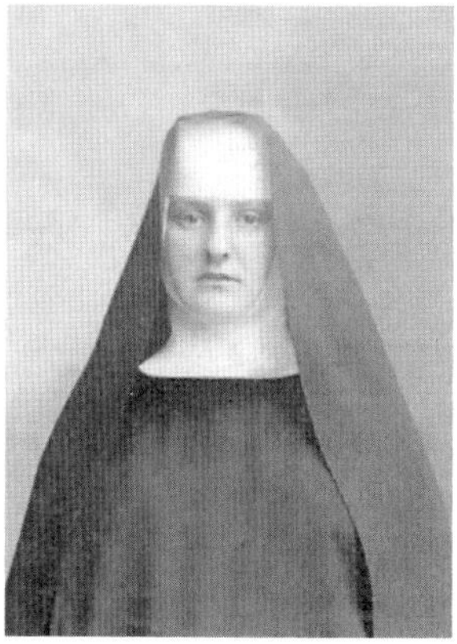
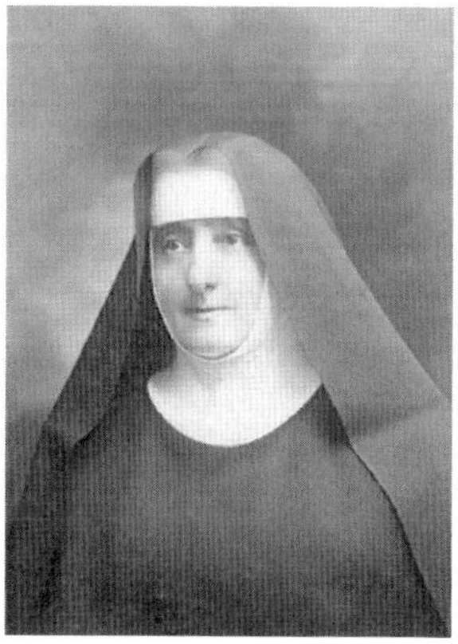
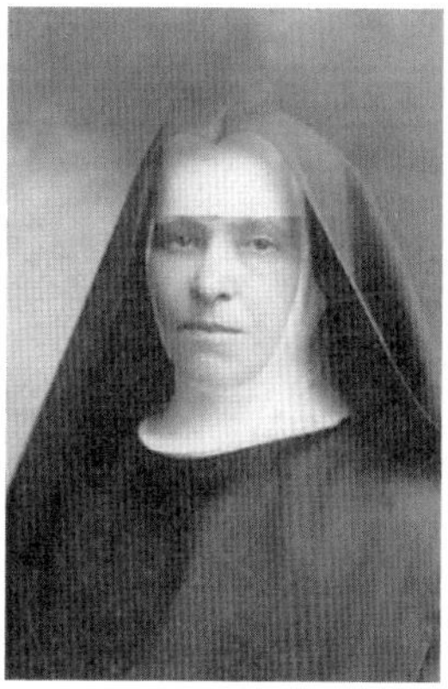

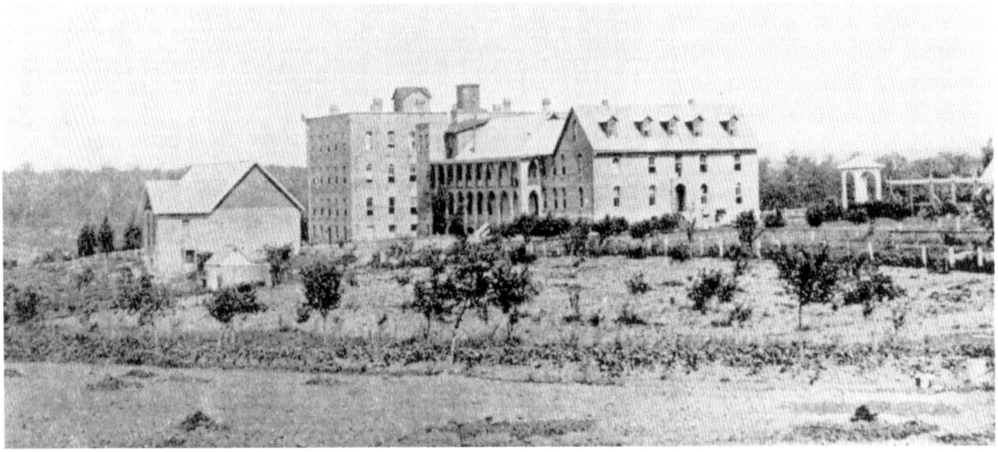

St. Bernard Abbey

Diocese officials agreed, a Benedictine monastery and college would be built in Cullman. Father Gamelbert Brunner, O.S.B., purchased acreage with monies loaned by the Brunner family, which was added to 360 acres purchased "by the generosity of Cullman citizens." He crossed the bridge that spanned Eight-Mile Creek below the Schmidt Farm and viewed a small clearing. It was decided St. Bernard Abbey would be built there. The first shovel of earth was turned in 1891, and by 1892, a two-story oratory with kitchen and living quarters and chapel were constructed. Focusing on male education, the first school enrollment was 48 students, 15 of which were from Cullman. Tuition, room, bedding, and laundry cost $180. The image above is of the Abbey in late 1800s, and the image below shows the founding fathers and their first students. (Both images courtesy St. Bernard Abbey.)

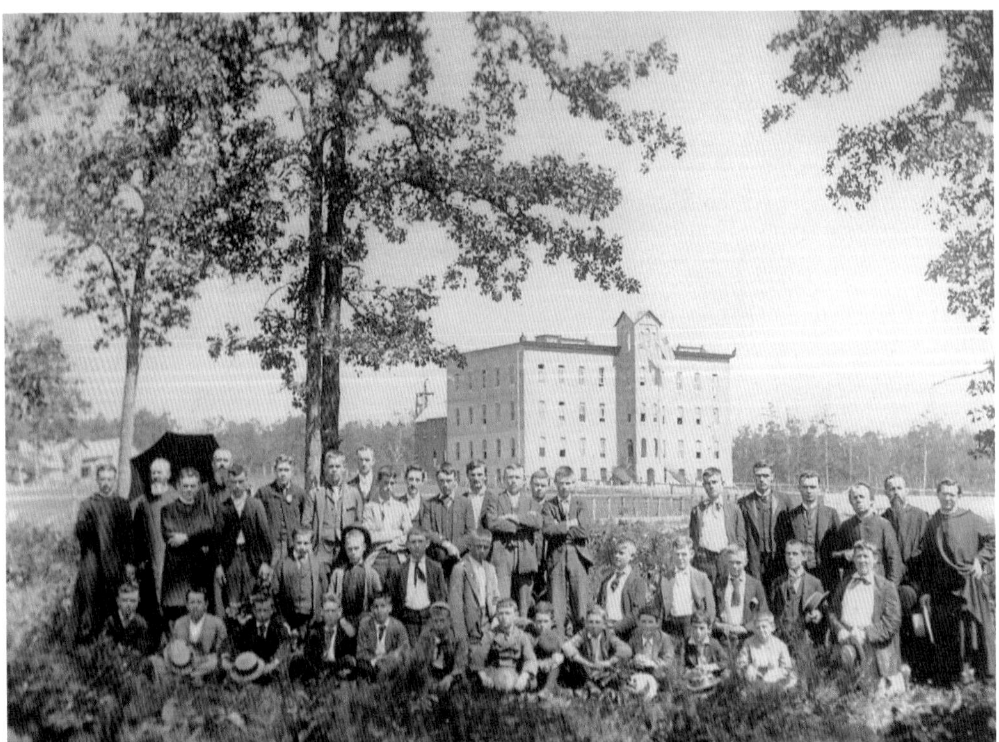

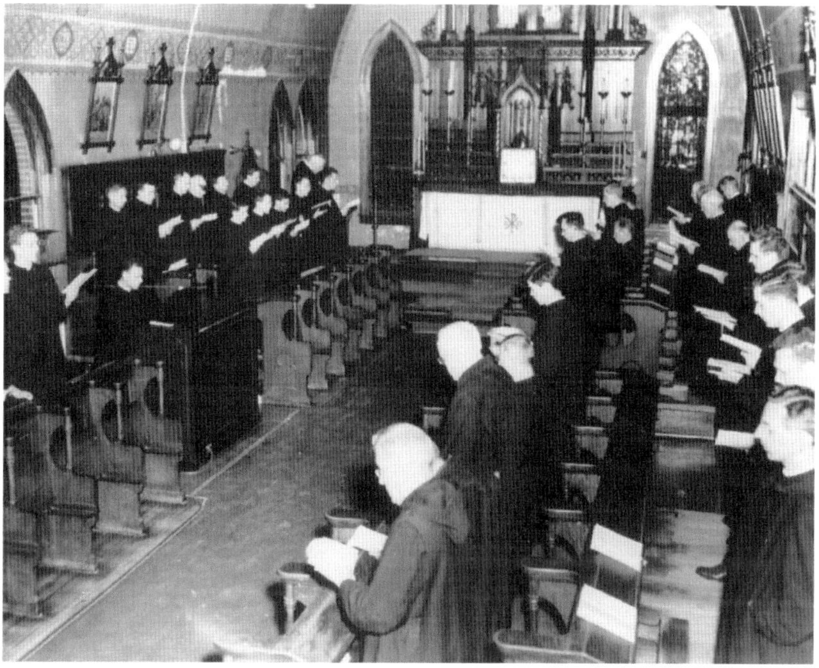

Spiritual Commitment and the Arts

The first chapel for St. Bernard Abbey had a primitive main altar, temporary side altar for the Blessed Sacrament, a pair of *prie-dieus*, a harmonium on a low platform, and hand-made pews. Pictured today, Benedictines worship in a sanctuary centrally located on the campus. Students at St. Bernard ranged from elementary to high school and junior college status by 1933. The curriculum included a rigorous and disciplined environment of learning, including music and the arts. After World War II, the campus and farming expanded. Currently, farm operations have ceased and the land converted to forestland. The college closed in 1979, and St. Bernard Preparatory School was opened in 1984 with the focus on college-prep levels of academic learning. (Both images courtesy St. Bernard Abbey.)

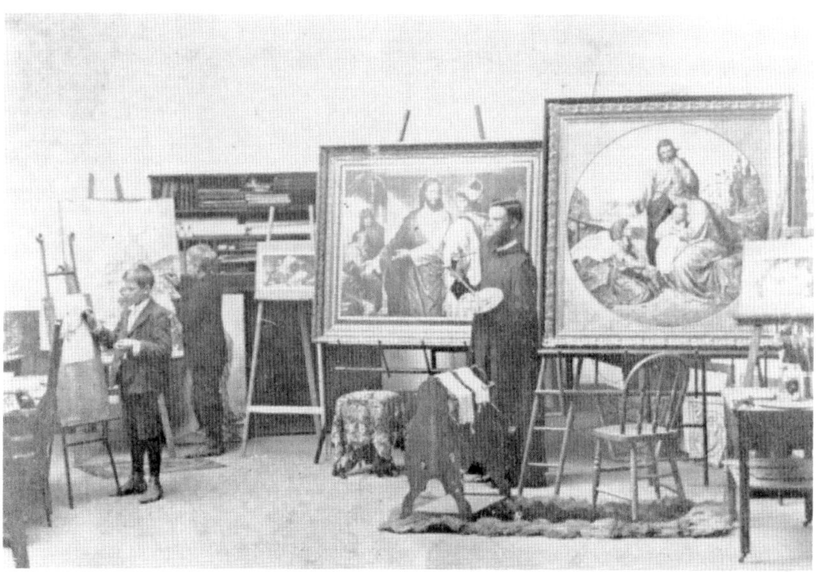

Shelton Grove Baptist Church

The Civil War, a wounded, young cavalry officer, and love for a pretty girl is the bond cementing the foundation of Shelton Grove Baptist Church. Henry Shelton, great-grandfather of Delane Shelton, was a Tennessee volunteer assigned to the Confederate Alabama Calvary. Henry's brother was the commanding officer. Henry was wounded on the trail, somewhere between what is now Johnson Crossing and Dodge City during Gen. Bedford Forest's pursuit of Colonel Streight. He could not travel with his unit and recuperated at the Dunlevy home. During that time, he fell in love with Margaret Dunlevy and could not stop thinking about her even after returning to his military headquarters. After the war, he returned and married Margaret, and from the Dunlevy area in Dodge City, the couple traveled to the top of the mountain, now known as Shelton Grove and built a cabin. The cabin site is where the church's current picnic shelter was built. The couple homesteaded several hundred acres of land, and every time a new child was born, a total three boys and three girls, Henry and Margaret acquired more acreage. The boys were Dave, Jim, and Joe. Joe was Delane Shelton's grandfather.

As the family grew and area became more populated, Henry and Margaret constructed a small building that was to serve as one structure for a worship center, school, and social meeting place. When Henry died, then Margaret a few years later, the children buried their parents in the back yard establishing a family cemetery. Those family plots are a part of the expanded Shelton Grove Church cemetery. The church became organized and named Shelton Grove in 1923 and it was agreed, communitywide, it should be named after Henry and Margaret Shelton, becoming Shelton Grove Baptist Church. (Courtesy Kay Cagle.)

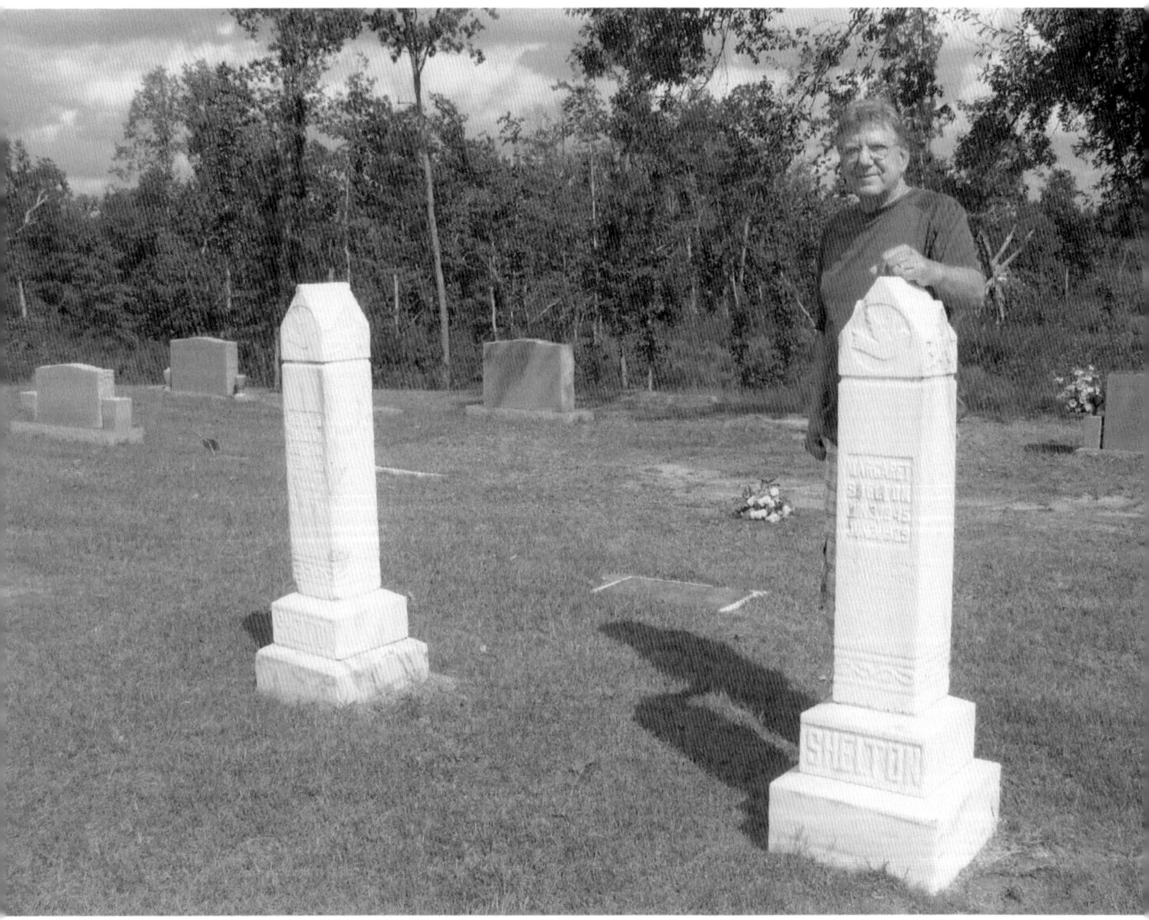

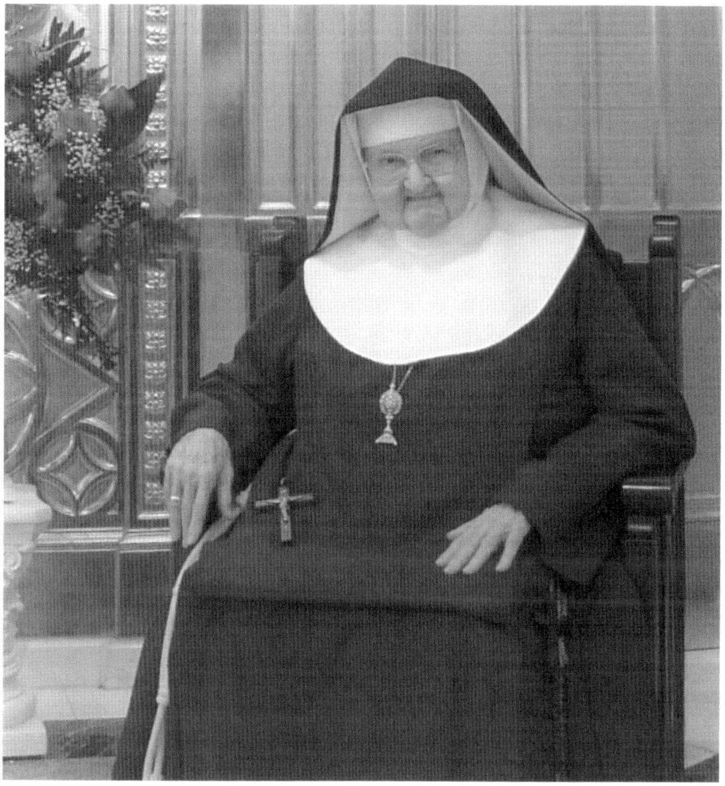

Mother Angelica

The nun known to millions on the television network EWTN, Mother Angelica's goal was to make the God she loves known and loved by others. Born Rita Rizzo in 1923 in Canton, Ohio, a severe stomach ailment as a teenager helped her realized God's immense love through an incredible recovery which lead her to resolve to give herself totally to God. She received her holy habit a year after entering the PCPA monastery in Cleveland, Ohio, becoming Sister Mary Angelica of the Annunciation. While cleaning at Sancta Clara Monastery, an accident caused a back injury and operation that threatened paralysis. She promised God that if she could walk after surgery, she would build Him a monastery in the South. With the aid of leg braces, several years later she was granted permission to fulfill that vow. Her promise to build a monastery in the Lord's honor was kept. Our Lady of the Angels Monastery was dedicated in 1962. She gave spiritual talks, wrote mini-books, hosted studio productions, and is the founder of EWTN, Eternal Word Television Network, a worldwide Catholic Multimedia Enterprise. Mother Angelica's show endeared her to people from every walk of life, disarmed the wry, and enabled her to befriend the lonely. As the Poor Clare Nuns at the Irondale, Alabama, monastery increased and EWTN grew, Mother Angelica decided to relocate to a rural place. Dedication of the Shrine of the Most Blessed Sacrament and Our Lady of the Angels Monastery was held in Cullman County in 1999. Mother Angelica continues to live at the monastery with her sisters. She suffered a severe cerebral hemorrhage on Christmas Eve 2001 but made a remarkable recovery, although never regaining full ability to speak. Although her life does not fully resemble days past, she is beloved Mother to millions through her programs, and her work is more significant in the heart of the church. She was named Abbess Emeritus and received the significant Pro Ecclesia et Pontificae in 2009, a tribute to a woman of great faith. According to Sister Mary Michael, PCPA, monastery vicar, Mother Angelica said she would live a long life and she has celebrated her 91st birthday. "She has always had a great deal of suffering and pain, but it never made her bitter or resentful. She knew God had a purpose for it and accepted it as a blessing." (Courtesy EWTN.)

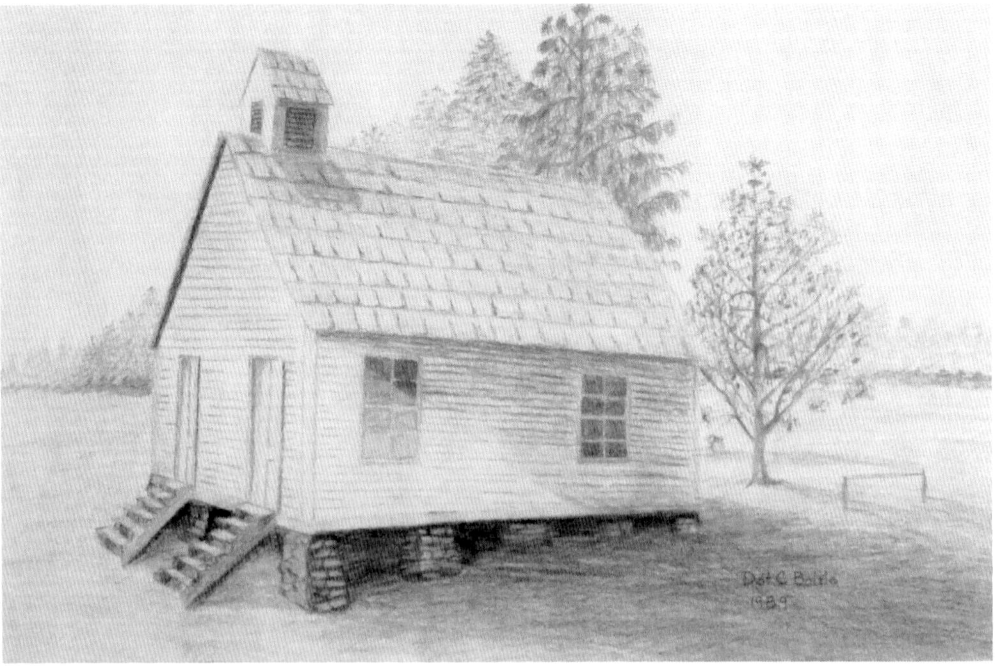

Longview Church of God

Longview Church of God owes its founding to a toothache. Around 1907, a daughter of W.C. Wilhite had to visit the dentist. He fixed her tooth and gave her a religious periodical and tract. The family ordered more and shared them with neighbors. They held prayer meetings in homes at first, and in March 1911 the group built a church in the Vinemont area. Its original building was dubbed "Old Thirteen" because there were 13 original members, or families. The church was moved to its current location in 1941. The site was chosen because it sat on what was then US 31, the main north–south route through the area. Since then, the church has been updated several times, and some of its leading families today are descendants of the first 13 attendees. (Both images courtesy Dot Bolze/Asa Brandon.)

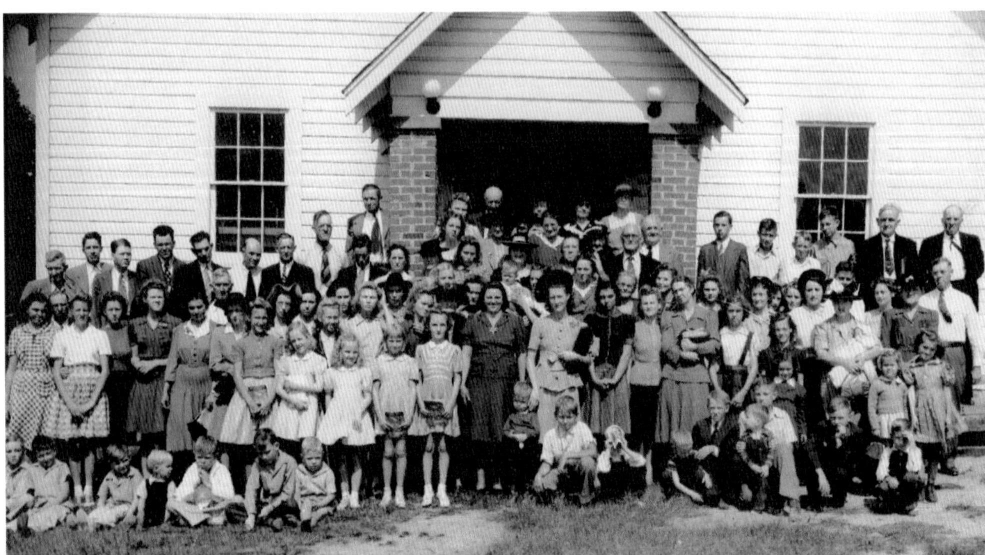

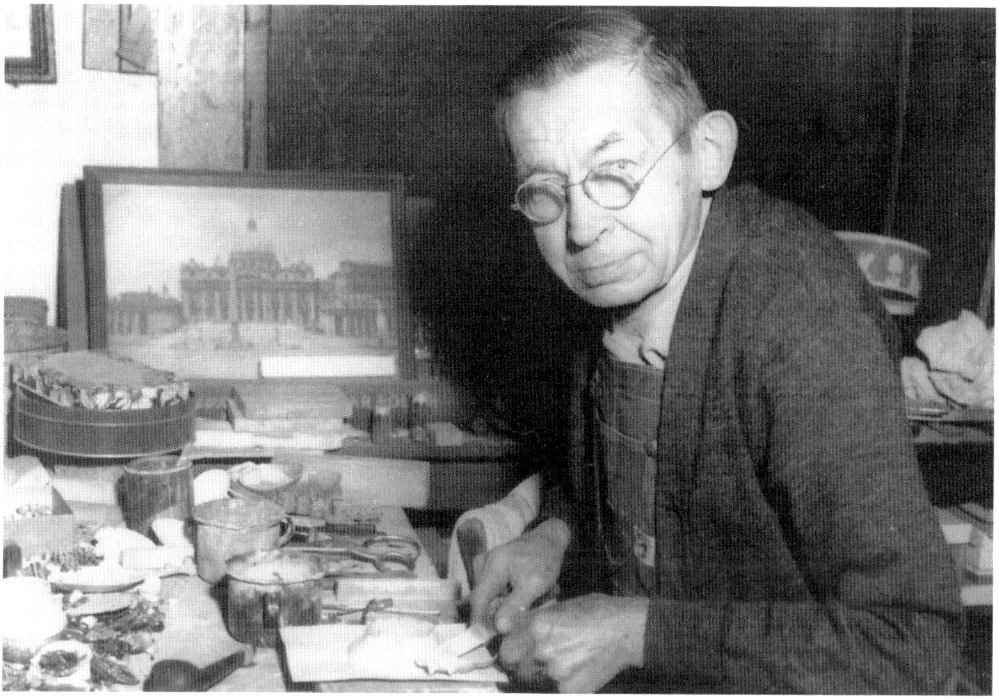

Brother Joseph Zoettl

Under the skilled hands of a partially disabled Benedictine monk, detailed miniature reproductions of Jerusalem and other holy shrines are captured in the Ave Maria Grotto at St. Bernard Abbey. It represents over 40 years of a work by Brother Joseph Zoettl. He was born, January 24, 1878. At age 13, he almost lost his life in the flu epidemic sweeping through Europe in 1891. Fr. Gamelbert Brunner, visiting Europe, was seeking candidates for the St. Bernard Abby. Young Joseph applied and was accepted. He departed for the United States from Landshut, Bavaria. Following other assignments, he was sent to the Abbey to operate the power station. His routine for 30 years was 17-hour days, seven days a week, barely allowing time to attend mass. He began to construct miniatures, as a hobby, in his workshop in 1918. The first attempt, still in existence, was a miniature church. Miniatures that followed became known as Little Jerusalem. His work gained attention. Father Dominic, who operated a store on the grounds, brought Brother Joseph's figurines, requesting he build a small grotto for each. They sold quickly, and more than 5,000 grottos later, the decision was made that Brother Joseph would build a grotto much larger. He began the work on the recreation grounds of the monastery, but due to the large amount of visitors a new location had to be found. On May 17, 1934, the Ave Maria Grotto was dedicated at its present location on Abbey grounds. Materials for the project came from donations all over the world, from colored glass to costume jewelry, all patiently worked into miniatures for a larger project of beauty. When an L&N train derailed near Vinemont, one of the cars carried marble, which was so broken up the owner donated it to St. Bernard. This was used to make the stalactites that hang in the grotto.

Brother Joseph's last project was the Bascilica in Lourdes when he was 80. This fairyland in miniature is on the grounds of Alabama's first and only Benedictine Abbey. It covers over three acres and contains miniature representations of over 125 churches and religious buildings and shrines. Brother Joseph Zoettl died October 15, 1961, leaving a legacy that the world still enjoys. He was never paid anything for his work, nor was it expected. (Courtesy St. Bernard Abbey.)

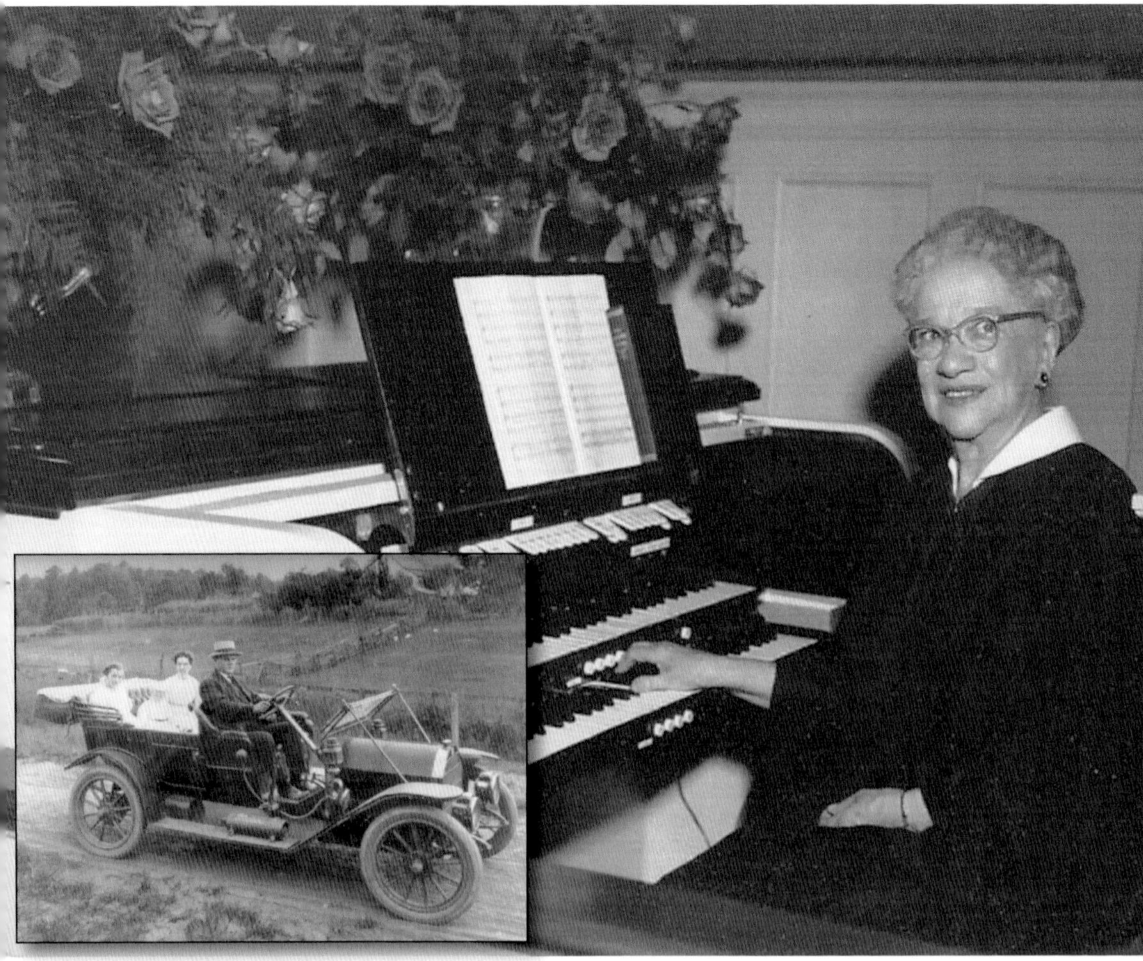

Nelle Fuller St. John

Nelle Fuller St. John held prominence at the First Baptist Church, not only in cultural affairs, but as church pianist and organist for 60 years, from 1893 to 1953. She was a charter member of the Symphony Club and served as president of the organization on several occasions. On the day of her retirement at 86 years old, she was presented a vase of 60 roses commemorating her service. She was the daughter of Judge and Mrs. S.L. Fuller of Cullman and wife of Finis E. St. John Sr., who served as state representative from 1923 to 1935. In the early-1900s Welch convertible are Finis St. John Sr., Nelle Fuller St. John, and their children Wynelle and Finis E. Jr. (a future Alabama state representative). (Courtesy Finis E. St. John IV.)

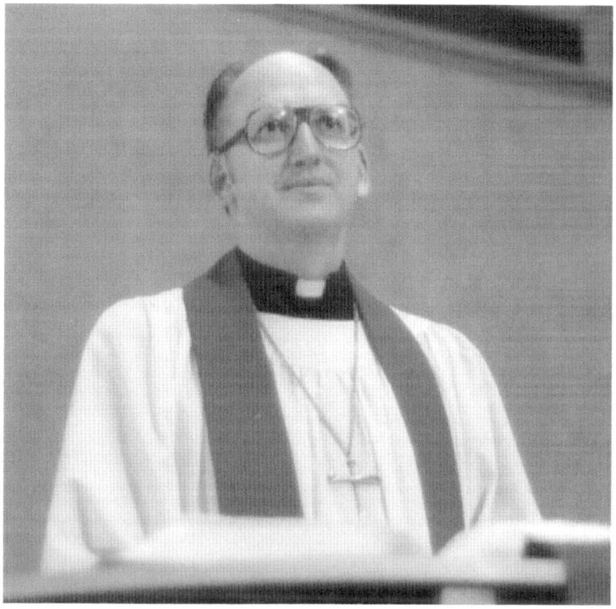

Rev. Harold Hermetz

Rev. Harold Hermetz was called to serve St. Paul's Lutheran Church in 1965. The 37 years that followed elevated him as the longest-serving pastor in the church's history (128 years), and as an extraordinary record of spiritual, community, and civic involvement. In 1970, he led the church congregation in the quest to construct and dedicate a new contemporary church sanctuary. The church congregational membership rose from 600 to 1,000. He also restructured the church's constitution and church administration. He helped sponsor immigrant families moving to Cullman from their homelands while mentoring new pastors, teachers, missionaries, youth leaders, and professional church workers. Prior to his death on October 12, 2010, he served for 10 years as interim pastor and in other capacities in Alabama and Mississippi Lutheran churches. In 1958, he was called to serve as founding pastor of Atonement Lutheran Church in Metairie, a New Orleans suburb. As a new pastor, he canvassed the Veterans Highway community, knocking on doors and inviting residents to attend church at a temporary location until a new sanctuary could be constructed. Today, Atonement Lutheran-Metairie is one of the Southern District LCM's largest churches. Within the community, he served on the Pilot Light House board of directors, on the Cullman Area Mental Health Authority, as president of the Cullman County Association for Retarded Citizens, on the Cullman Area Chamber of Commerce, and on the Cullman Oktoberfest and Community Concert Association boards. He also served as president of Cullman High School PTA, Quarterback Club, Swim Team Parents Association, County Ministerial Association, founded Cullman Toastmasters International, and was selected to be Burgermeister of Cullman's Oktoberfest 1998. His involvement in the community from spiritual to medical groups reaches into many areas.

Pastor Hermetz has been honored by the Cullman Boy Scouts for decades of volunteer service and countless hours to help build character and religious influence in hundreds of boys, teaching young men to "Be Prepared for Tomorrow." In 1983, he was honored by the Alabama House of Representatives and Senate for 25 years of outstanding service to the Lutheran ministry and again in 2010 for his service to his church and ministry and being a powerful influence of good in the community for 50 years. Pastor Hermetz provided invocations for countless community events, including sharing the stage with former California governor Ronald Reagan during his visit to Cullman and campaign for president. He was also present when Alabama governor George Wallace, Rev. Norman Vincent Peale, Rev. Dr. Robert Schuller, Vice Pres. Walter Mondale, Congressman Tom Bevill, and other political dignitaries visited Cullman. (Courtesy Hermetz family.)

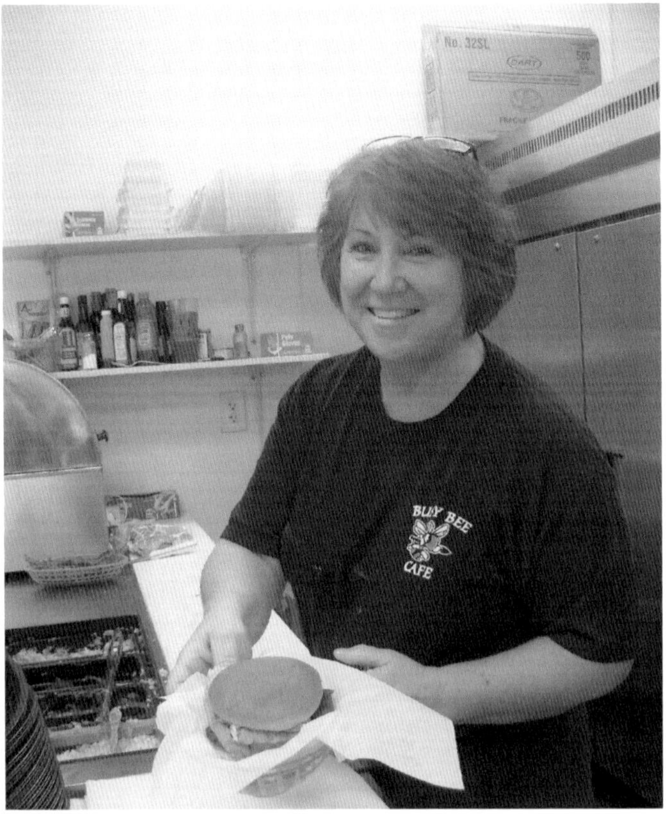

Kitty Spears

"I should be dead," Kitty Spears said after tornadoes wreaked a path of destruction through North Alabama on April 27, 2011. Hanceville, 15 miles south of Cullman, was hit hard that morning. The horror was repeated that afternoon in Cullman. Kitty Spears, owner of the Busy Bee Restaurant, a memorable landmark for generations, never dreamed it would happen. "I let my girls off early." Many businesses closed early because of storm forecasts. She was removing money from the cash register and felt intense pressure in her ears. She looked up and was face-to-face with an EF-4 tornado. "I jumped under the counter. I never dreamed the building would explode." She was trapped. "I couldn't move. The first thing I said was, 'Thank you Jesus,' because I was still alive. I could hear people. I started screaming and they found me, dug me out. I realized I was hurt." The business she and her husband, Steve, operated since 1962 was a pile of rubble. Even when she was in the hospital, they made plans to rebuild because of its history and what it meant to so many families. Two weeks after the restaurant was destroyed, Steve was diagnosed with terminal cancer, but he started treatments to prolong his life, wanting to see the restaurant re-open. It did on April 27, a year after it was destroyed. Steve died on May 27, one month after it reopened. This was the second location of the restaurant, the first constructed in 1919 on Third Avenue, next to a mule barn, operated by Milford Ford and later by Carl Lassiter when it was relocated at its present site, then purchased by the Spears family. It is not unusual for families to visit the restaurant and take five-generation pictures. Residents refer to it as the oldest new restaurant in town. On any given day and during lunch, The Busy Bee is filled with customers ordering the Depression burger, a mixture of bread and hamburger meat. Hamburger was mixed this way during the Depression to make it go further. The restaurant serves around 500 Depression burgers each day. The restaurant is busy as a bee. "You may come in as a stranger, but before you leave, you'll have a friend," Mrs. Spears says. Her children Kyle and Stevie work at the restaurant with their mother, the next generation to operate the Busy Bee and carry on the tradition. (Courtesy Kay Cagle.)

CHAPTER FOUR

Agriculture Leader

Cullman County is the state's number one agriculture producer, leading the poultry industry with broilers, breeder hens, tops in cattle production, and is second in the state for sweet potato production. Four major poultry industries have interests in Cullman County: Pilgrim's Pride, Ingram Farms, Tyson, and Kocks. Historically, Cullman County has always been an agricultural area. However, in the late 1800s, planters avoided what they considered soil too thin and sterile to be productive. Colonists began to experiment with the soil. The 17 soil types found across Cullman County were to prove adaptable for a wider variety of crops. Cullman County was propelled to the prestigious ranking of the top agricultural county. Legumes were planted, despite much scoffing, and thrived, setting the stage for dairy and beef cattle production. When the luscious, strange, red berry that Germans called *erdhebren* (strawberry) was introduced, markets opened from Birmingham to Cincinnati and other northern areas. P.H. Kessler, who brought the first strawberry plants to the Cullman area, was known as "Father of the 'Berry' Culture."

Early settlers realized survival meant having knowledge of more than a few vegetable crops. Colonists experimented with crop diversification. According to an 1874 article in the *Southern Immigrant*, "The hillsides are covered with grapevines, the summits with promising young orchards, while the valleys and coves are full of waving grains. Land is now selling readily at $5 to $20 per acre where only a few years ago, a whole farm of 40 to 80 acres could be had for a wagon and yoke of steers."

There are families in cattle, poultry, sweet potato, and truck farming who have harvested their livelihood from the land for generations—from the Parrish family who opened a livestock facility, known as the Cow Palace, to families managing herds. The Mobleys and Meeks were in the poultry industry, and acres and acres of sweet potatoes were being shipped to markets. The Peinhardts have a working farm toured by youths to discover their heritage.

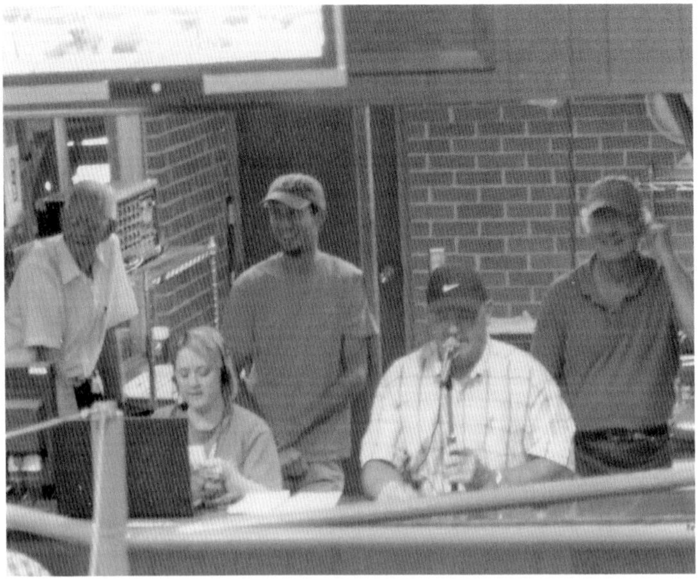

Keith Parish

Cullman Livestock Barn, the Cow Palace, opened in 1969, operated by Keith Parrish and family. His father, S.E. "Tuck" Parish, traded a farm for the old livestock barn on Highway 278 East. Keith has been in the cattle auction market 62 years. On the auction floor are Keith Parrish, grandson Callahan, and son Hoagy, along with clerk Amy Ray, and auctioneer Scott Aaron. (Courtesy Parish family.)

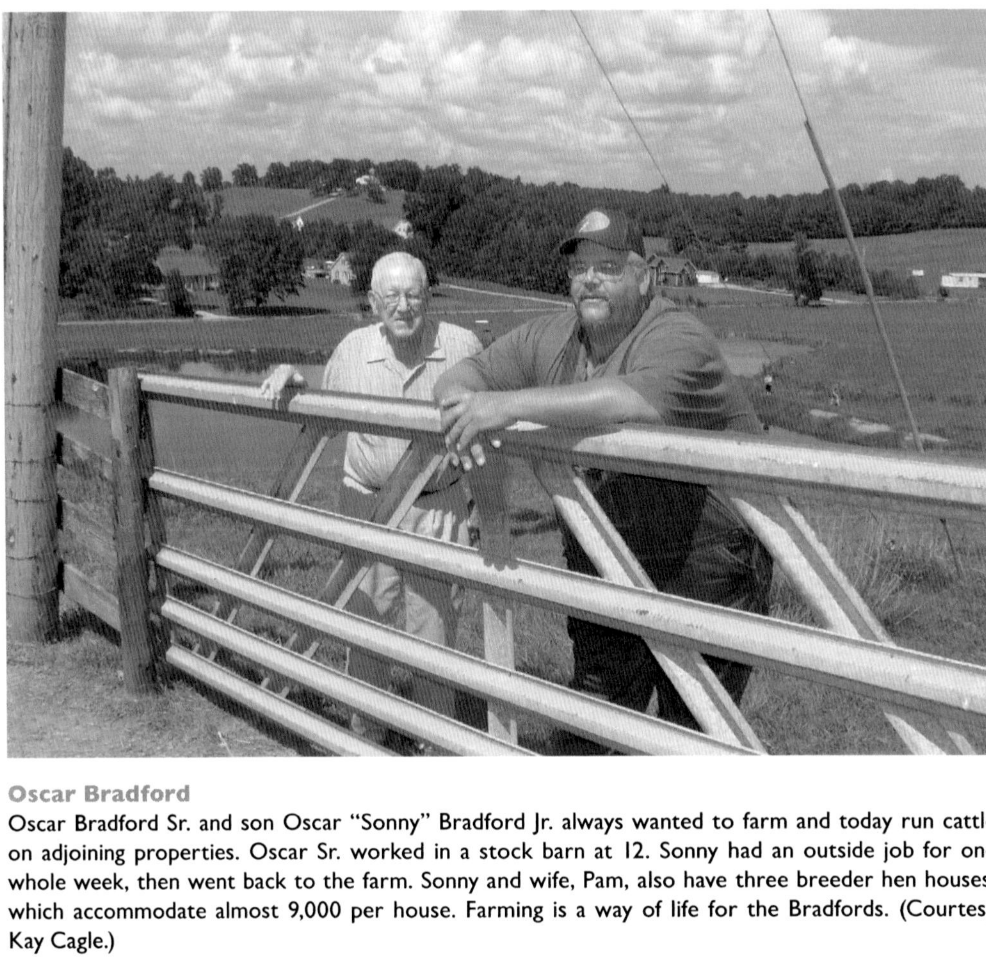

Oscar Bradford

Oscar Bradford Sr. and son Oscar "Sonny" Bradford Jr. always wanted to farm and today run cattle on adjoining properties. Oscar Sr. worked in a stock barn at 12. Sonny had an outside job for one whole week, then went back to the farm. Sonny and wife, Pam, also have three breeder hen houses, which accommodate almost 9,000 per house. Farming is a way of life for the Bradfords. (Courtesy Kay Cagle.)

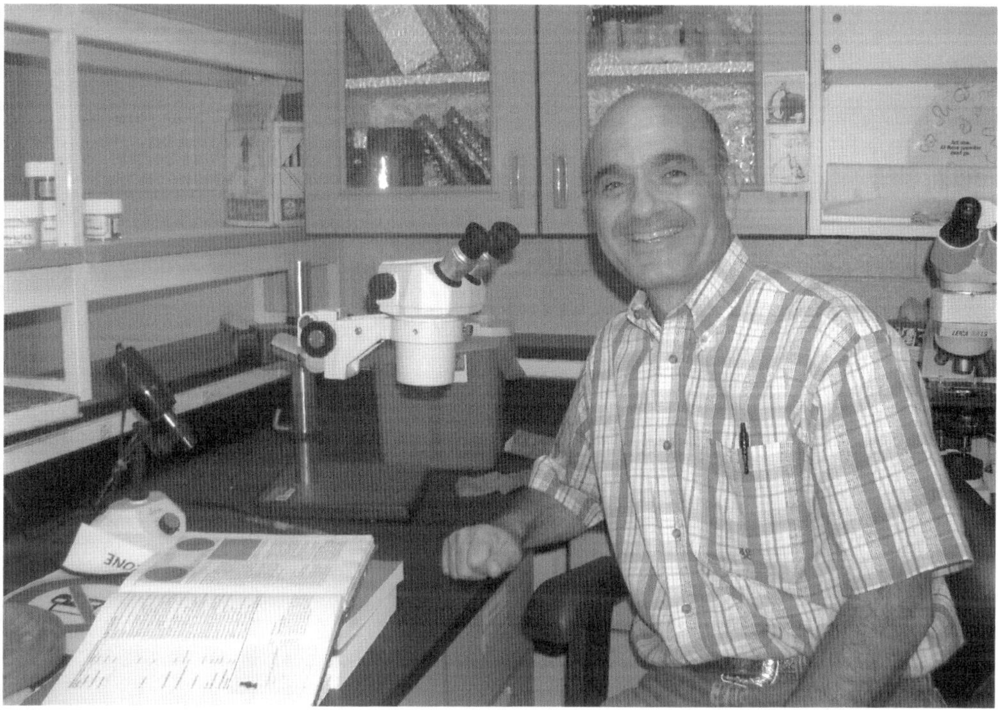

Dr. Terry Slaten

Dr. Terry Slaten's, passion for agriculture led him to veterinary medicine and the cattle industry. Under his leadership, the local cattleman's association became the best in the state. His wife, Lana, was the first Alabama woman to serve as president of the National Women's Association. A hobby farmer, he manages the state veterinary diagnostics lab at Wallace State, researching and diagnosing poultry and livestock problems and advising treatments. (Courtesy Kay Cagle.)

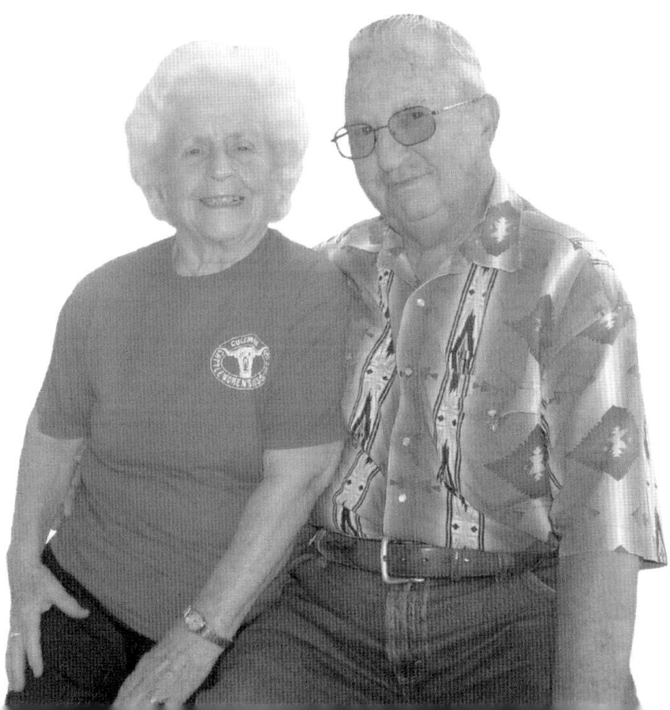

Edwin and Betty Calvert

Edwin and Betty Calvert bought land after they married and paid for it by growing chickens, then opted to go into the cattle business. They still manage a cow and calf operation. During the holidays, the Calvert farmhouse is filled with family activity. Edwin runs the soil and water testing lab at Wallace State College, Betty calls herself, the "cow mama," caring for all of the cows. (Courtesy Kay Cagle.)

W.C. and Charlotte Kress
W.C. Kress, his grandfather Conrad, and father, George, all grew sweet potatoes marketed to local dealers and brokers. But their 200-acre farm was diversified with Irish potatoes, strawberries, vegetables, and livestock. W.C. says the soil is the sweet potato miracle worker that put his children through Auburn University. His nephews work the sweet potato farm, which has among its structures a 100-year-old barn with hand-hewn logs that was constructed with wooden pegs. (Both images courtesy Kay Cagle.)

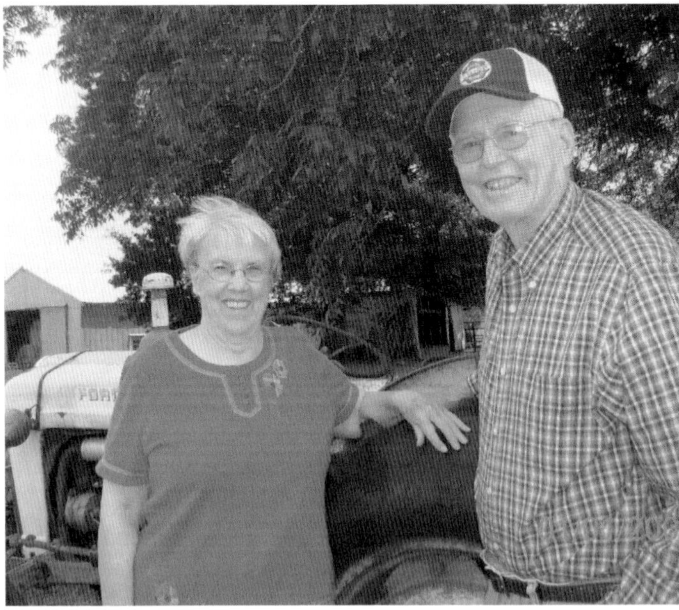

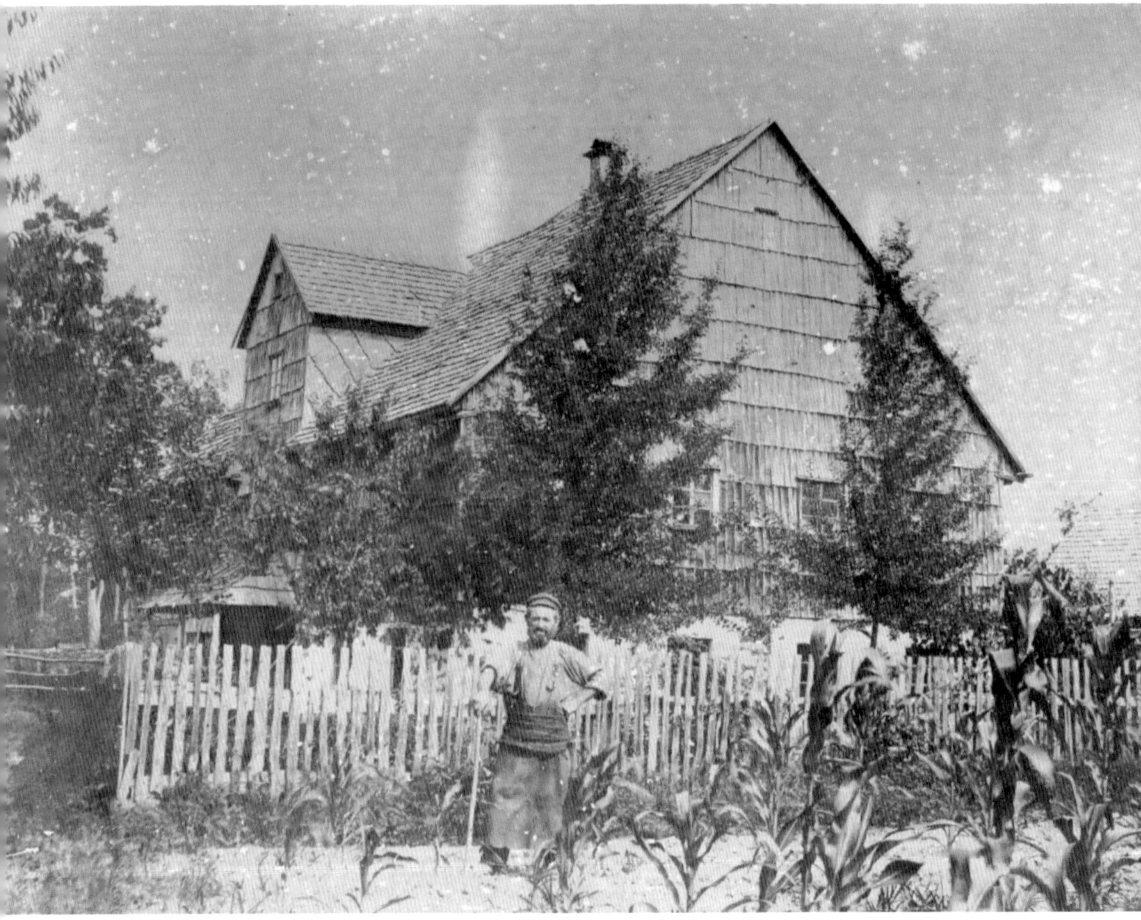

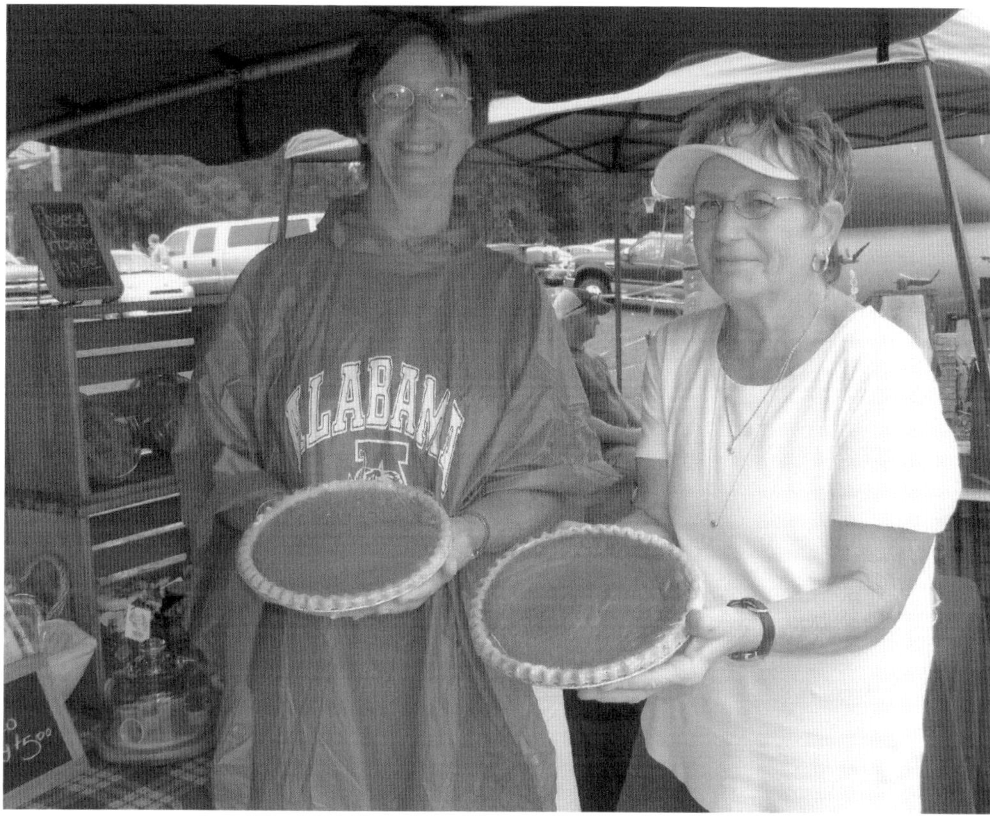

Sweet Potato Festival
On Labor Day, hundreds attend the Sweet Potato Festival for entertainment and sweet potato pies. Seventeen years ago, Dowling Elementary School burned on Labor Day. A park was rebuilt in its place. Festival proceeds maintain the park. Jeanette Duke and Jane Gammon show off sweet potato pies made by Seven Winds Kitchen. Pies and a large variety of other sweet potato delicacies are favorites among festival attendees. (Courtesy Kay Cagle.)

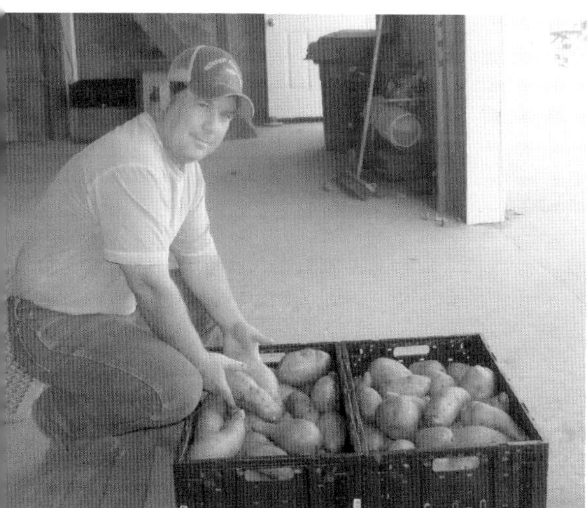

Clark Haynes
Clark Haynes is a third-generation sweet potato producer. He also produces soybeans, seedless watermelons, cotton, and runs some cattle on his 600 acres, as well as farms sweet potato acreage in Butler County. He follows in the footsteps of his father and grandfather, together covering a century of farming. Being a producer has always been his goal, and today he still resides on the family farm. (Courtesy Kay Cagle.)

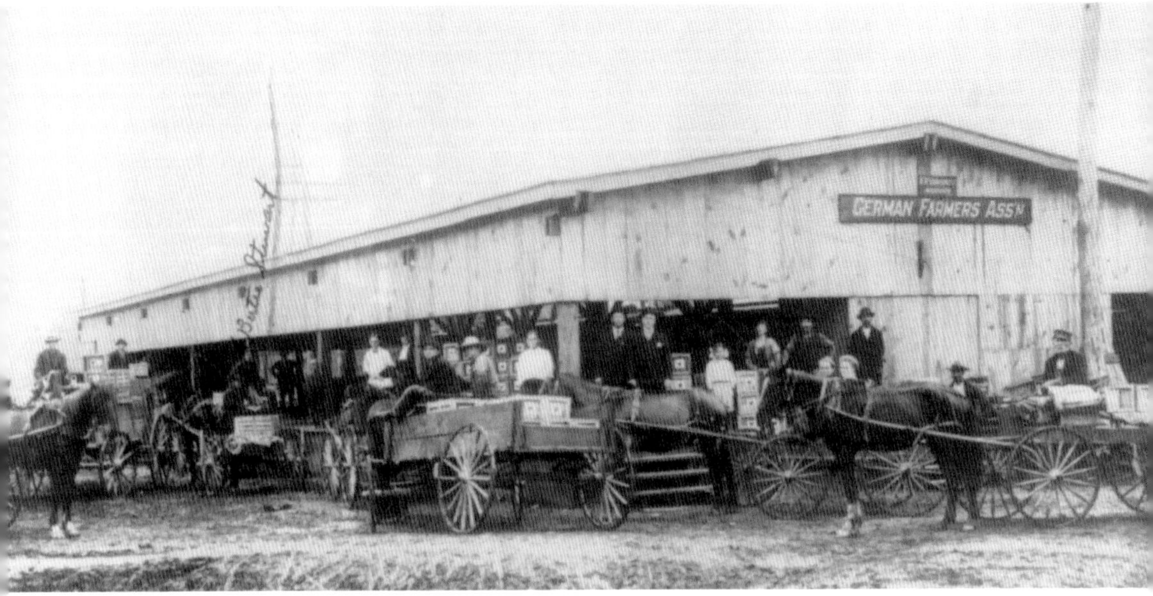

German Growers Association

Under the German Growers Association, strawberries became a main crop. Growers filed suit against the L&N Railroad to lower freight rates. After an investigation, Cullman received the same rates as Decatur. The decision meant a $100,000-a-year savings to growers. The organization was doing an annual business of $100,000 six years after the lawsuit. (Courtesy Cullman County Museum.)

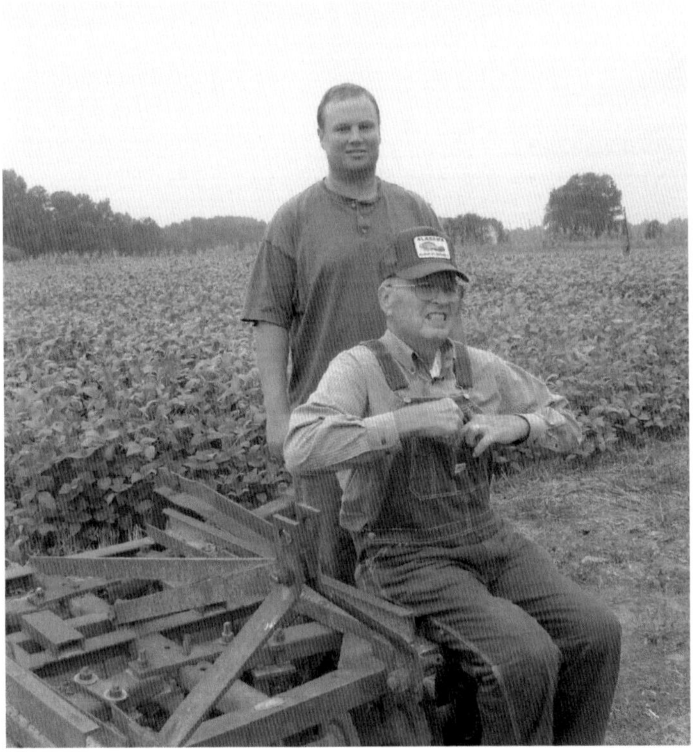

Jim Boyd

Jim Boyd's grandfather walked beside a wagon, bringing his family from Georgia to Fairview, searching for good farmland. Today, as a retired, five-term Cullman County Superintendent of Education, Jim is a hobby farmer and, during the growing season, a regular at the local farmer's market. His son Trent owns Harvest Farm and participates in the Community Supported Agriculture Program, delivering fresh fruits and veggies to Birmingham restaurants. (Courtesy Kay Cagle.)

Sammy and Brenda Mobley

It is a revolving environment of activity getting poultry to the market and to America's dinner table, but one phase begins at the breeder-hen farms like the one owned by Mr. and Mrs. Sammy Mobley. They are part of a leading farming industry and the area's claim to being the state's top poultry producing county. Sammy's parents owned a chicken farm. He jokes about being "born in the field," and remembers his father was not required to enlist for service during World War II because he, like many farmers, was producing food for America. That was also the time when famers were self-sufficient, providing for their own families. Even when Sammy was employed at Hays Aircraft in Birmingham, he was still a partner with his father in the commercial hen business. They sold and delivered the white eggs for resale in grocery stores. Today, Sammy and his wife, Brenda, maintain two poultry houses with 18,000 breeder hens and 1,700 roosters.

Chickens at 20 weeks old are trucked to the Mobley farm from the hatchery. Sammy manages one flock a year over a period of 65 weeks. These breeder hens lay brown eggs, which are picked up and transported to incubation rooms at the hatchery. When hatched, the baby chicks are then shipped to county poultry broiler producers. Brenda always pitches in when she is needed, but her primary job is a registered nurse at Cullman Regional Medical Center. She works in the obstetrics ward. In the photograph, Brenda and Sammy push the "egg buggy" through the breeder hen farm, collecting eggs. (Courtesy Kay Cagle.)

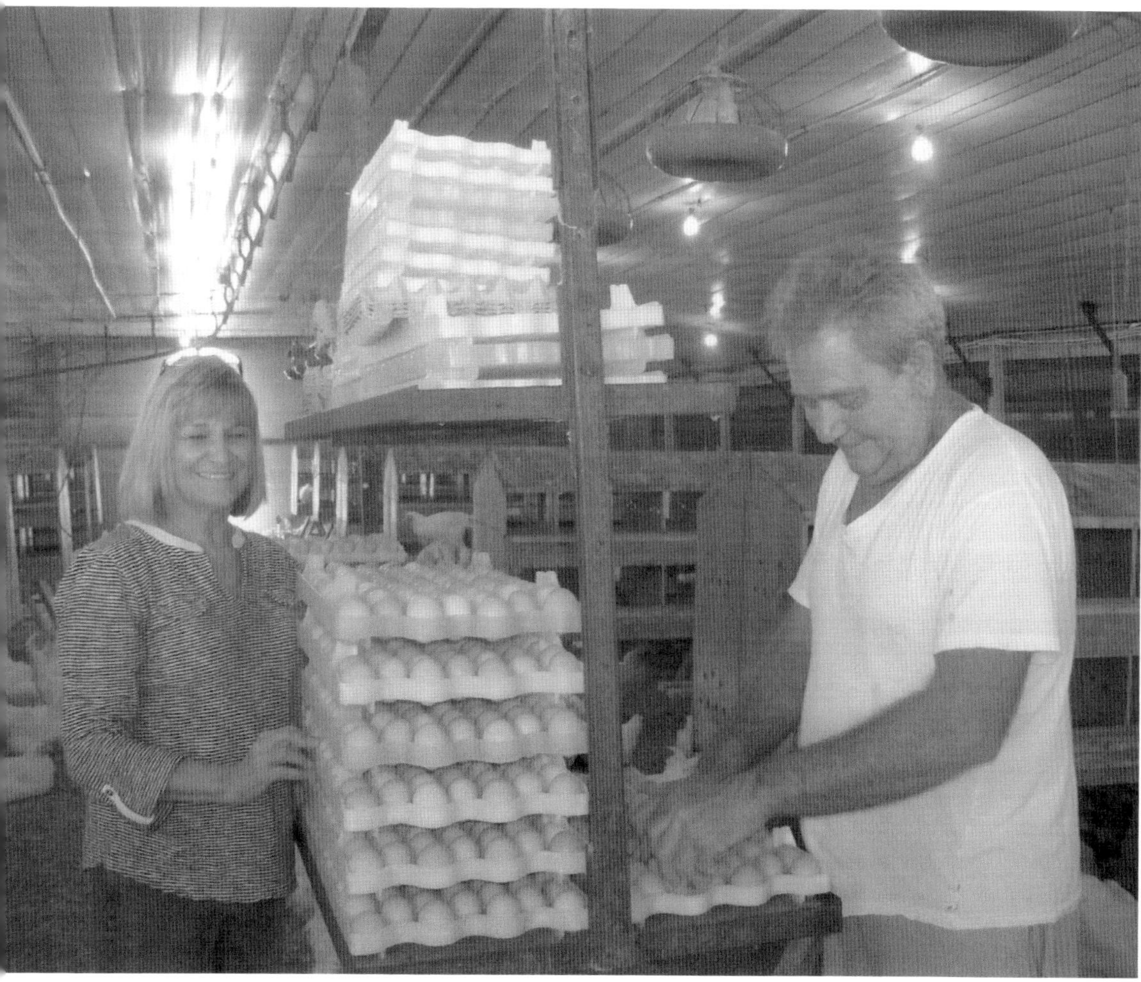

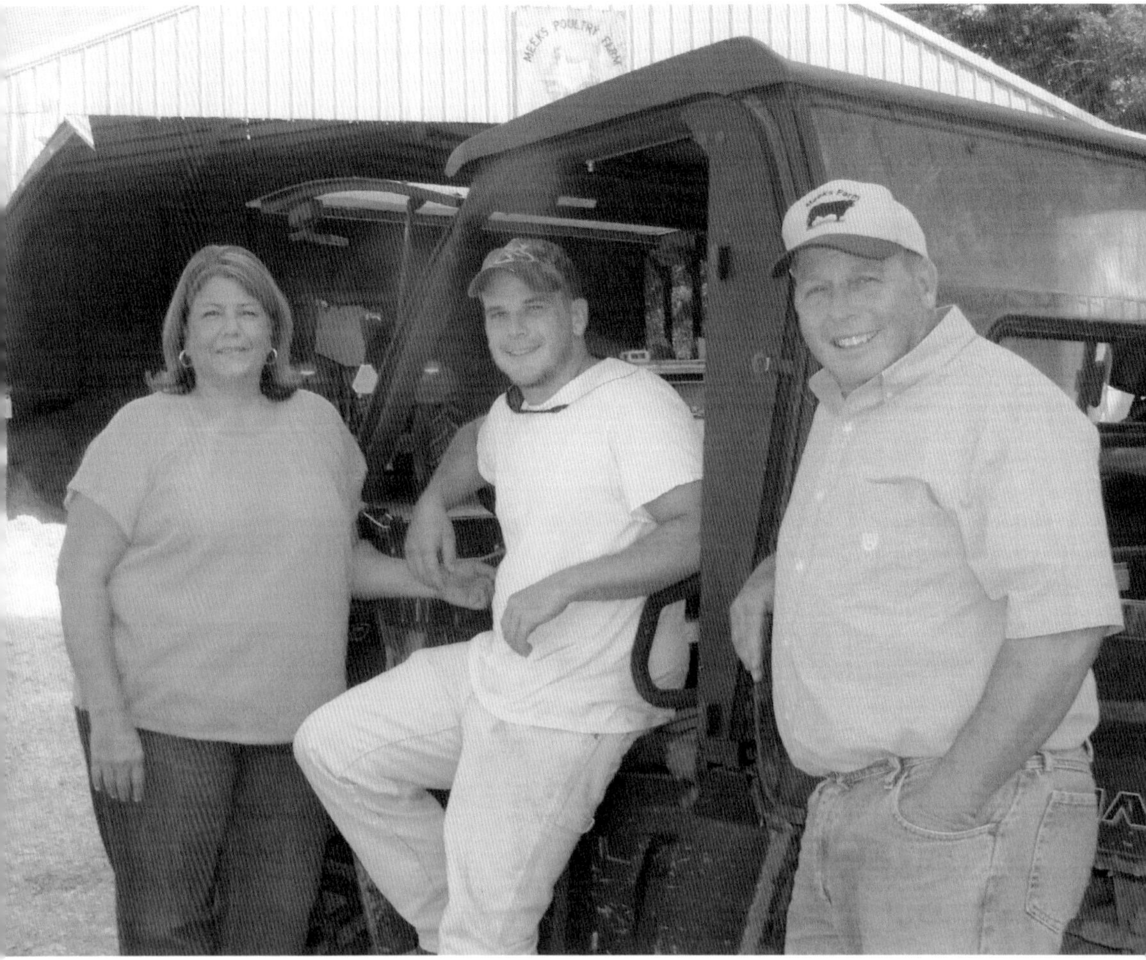

Billy and Donna Meeks

It takes a lot of hard work just to prepare for a new batch of chickens, but Billy and Donna Meeks are accustomed to hard work. Raising broiler chickens has been their family livelihood for 23 years, and today, Billy owns or manages approximately 800 acres, which does include acreage for cattle and soybeans. Billy and Donna have farm-family backgrounds. They are producers in an industry that has cut a path to the top and helped to make Cullman County the state's leading agricultural area, maintaining the No. 1 ranking as poultry producer for years. Billy Meeks has eight poultry houses, but to get ready for a flock of chickens the houses have to be cleaned, fresh shavings spread, and equipment checked out, which takes several days. They also have to make sure the chickens are sufficiently fed and watered until they are ready for harvesting. Today, Billy buys feed for the chickens, which adds to local economic benefits of a thriving poultry industry. The family will grow out approximately 200,000 broilers over a five-week period. This is repeated up to seven times a year. That puts a lot of chicken on America's dinner tables. Donna does their accounting. Pictured with Donna and Billy is their son Brad, who, for the time being, is following in his father's footsteps. They have a daughter, Stephanie, who lives nearby. (Courtesy Kay Cagle.)

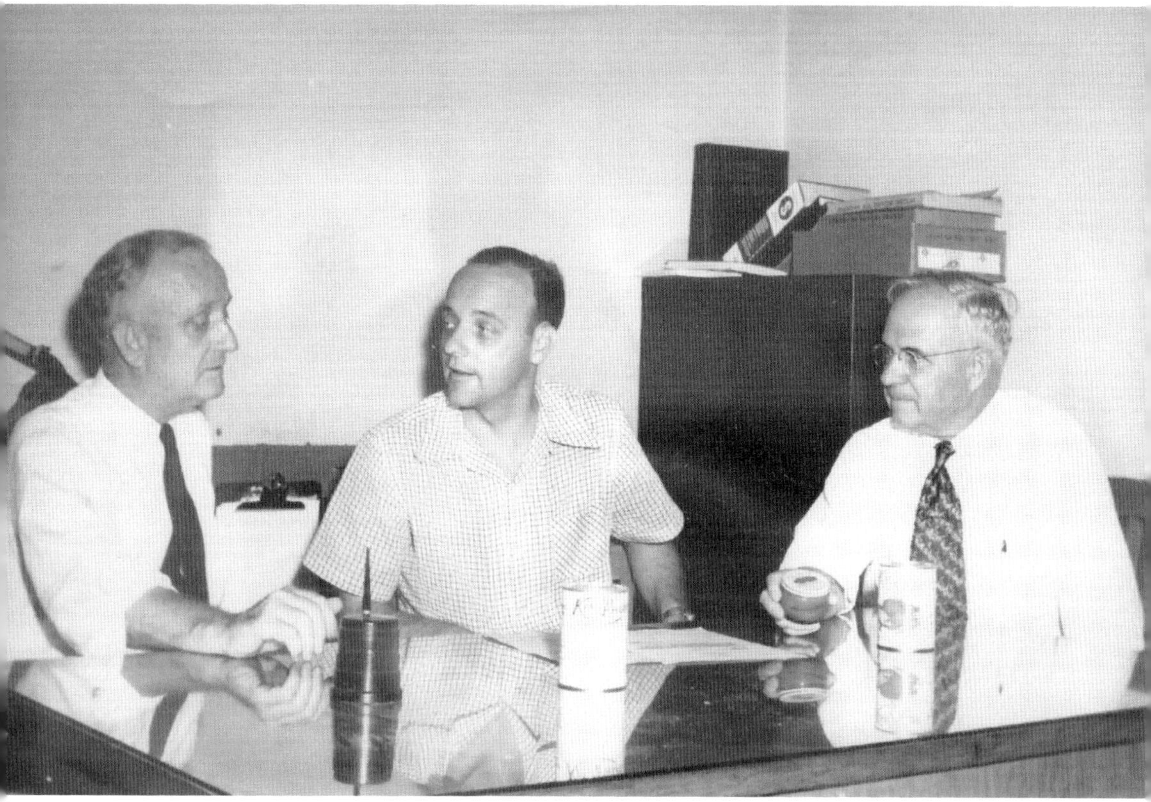

King Pharr Canning Company

As Cullman County boomed in agricultural production, it was a natural economic decision to locate a vegetable processing business in the area. The McPhillips family answered that need, and in 1945 King Pharr Canning Company was located a few blocks from downtown Cullman. Their base of operations was Mobile, Alabama, with four other plants: Selma, Alabama; Uniontown and Zebulon, Georgia; and one in Louisiana. Two needs were served—providing a buyer for local farmers who had no market for ripened tomatoes (an alternative to letting them rot in the field) and producing a product that would be sold throughout the nation. Julian L. McPhillips was president of King Pharr from 1945 to 1959. It was between the mid-1940s to early 1950s that McPhillips rode narrow, dusty county roads, visiting and contracting with local farmers to buy tomatoes and vegetables. Cans with the King Pharr logo were filled with a variety of peas, tomatoes, whole green beans, potatoes, and okra, just to name a few items. During harvest season, local farmers lined up for blocks in pickups and larger trucks laden with farm-fresh vegetables. As early as 1958, more than a thousand county farmers sold annually to the King Pharr operation. When McPhillips Sr. left for Episcopal Seminary in 1959, becoming an Episcopal priest, his brother Warren McPhillips, also son of Julian Byrnes McPhillips, board chairman of the Mobile-based corporation, became president, running the Cullman location until 1976 when King Pharr went out of business. The food industry was changing, enhanced by expanding fast food operations. King Pharr self-liquidated in 1975. At their peak, King Pharr employed over 1,000 people and shipped 33 different canned vegetables all over the United States. Pictured in the late 1940s in Cullman are Julian Byrnes McPhillips, board chairman, his son Julian L. McPhillips Sr., and stockholder Arnold Brush at a King Pharr meeting. (Courtesy Julian L. McPhillips Jr.)

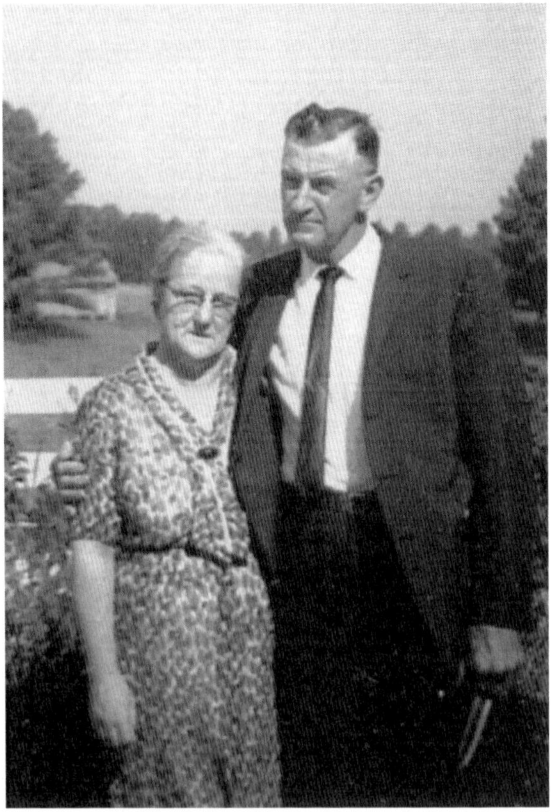

Carl and Irene Peinhardt

Discontent under the Bismarck and Kaiser rule spurred Karl Peinhardt to migrate from Germany to the fledgling colony of Cullman in 1873 where he farmed. His son Otto followed in his father's footsteps, also running a small, diversified farm with row crops, cattle, and milk production. It was his son Carl who studied agriculture at Auburn University and continued the same diversified farming, developing a registered Guernsey Dairy herd as his main focus. He was also a carpenter, musician, rock mason, and worked diligently with soil conservation. Carl Peinhardt's family lived outside the city limits, Irene Ehrensperger's family inside the city. They both attended St. John's Church, founded by Colonel Cullmann. They married after she graduated from Judson College, and she joined her husband for a lifetime in the agriculture industry. They had five children. Today, that acreage is called the Peinhardt Living History Farm. It is an educational family farm, focusing on rural life in the 1930s and 1940s. One of the main goals is to help fill a void in children's agriculture literacy. Peinhardt Living History Farm is a member of The Association of Living Historical Farms and Agricultural Museums. Members of the Peinhardt family and farm supporters formed a 501(c)3 public foundation with a mission to promote agriculture, historical, and conservation education. The farm is a living history classroom with an 8,000-square-foot museum, filled with agriculture, household, and forestry tools of the late 19th and 20th century, including items made at the Ruehl Wagon Factory and individually fashioned stalk cutters used before the invention of mowers. Among the items is a loom used by the Peinhardt children's grandmother, Pauline Ehrensperger. The fourth Saturday in October is designated Public Farm Day. The four remaining children keeping the farm together, emphasizing life on a family farm in the 1930s and 1940s are Bill Peinhardt, a Cullman Internal Medicine physician; his sister Carolyn, a retired schoolteacher; his sister Pat, a retired physical therapist who lives on the farm, and his brother Eddie and his wife, Becky, who farms for a living, have chicken houses, cattle and corn, soybean, and hay acreage. All of the children live on or near the farm. (Courtesy Peinhardt family.)

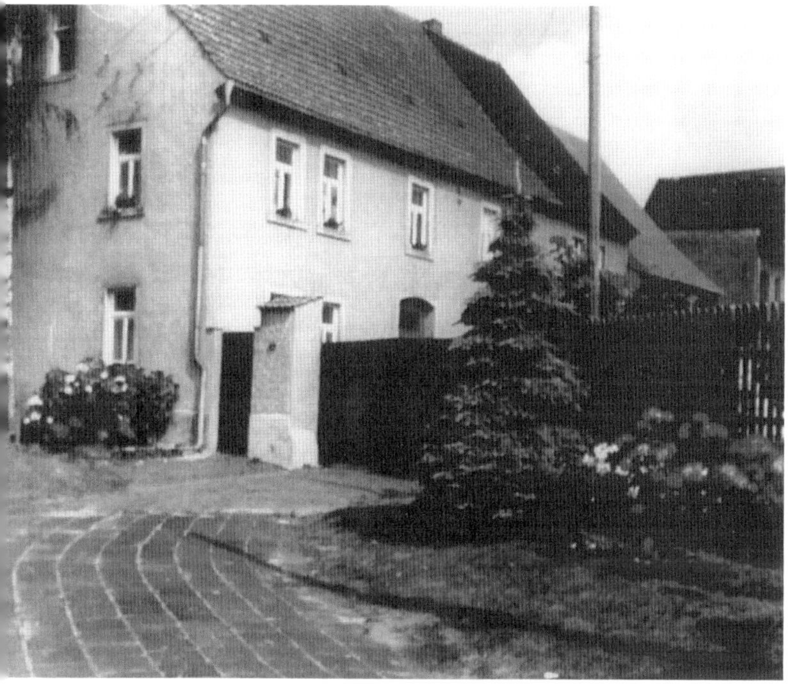

Karl Peinhardt Home, Germany

Karl Peinhardt left his home in Germany (pictured) for America when the West was being developed and the South was recovering from the Civil War. From New York, he traveled on to Cincinnati where he worked several years. He heard of the new town of Cullman being settled and traveled south, where his descendants remain. (Courtesy Carolyn Peinhardt Johnson.)

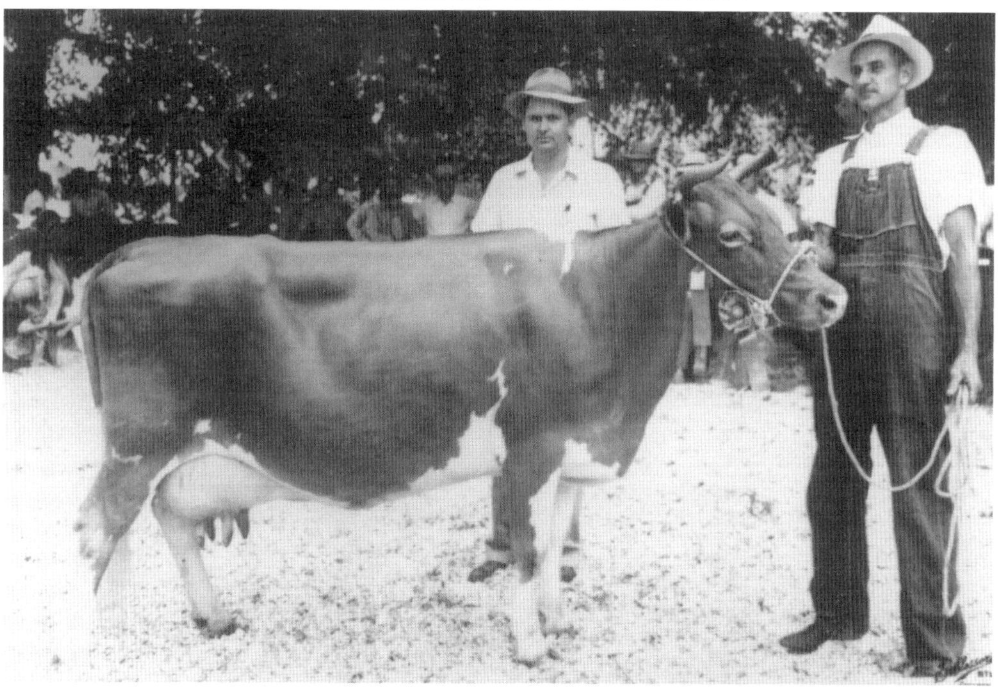

Carl Peinhardt, Dairy Farmer

Dairy farming was Carl Peinhardt's livelihood, but he did include beekeeping later. Carl Peinhardt is shown with a Mr. Alverson, cattle judge, and Promise, the prize dairy cow. Promise, owned by Carl, was named grand champion in a late-1940s dairy competition and shown on Fourth Avenue near D.T. Kinney Mule Barn. (Courtesy Carolyn Peinhardt Johnson.)

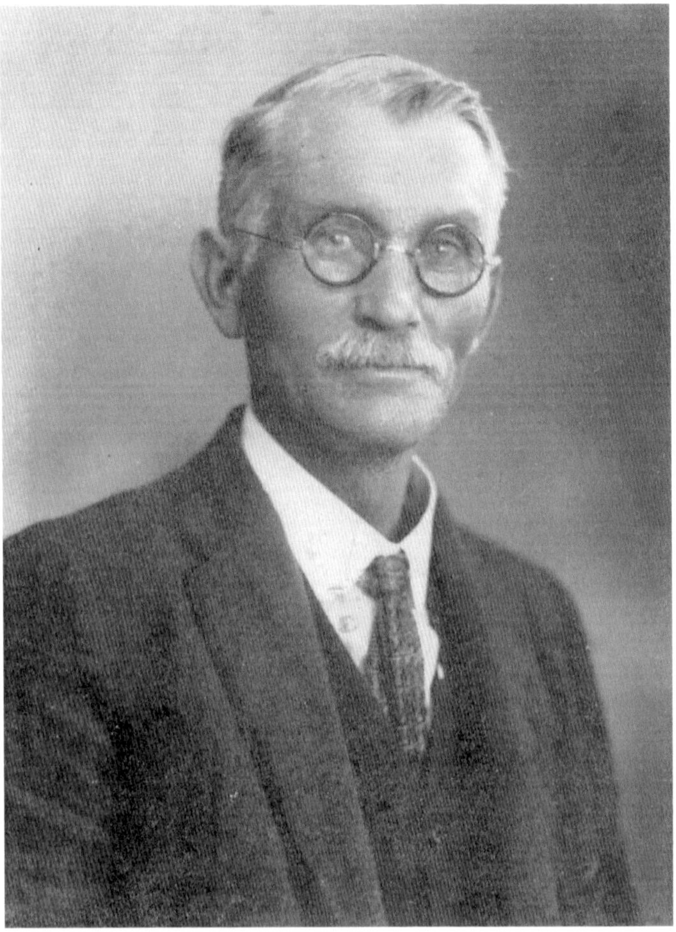

P.H. Kessler, "Father of the Berry"

German colonists, accustomed to the rich soil of the Rhine Valley, were not excited over southern crops of cotton and tested Colonel Cullman's claim that Brindley Mountain would be the new garden spot of the world. Adam Kessler and his son P.H., among the colony's first immigrants in 1880, bought a few strawberry plants from Kentucky. The luscious red berries were called *erdhebren*. Having knowledge of fruit crops enabled them to produce and then grow them commercially. P.H. Kessler became known as the father of berry culture, introducing the red and black raspberry and dewberries to the agriculture community. Within a few years, he, with George Grob and Mr. Goehler, on farms adjoining the Kessler property, Welti Road, were the first Cullman County farmers to grow strawberries commercially. As harvests increased, acreage expanded for more strawberry production. According to records, by 1931, a total of 279 carloads of strawberries were shipped out of Cullman County at a value of $250,000, and by 1935, strawberry acreage had expanded to 2,200 acres. The economic influence as early as 1905 was celebrated with a Strawberry Jubilee, with more festivals by May 13, 1939. Henry F. Arnold was chairman of the festival, which featured a 50-float parade, fiddlers' contest, street dance, and crowning of the strawberry queen, climaxed by a grand ball. Since that time, strawberry acreage has fluctuated and the last festival was held in 1950. However, a one-day festival was revived in the late 1990s, headed by Randy Britt. Jimmy Sims, who works with the Festalle Market, Department of the Parks and Recreation, went to the county commission and city council to get their support for a two-day festival, which began in 2009 at the Festalle Market, and today the event is held the second weekend in May. (Courtesy Karen Hassell.)

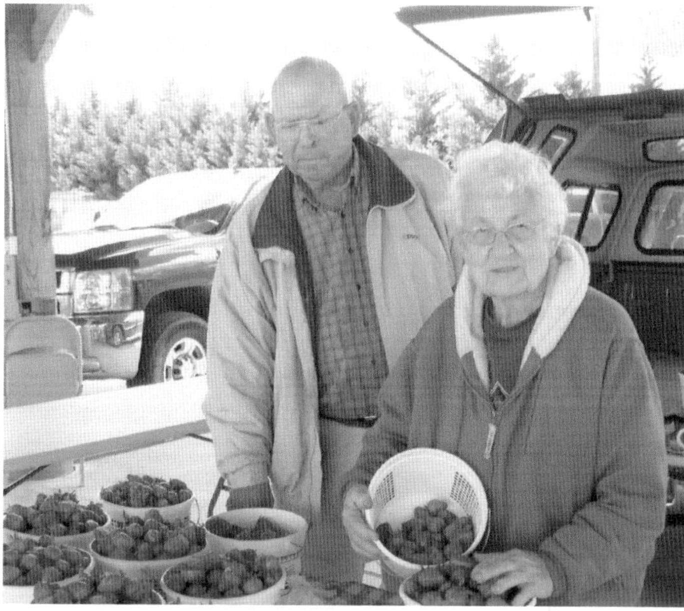

Sonny and Betty Voight
Betty and H.A. "Sonny" Voight Jr. are vendor favorites at Festalle Market. His father, Herman, migrated from Germany and purchased land in the southeast part of the county. When his father died, Sonny continued farming. When the Festalle Market bedding plant, strawberry, and vegetable season opens one can find the Voights traveling into the city with a truckload of whatever vegetables are in season. (Courtesy Kay Cagle.)

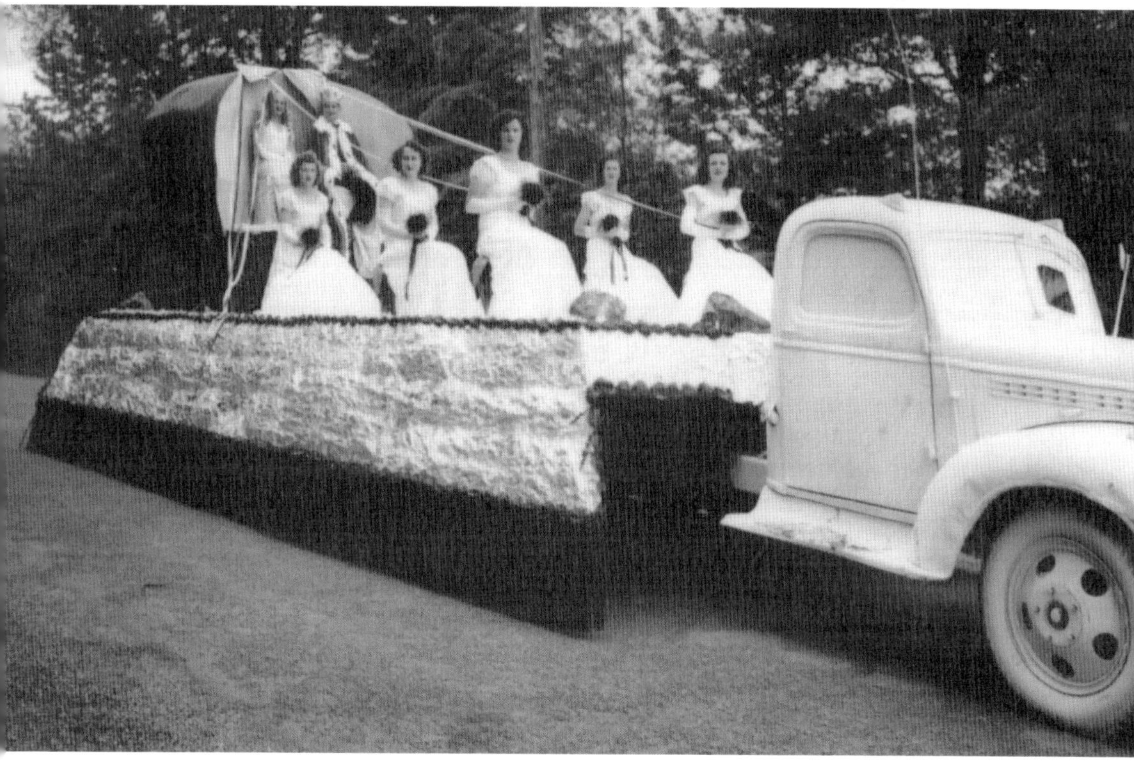

Strawberry Festival Parade
Cullman County residents love a parade, and by 1939, celebrating strawberry harvests, Henry F. Arnold was chairman of the festival, which featured a parade with 50 floats, a fiddlers contest, street dances, pageants, strawberry exhibits, a flower show, and a grand ball with the strawberry queen. (Courtesy Cullman County Museum.)

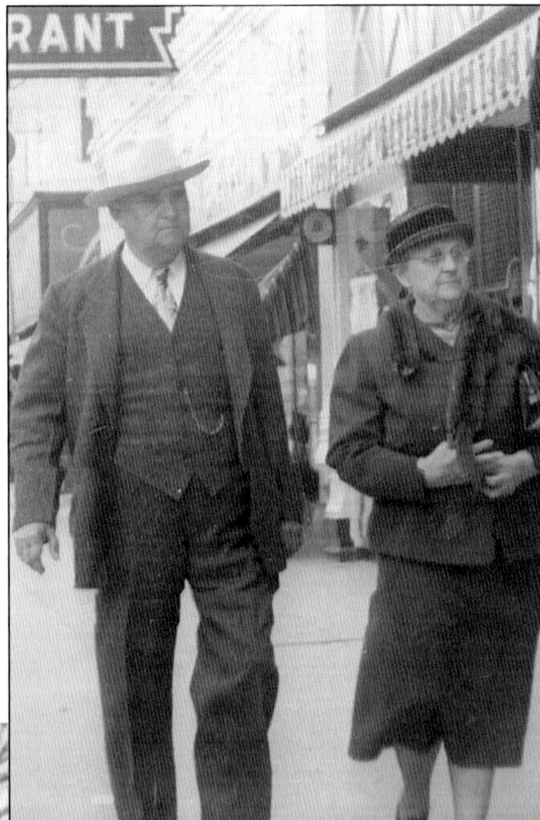

D.T. Kinney

By 1900, Cullman was a leading mule market. Horse and mule swapping events were held over several days. Herds were driven or shipped to Cullman. Keith Parrish, owner of Cullman Live Stock Barn, said mules shipped into Cullman were unloaded and led by a man named Richards, on horseback, to the auction site located on Highway 278 East. In 1911, F.C. Kinney built the largest mule barn north of Birmingham. There were other dealers, D.T. Kinney, Jim and Tom Bright, and Al Peinhardt. D.T. Kinney's mule barn, on Fourth Avenue Southeast, was built shortly after World War I. The big oak tree out front became a famous place for local politicians to caucus, and it was later named the "Political Tree." (Both images courtesy Steve Griffith.)

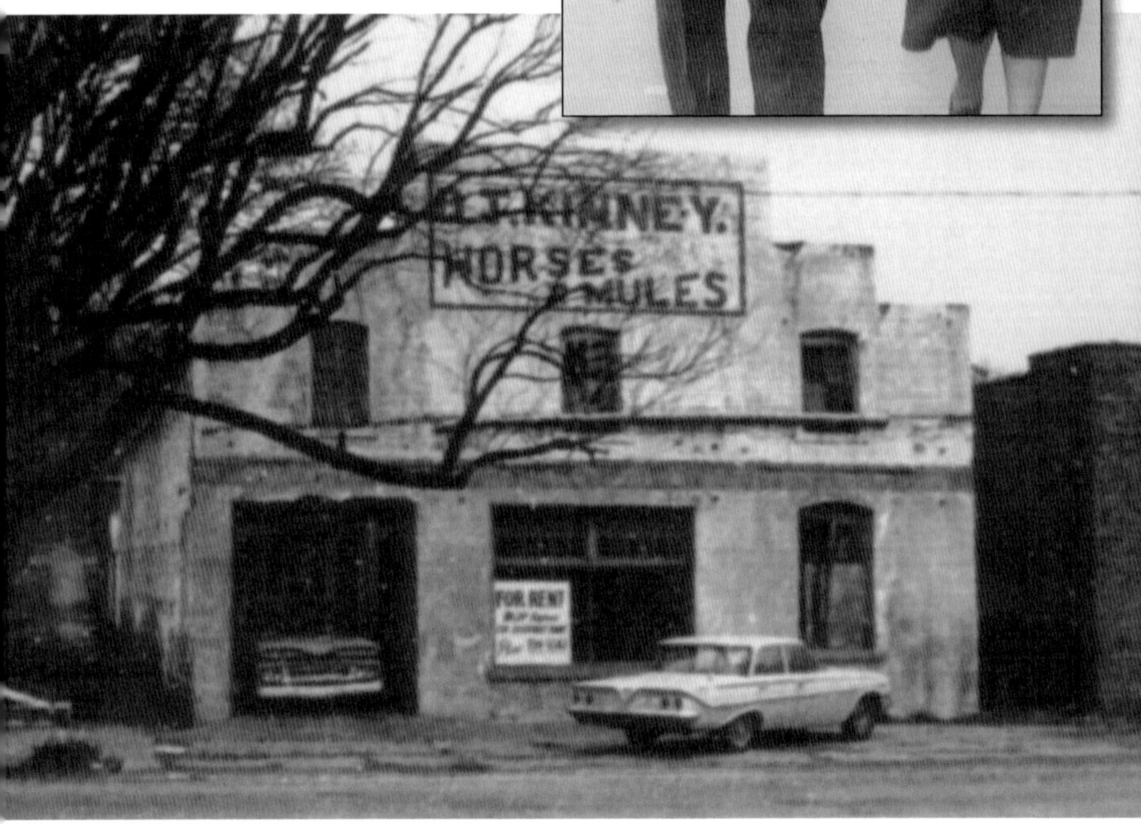

CHAPTER FIVE

Health and Wealth

As forests were cleared, lands cultivated, and farms dotted the landscape, settlements grew and attention turned to other important needs—medical and financial. No deaths were reported in Cullman during the first two years of colonization. Thirty-five years later, statistics showed the area had the lowest death rate in the country. The Cullman area was spared the 1878 nationwide epidemic of yellow fever, but the event pointed out the need for medical facilities.

By the turn of the century, Cullman had 23 practicing physicians who organized a medical society to serve the people's needs. Many of these physicians had small private hospitals with three or four beds, adjoining their homes, located throughout the county, including Joppa, Arkadelphia, and Bremen. H.C. Arnold had a dream of building a modern hospital. Following his death, Mrs. Alma Arnold donated a block of land, located in the heart of the city, in her husband's memory, and Cullman Hospital was constructed, receiving the first patient in 1939. Serving on the first board were the following: J.W. Arnold, Dr. J.G. Davis, Dr. J.C. Martin, Walter Herrell, and Conrad Howard.

While physical health was important, so was financial health. As Cullman began to grow, banks were created to finance businesses and homebuilding. Many banks that later became lasting institutions were started by individuals who started their own banks in the stores they operated. Others began lending money out of their own pockets.

Essentially, someone could hang up a shingle and become a bank—with proper capitalization, of course. George Parker and Scott Leeth were among those who started banks named after themselves, and their legacies live on today as their banks were later sold to larger institutions.

Not all banks survived. An embezzlement scandal brought down the German Bank after only 11 years of operation, and many depositors—including Sacred Heart Catholic Church—felt the sting.

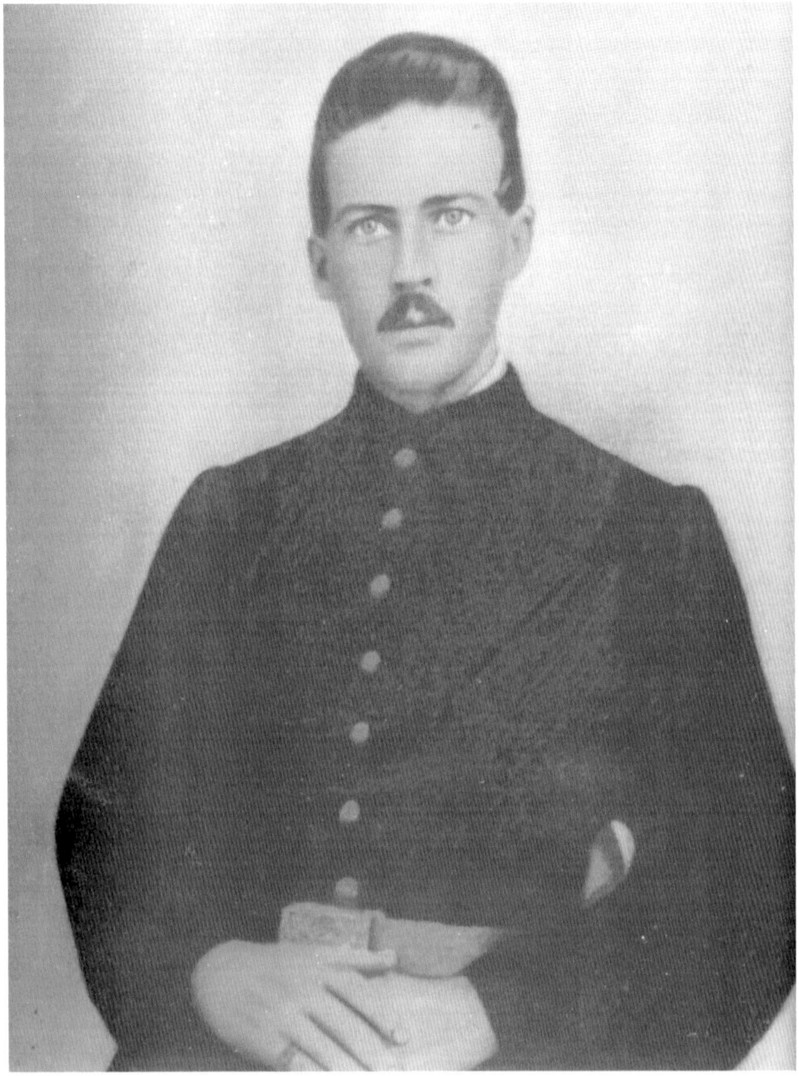

Dr. Luther Blair Hays

As the community flourished and basic needs were met, attention also turned to the medical facility expansion. By 1915, Dr. Luther Blair Hays and Jim Culpepper leased the old Frank Arndt home and converted it into the Cullman Hospital. This was the first step toward a physician association that would lead to the construction of a hospital. Unfortunately, Dr. Jim Culpepper was fatally injured in an automobile accident, and it was the spring of 1916 before the subject of a hospital facility was again pursued by Dr. Hays and other physicians. Dr. Hays, nicknamed "Lute," earned his pharmacy degree in 1896 and served in the Spanish-American War. He was the second son of Asa B. Hayes, first elected probate judge in Cullman County. Contributing to the early development of medical facilities and attending to the needs of an expanding population, Lute Hays, single at the time, made the difficult journey in the early 1900s to North Jefferson County where he served as physician to that county's burgeoning coal-mining industry. He was to meet and marry a woman who became affectionately known as "Miss Dollie." She would travel to Vinemont to partake in spa-like waters, and meet and marry "Lute" Hays as a result. An artist, she contributed to the early culture of Cullman and was a charter member of the Symphony Club. (Courtesy Dan Keel.)

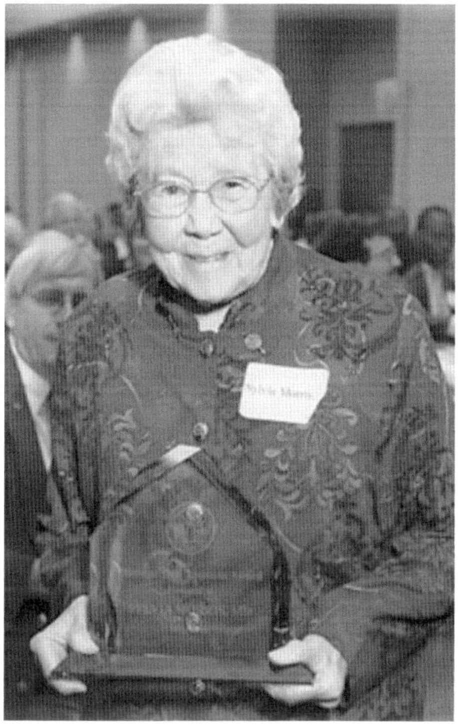

Dr. Sylvia Morris

Dr. Sylvia Morris, a pediatrician, was a promoter of diligence and hard work. Her life was infused with humor and wit, and she was destined to become a powerhouse in the medical community. She attended the University of Iowa when professors accepted the premise that girls did not belong in medical school. This tenacious character evolved by rolling up her sleeves to overcome difficulties, representing the very best in feminism, but she also was capable of walking into the kitchen and baking a mouth-watering loaf of bread. She followed in her father's footsteps and became the fourth generation in the family to practice medicine. She married John Thomas Morris, and the couple moved to Hanceville in 1949. When their Hanceville medical partner moved to Mississippi, Dr. Morris stayed to become the only licensed practicing female physician in Cullman County. The couple moved to East Cullman in 1955, and her lifelong home was established. Dr. Morris returned to practicing medicine after her children were school age, becoming assistant medical director for the Tri-County Health Service and going back to school for her MPH in epidemiology. Her son, Dr. John Morris, CRMC hospitalist and fifth medical generation, says his mother's primary concern was her adopted community. He remembers visiting the Cullman Health Clinic and not one child crying. "From pint size to adult, she had a real knack for bedside manner. She saw kids mostly, was dedicated to getting parents to sign on and help work with the health of children," he said. "Nothing got in the way of helping her patients." Dr. Morris pushed for children's immunization programs, lunch, and breakfast meals in schools. Her love for community kept her deeply involved; she was president of the Women's Medical Auxiliary, Mental Health, and worked to create the kind of community her children would want to live after their education was completed, and they did. Dr. Morris helped establish scholarships for schoolteachers and build the public library and high school complex. She established the hospice program in Cullman. She authored a novel *Jerome: To my Beloved Absent Companion*, a publication on her great-grandfather. The book was based on letters of the Civil War surgeon to his wife, followed by a book about Cullman County doctors before the 1900s. She also wrote short stories and made her beloved cat Jennifer famous in three books. Dr. Morris was a First United Methodist senior adult Sunday school teacher, or, as she often said, a referee for the classes. (Courtesy Dr. John Morris.)

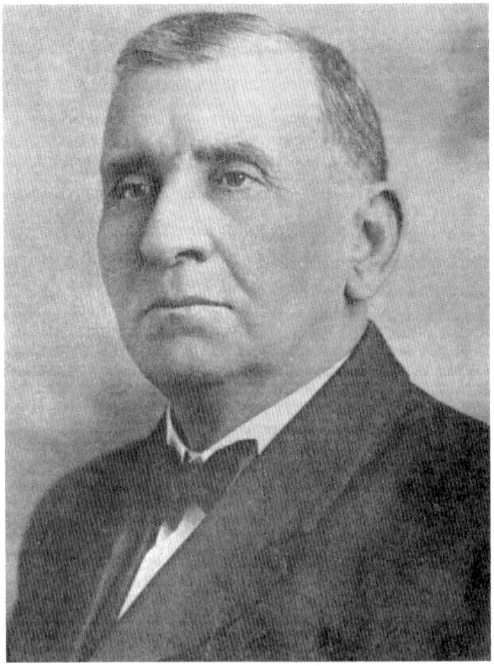

Dr. J.I. Armstrong
During the tragic 1918 flu epidemic, a call came for volunteer doctors to go to Huntsville and aid other doctors working among the Merrimac Cotton Mills employees. Conditions were serious and the death rate was high. Dr. Armstrong spent several weeks working with government doctors who were sent to help. He was presented a citation by the federal government for his services. (Courtesy Cullman County Museum.)

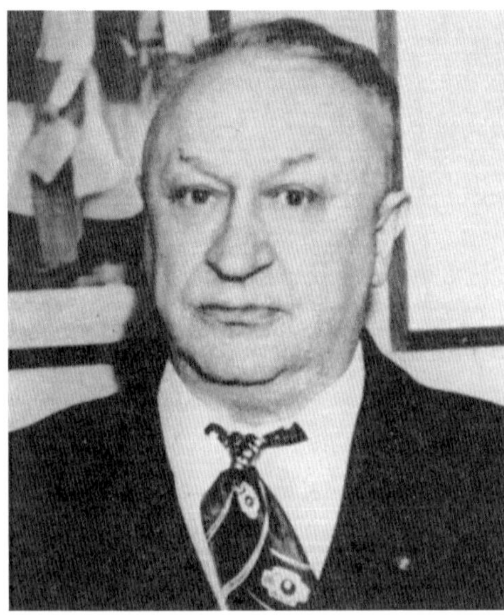

Dr. Phillip "Phil" Hartung
Phillip Hartung was known as "Dr. Phil" when he ran the People's Drug Company, popular for medicines and notions, for approximately 40 years before his death in 1955. With medical backgrounds, the Hartung family was established with the marriage of Gottlob Hartung to Julia Elizabeth Cullmann, niece of Col. Johann G. Cullmann. Phillip Hartung was one of eight children of Gottlob and Julia. (Courtesy Cullman County Museum.)

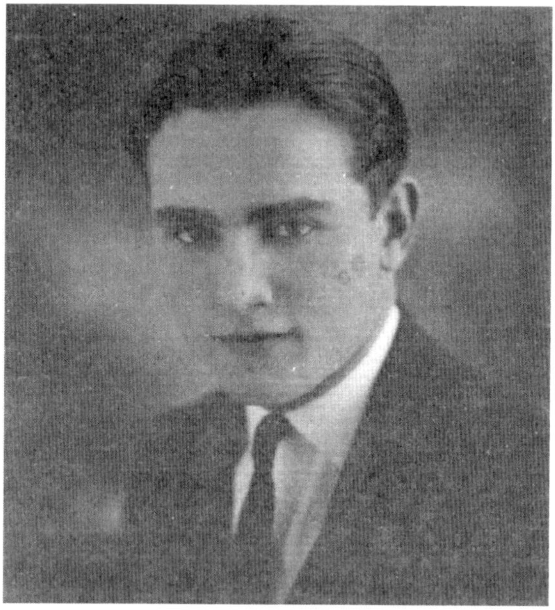

Horace Wells

Horace Wells, pharmacist, opened Mays and Wells Drug Store when soda fountains were part of drugstore décor. Medicine accounts were paid at harvest time. The business failed in 1931 when he kept filling prescriptions for people who could not pay. Before retiring in 1969, he worked for Super Drugs, managed the A&P store, worked for the Ford dealership, and worked in People's Drug Store. (Courtesy Cullman County Museum.)

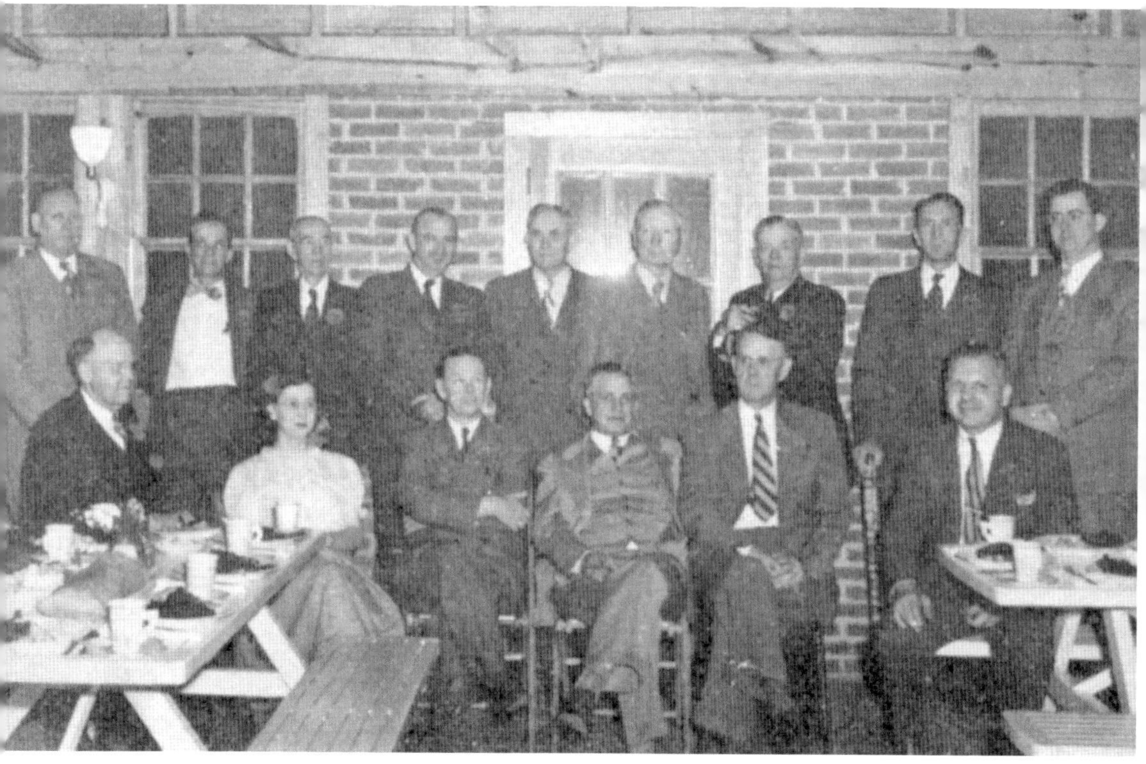

Medical Society

The 1940s and 1950s Medical Society members are, from left to right, (first row) Dr. R.B. Dodson, Dr. Sylvia Morris, Dr. Hughes, Dr. George Rowe, Dr. M.W. Whitesides, and Dr. E.B. Barnes: (second row) Dr. Mike Crawford, Dr. John Morris, Dr. J.C. Martin, Dr. Frank Stitt, Dr. J.G. Daves, Dr. R.A. Culpepper, Dr. E.D. McAdory, Dr. Tom Beatty, and Dr. J.C. Chambliss. (Courtesy Cullman County Museum.)

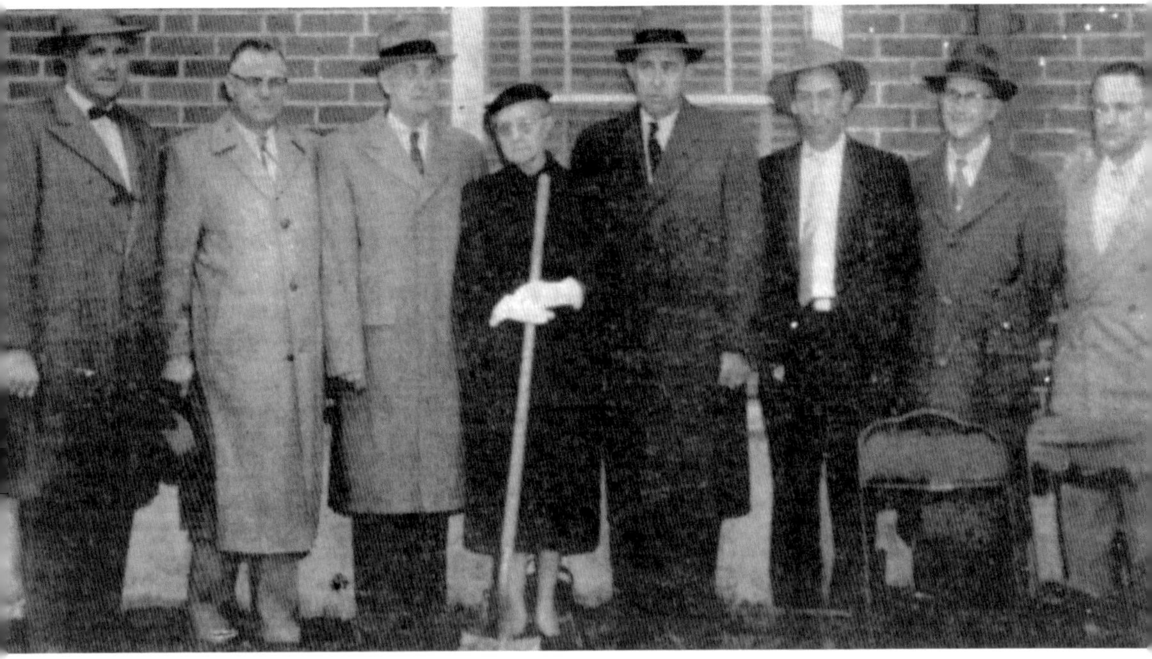

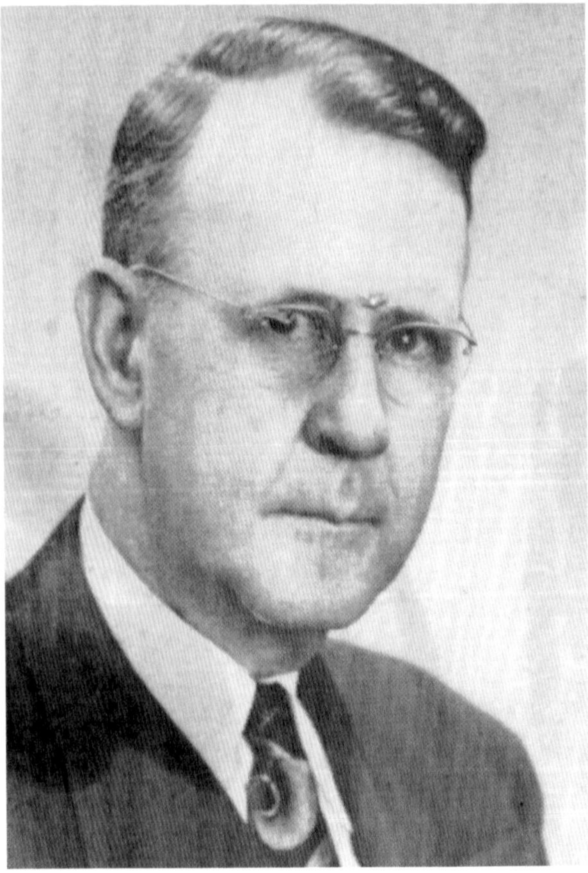

Alma Arnold

H.C. Arnold, leading local industrialist, made provisions to donate land in the heart of downtown Cullman to construct a hospital. He died before the transaction could be completed. His widow, Alma Arnold, fulfilled his wishes. She is shown with other Cullman dignitaries breaking ground for the new 54-bed hospital. This was the beginning of a march toward medical expansion. (Courtesy Cullman County Museum.)

Dr. M.S. Whiteside

At a time when typhoid fever, diphtheria, scarlet fever, and other communicable diseases were a concern, Dr. M.S. Whiteside became county health doctor and director of the health center, constructed in 1927, across the street from the hospital. Constant vigilance through education, the county's health vital statistics propelled Cullman County in the top echelon statewide for health. (Courtesy Cullman County Museum.)

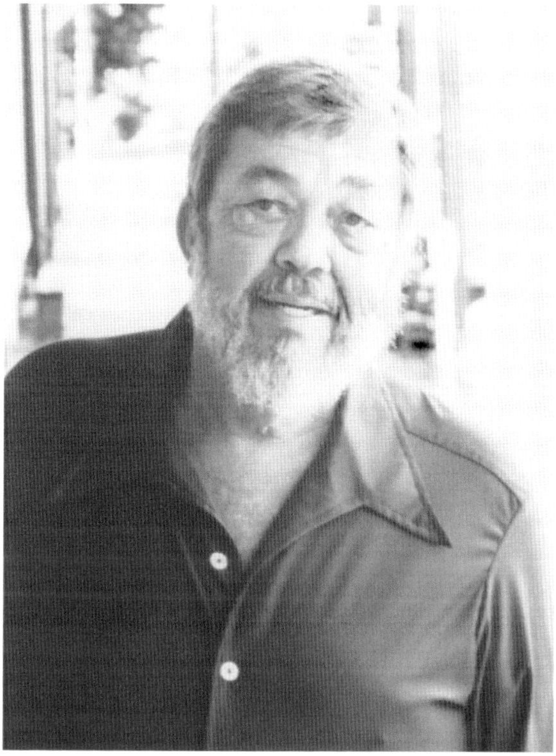

Dr. Lowell H. Clemmons Sr.
A dedicated physician and humanitarian, Dr. Clemmons had magnetic people appeal and left a lifetime of accomplishments. One of the Flying Fifty, he was medical director of the tuberculosis hospital in Decatur, recognized for his services by the Douglas L. Cannon Medical Journalism Award, published two books, wrote for the *Saturday Evening Post*, *Sports Illustrated*, and numerous medical journals. (Courtesy Clemmons family.)

Cullman Doctors Honored
In 1970, the Cullman Medical Society honored prominent local doctors for more than 50 years of service. From left to right are Dr. M.S. Whiteside, Dr. J.G. Daves, Dr. E.D. McAdory, and Dr. R.B. Dodson. (Courtesy Cullman County Museum.)

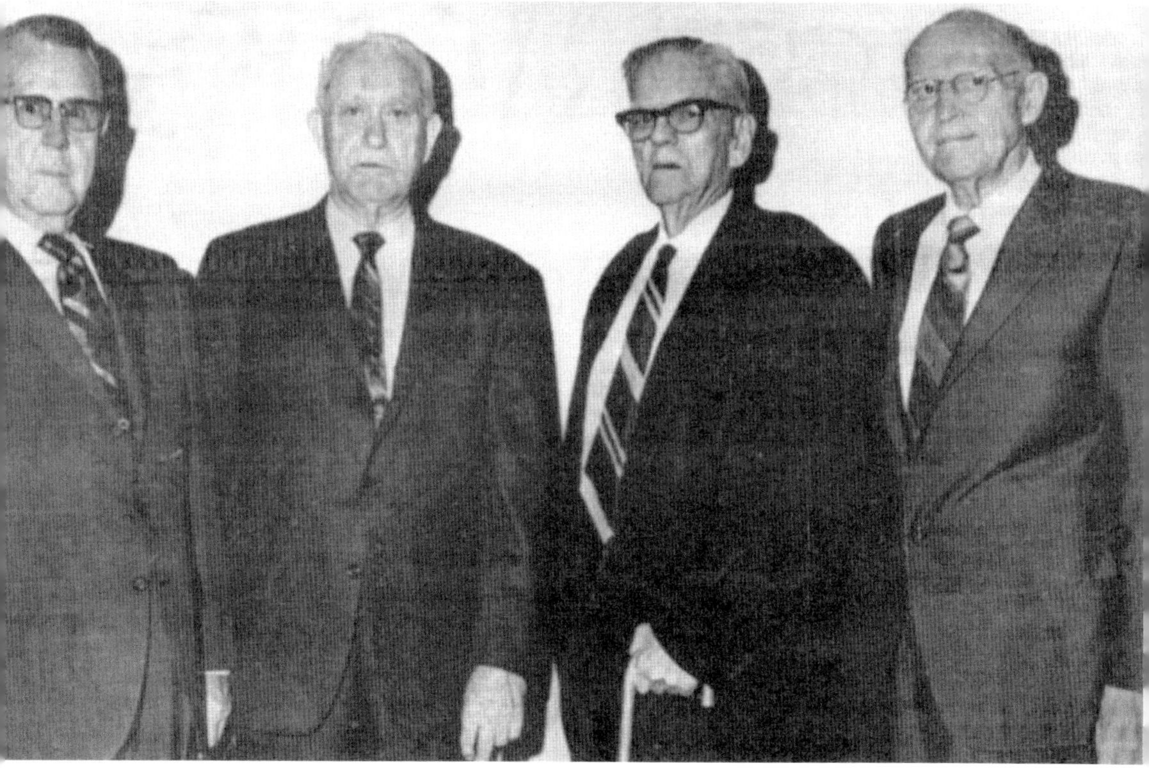

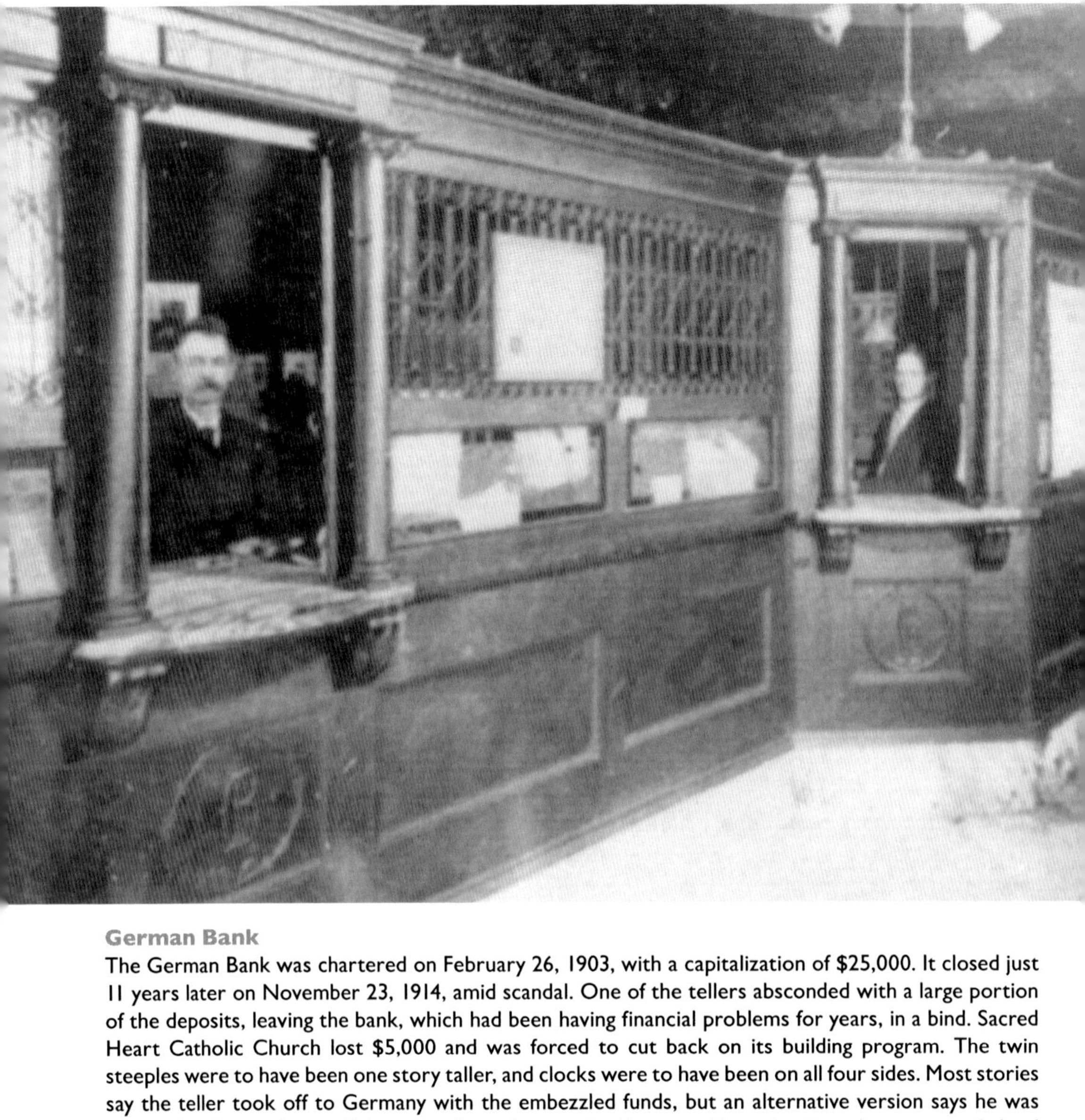

German Bank

The German Bank was chartered on February 26, 1903, with a capitalization of $25,000. It closed just 11 years later on November 23, 1914, amid scandal. One of the tellers absconded with a large portion of the deposits, leaving the bank, which had been having financial problems for years, in a bind. Sacred Heart Catholic Church lost $5,000 and was forced to cut back on its building program. The twin steeples were to have been one story taller, and clocks were to have been on all four sides. Most stories say the teller took off to Germany with the embezzled funds, but an alternative version says he was arrested and served time. Either way, the action resulted in several lawsuits since there was no federal insurance for banks at the time. Hanover Bank of Germany, and its American counterpart, Hanover Bank of New York, funded the German Bank and demanded payment from customers who had already paid back the German Bank for their loans. There was a total of $169,000 in outstanding loans at the time. The bankruptcy judge turned the records over to a teller at Parker Bank, though Parker did not officially take over the accounts. (Courtesy Cullman County Museum.)

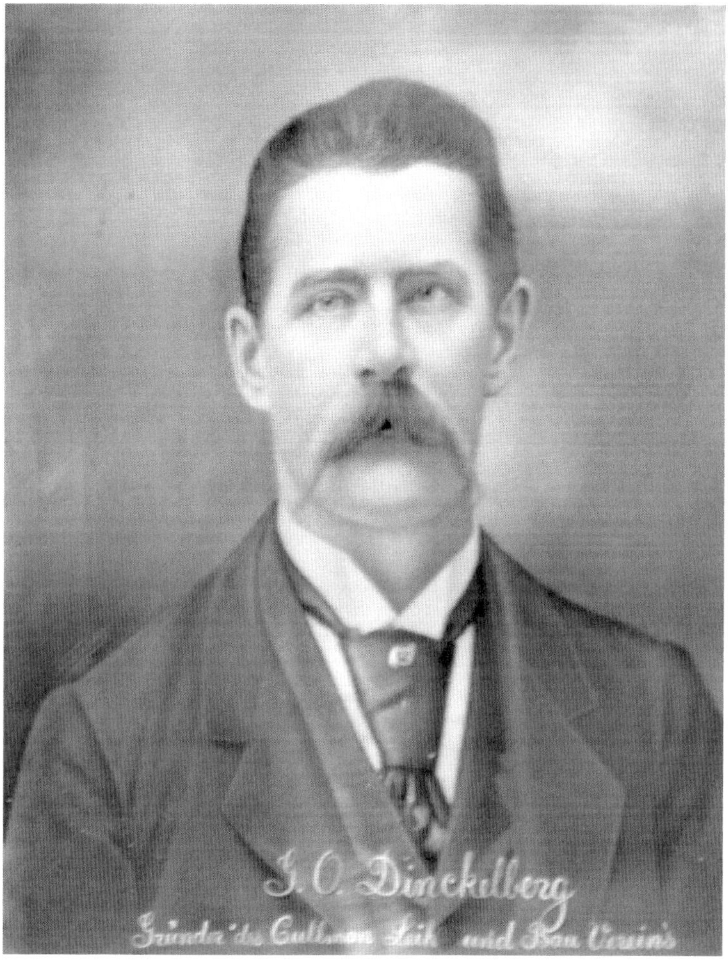

G.O. Dinckelberg

In the early days of Cullman's growth, men not only managed and operated businesses, but also served the community in other vital capacities. G.O. Dinckelberg was the first president of Cullman Building & Loan and also a volunteer firefighter. A native of northern Germany, he was recruited by Col. Johann Cullmann and came to the fledgling town with his wife, Amalia. When the bank was founded on October 1, 1887, by the original 30 settlers, Dinckelberg, as president, had a plan: Each member of the building and loan facility would deposit a small sum of money, and members would lend the money to each other as needs arose in home construction. The 30 charter members had a total of 130 shares. The investment represented $5,200. The bank made its first home loan to Peter Winkerbach for $200 for a loan period of five years, which was longer than other banks in the community did at the time. The bank was first located in the upstairs area of Kullman Hall. At that time, there were no regular office hours, and members assembled each Saturday night for the transaction as business. In the mid-1890s, Dinckelberg responded to a large fire in downtown Cullman. The fire destroyed a large section of the town, including the courthouse. Dinckelberg died fighting the blaze. His business acumen lived on. By 1900, bank assets had reached $50,000, and the institution held loans totaling $40,000. In 1941, the bank changed its name to Cullman Savings & Loan and started having regular office hours in the Imbusch Building. Total assets were $136,000. From there, it moved to the Fuller Building and to its current location at Second Avenue in downtown Cullman. It changed its name to Cullman Savings Bank in 1994. (Courtesy Cullman Savings Bank.)

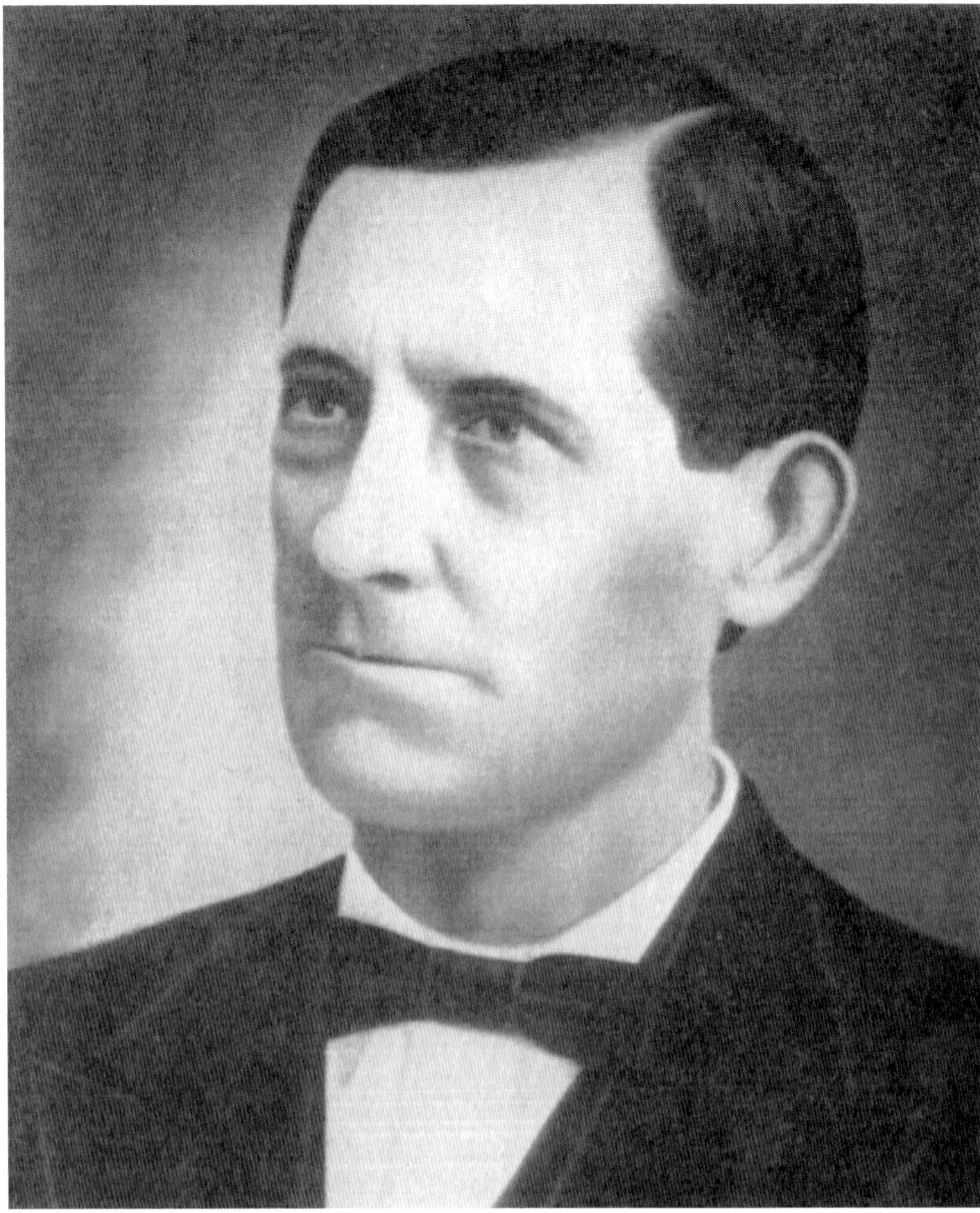

George Parker

George Parker came to Cullman in 1874 from his native Cincinnati. He had obtained a law degree a year earlier and set up a law practice in the new colony. Parker started loaning money out of his own pocket, eventually opening the banking business Parker & Co. in the basement of Cullman's first courthouse. Despite the name Parker & Co., George Parker was the sole owner. Eventually, Parker Bank & Trust was opened on Second Avenue South. The building still stands. For a while, it was the only banking establishment between Birmingham and Decatur. Parker Bank's final home was on the corner of Alabama 157 and Second Avenue South, and that building, too, still stands. Parker Bank eventually sold to AmSouth, which closed the location when it merged with Regions in 2007. Parker served as Cullman's mayor from 1889 to 1896. (Courtesy Cullman County Museum.)

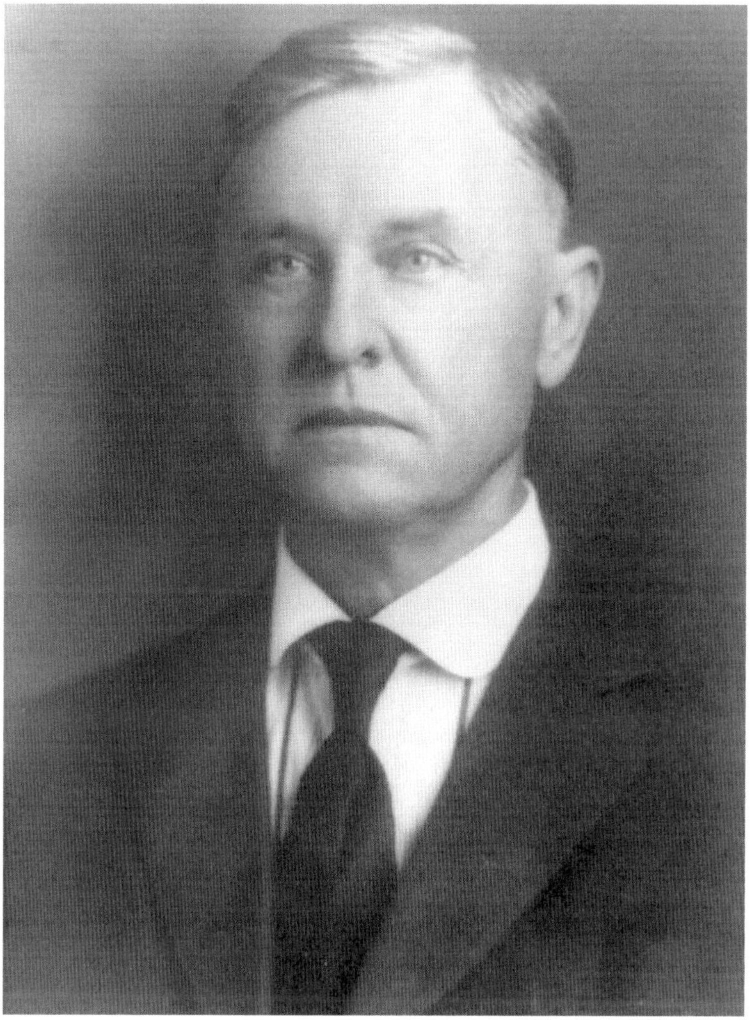

Scott Leeth

George Scott Leeth began his career working on his father's farm in Arkadelphia. As he reached adulthood, he began assisting a man who owned a store in Arkadelphia, and after three years, he moved to Cullman and started his own mercantile store. He gave out pocketknives with his store's motto: "Everything for the living and the dead—except whiskey." Leeth founded the National Bank of Cullman in 1906, running it from the back of his store. He closed the bank in 1909, saying he knew nothing about banking. He clearly regained his confidence and founded Leeth National Bank in the same year with $50,000 at the current site of Wells Fargo. The current building, which has been remodeled a few times, was built in 1952. Two drive-in windows were added in 1960 during expansion, which also added off-street parking. The Northside Branch was built at the Cullman Shopping Center in 1968. A mural of the original Leeth Bank was commissioned by Betty Leeth Haynes as part of the Cullman County Historical Society's mural project in 2010. Other presidents included H.C. Arnold, J.P. Young, J.A. Dunlap, and W.O. "Oscar" Dunlap. Leeth National Bank was acquired by SouthTrust in 1983, which merged with Wachovia in 2004. In 2008, Wachovia was acquired by Wells Fargo. Leeth remained the head of the bank he founded until his death at age 65. In addition to his multiple business holdings, Leeth also supported his community by funding schools and by helping individual students. (Courtesy Betty Leeth Haynes.)

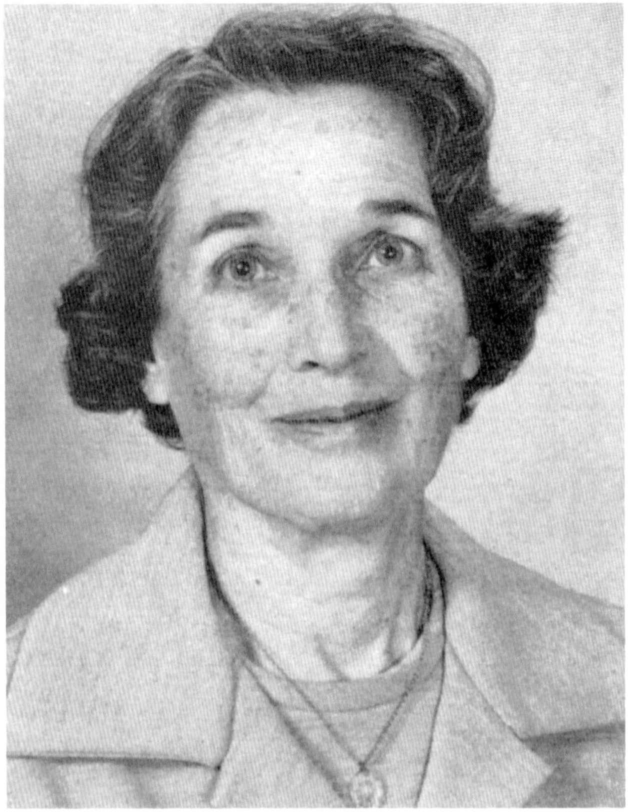

Edna Earle Arnold

In 1968, the board of directors of Improved Savings & Loan asked Edna Earle Arnold to compile a history of the bank to be put into "a folder or pamphlet or booklet or whatever you may call it." No copy of that final document exists, but Edna Earle's handwritten history does. Beginning with the institution's founding in 1905, she describes what the town was like at the time: no paved streets (but a lot of sidewalks for foot traffic), blacksmiths, livery stables, mule dealers, saloons, and an opera house. In a city of 1,500 inhabitants, the fledgling lending institution drew a total of 55 initial members. The original name, Improved Building & Loan was adopted a month after its founding. At first, members met every Saturday night. Business was discussed, but so were politics, local happenings, and the weather. "Thrifty citizens would come with a few dollars saved during the week to invest, while other 'members' would bring a dollar or two to apply to the loans they had made from the association," Edna Earle wrote. In May 1907, assets were listed at $9,300. In 1941, Finis E. St. John Jr. was appointed as the attorney to reorganize the institution. He was elected director later that year. Assets were $152,024. Improved Savings & Loan was housed in various buildings in town throughout its history, but by 1968, it was ready for a home of its own. Edna Earle noted that the city had grown by tenfold to a population of 15,000. There were paved streets as people had taken to auto travel. And instead of businesses dealing with mules, there was cable television. In 1974, the name was changed to First Federal Savings & Loan as the institution switched from a state to a federal charter. In 2011, it was forced under the Dodd-Frank law to return to a state charter, and had to remove "federal" from its name. Since then, it has been known as First Community Bank. Despite charter and name changes, bank president Billy Faulk says the bank is doing the same thing today as it has been since its founding, loaning money for homes and being a banking institution for people from childhood throughout their lives. And the history of the original Improved Savings & Loan is on record due to Edna Earle Arnold's persistent research. (Courtesy First Community Bank.)

CHAPTER SIX

Notables and Niches

Before Col. Johann G. Cullmann founded Cullman, other men and women trekked into local areas, establishing homes and communities. The Speegle family traveled into southwest Cullman County in the early 1800s, then a part of Mississippi. Mace Brindley forged into the northeast part of Cullman County.

They emerged from all walks of life and found themselves serving their fellow man, protecting a nation, founding civic organizations. Winifred Cranford walked over rutted paths into dense forests with wild animals to perform services as a midwife. She was known as an "Angel of Mercy." They are the individuals who put their community, not themselves, first, dedicating their time and talents to make it a better place for their family and future generations. These homegrown men and women stepped forward and became committed to serving in various capacities. There are notable individuals who fill a niche within the community; heroes of World War II, Korea, Vietnam, Desert Storm, and Iraqi Freedom. They served with honor and distinction. Foreign lands were not unknown to young men like Whit Warren who was a missionary to Kenya and filled the air and children's hearts with song, and as part of his legacy, Whit's Place in Kenya still remains and every song that is sung by the children is called Whit's song.

Communications flourished with men like Carroll Eddins, a chamber of commerce thrived under the guiding hand of Raymond Yost, and Pastor Bob Kurtz utilized his passion for golf to benefit children's charities.

We learn of the heroism of Catherine Clark Voss when the State Bank was robbed, and of individuals who have made it a life's work to preserve the history of the county in which they live and document it for future generations like Earlene Johnson, who became the first female mayor in the colony in over a hundred years. There is an unending chain of notables who fill niches, and each individual forms a strong link in the bond that makes Cullman County a great place to live.

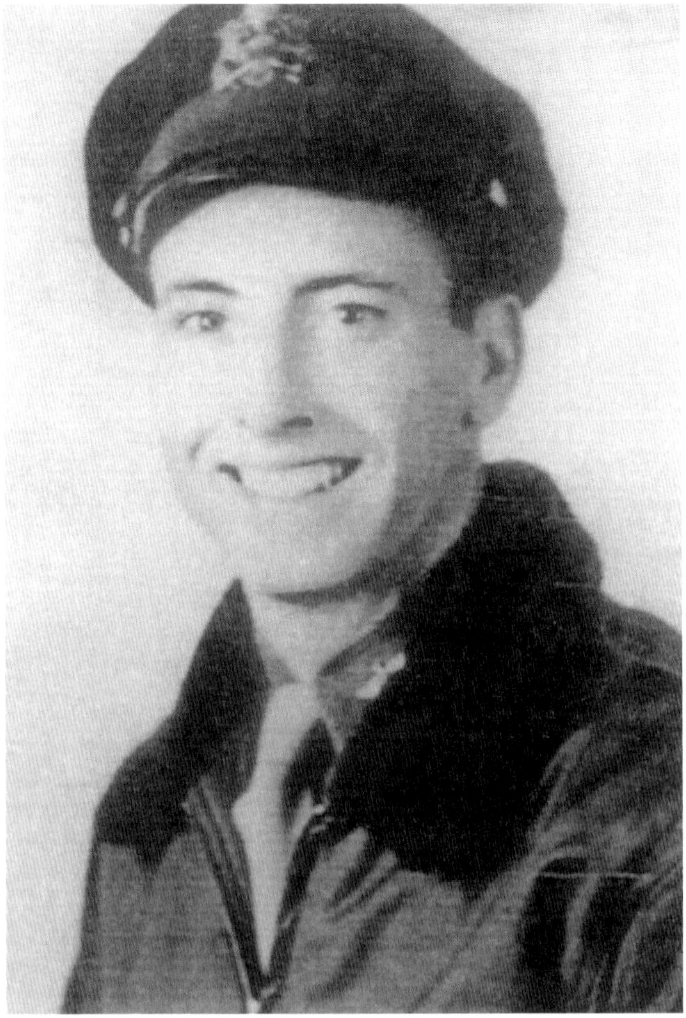

Julian Campbell, World War II

Drafted into the Army at 21 years old, Julian Campbell, who had grown up on a farm, thought he would be going out to see the world. He saw the world, piloting 40 separate B-26 bomber missions during World War II, hitting targets in Sicily, Italy, and Southern France in 1943. These missions were flown from bases in Algeria, Tunisia, and the Island of Sardinia, which supported the invasions of Sicily and Italy. He went on to fly transport missions into occupied Japan and combat missions into Vietnam. Receiving his early aviation training at Maxwell Field in Montgomery, he climbed steadily to upper classman status, a big step from plowing a field in Arley, Alabama. "I'm glad I contributed to the war effort," he says about flying a Martin B-26 on World War II combat missions. He flew the C-54 across the Pacific and the Douglas B-26 with the Alabama Air National Guard. When he mustered out, Julian served in the Air National Guard and was recalled to duty for a stint in the Korean War. He served his country 28 years, first with the Army Air Force. He retired from the US Air Force in 1969. Julian says when he was originally drafted they called him private, but he did not feel any anything was private, sharing "one" bath and bedroom with "all those men." Now, at 93 years old, part of a class referred to as the "Greatest Generation," he has authored a book, *Memories That Must Not Vanish*. During his military years, he completed some non-flying assignments, was squadron commander, Air Force ROTC instructor, and managed other staff responsibilities. (Courtesy Julian Campbell.)

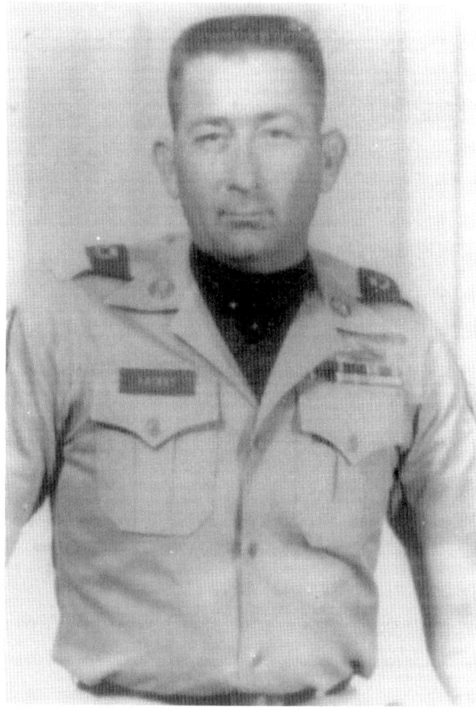

Wayne Lackey, Korea

Wayne Lackey, Baileyton, enlisted in 1947, assigned to the Honor Guard of Arlington National Cemetery. With the 7th Army Infantry, he was in the Inchon landings, Seoul, and North Korean coast invasion. He earned the Purple Heart, Combat Infantry Badge, and Bronze Star and was promoted to corporal. He retired sergeant first class in 1974. Wayne designed and supervised construction of Cullman's VFW, serving three terms as commander. (Courtesy Cullman VFW.)

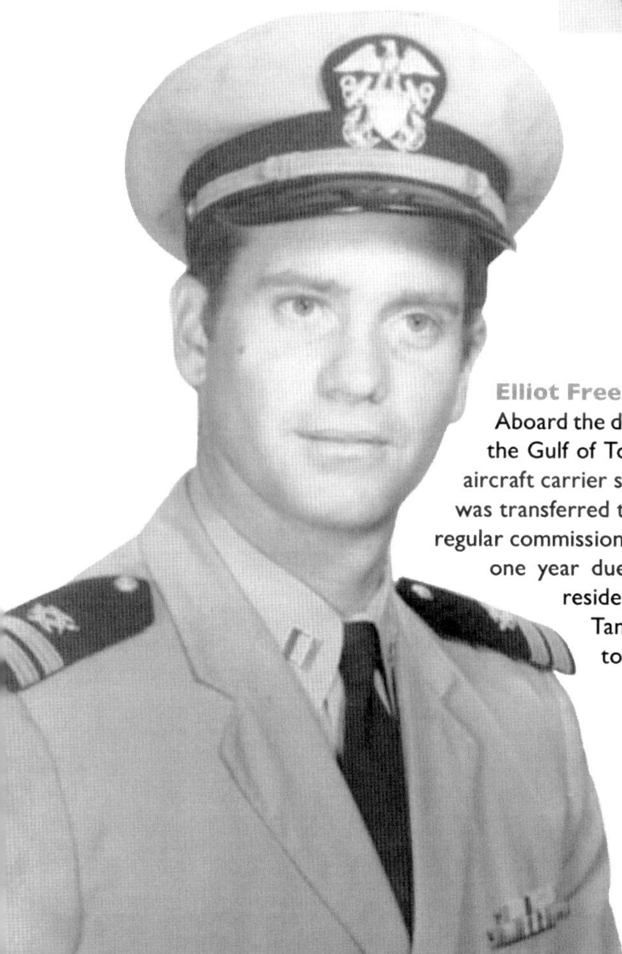

Elliot Free, Vietnam

Aboard the destroyer, USS *Beale*, Elliot Free deployed to the Gulf of Tonkin, participating in offshore gunfire and aircraft carrier support. Returning to the United States, he was transferred to the Civil Engineering Corps and notified regular commissioned naval officers' enlistment was extended one year due to the Vietnam War. He was assigned resident officer in charge of construction Dong Tam for main road construction from Saigon to the Mekong Delta. (Courtesy Elliot Free.)

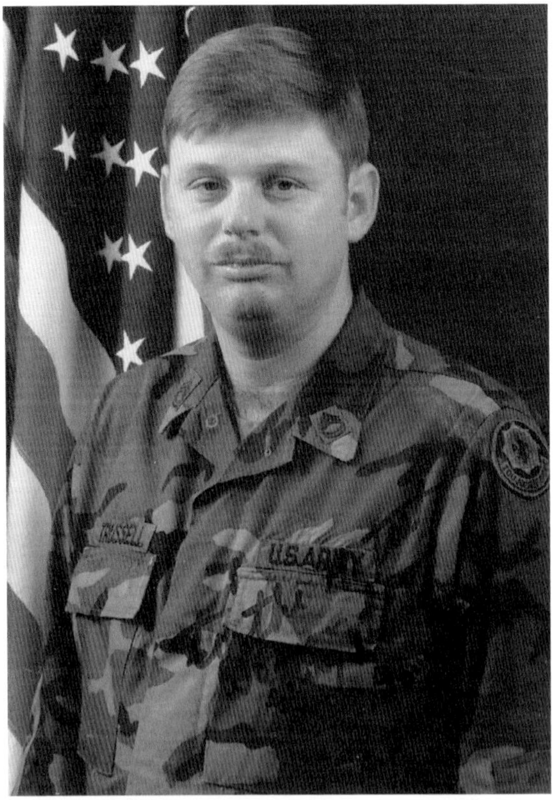

Joe Trussell, Desert Storm
After sitting in the sand six months, Sgt. Maj. Joe Trussell's little four-tank platoon spearheaded penetration with the 24th Army Infantry Division, cutting Iraq in half with a "hammer and anvil" attack maneuver. Troops in the north and south were the anvil, and the 24th Division was the hammer. He was commander of the M-1 Abrams tank platoon, the Army's only trained desert fighters at that time. (Courtesy Joe Trussell.)

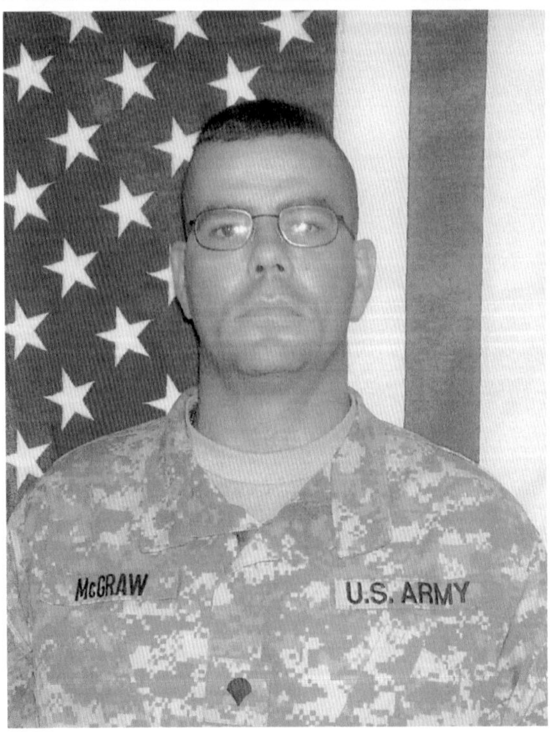

Randy McGraw, Iraqi Freedom
McGraw was deployed to the Horn of Africa in Operation Enduring Freedom, then wounded in an al-Qaeda firefight in Somalia. After recuperation, he was retrained and assigned as officer to the 99th Movement Control Team in Italy. He was injured again following another deployment to Iraq and medically unable to stay in the military, so he was assigned to the Wounded Warrior Transition Battalion. He retired in 2011. (Courtesy Randy McGraw.)

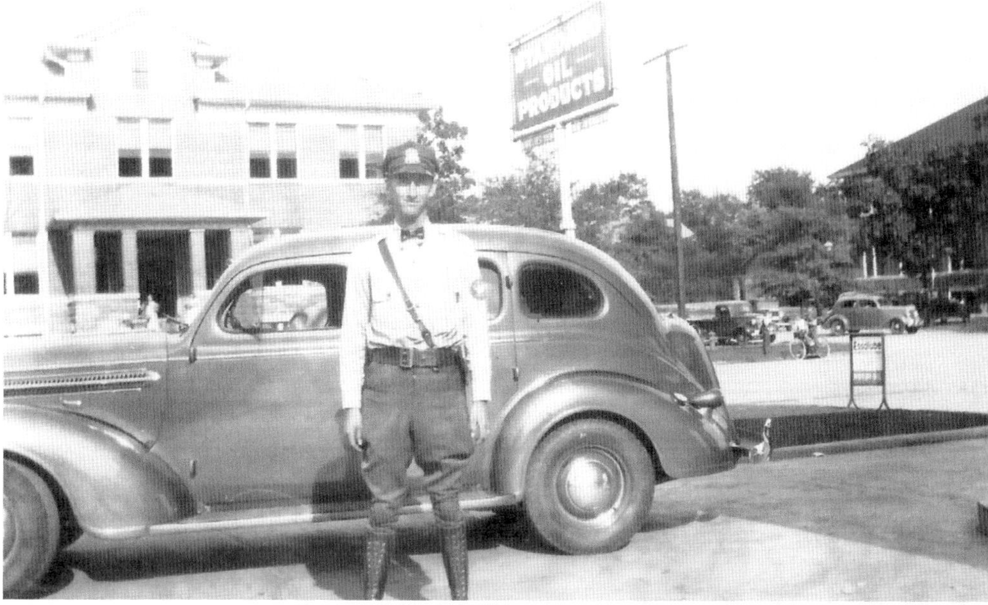

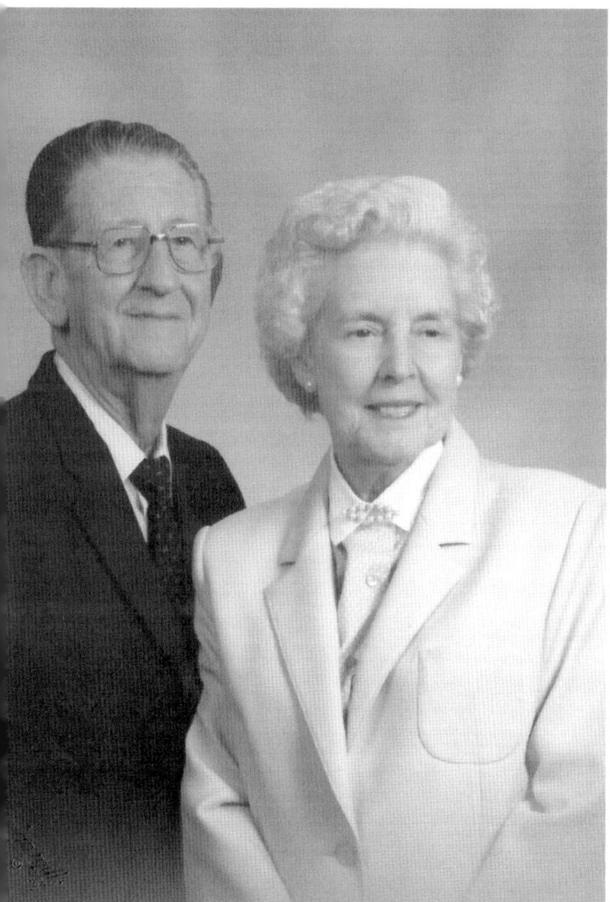

Carroll Eddins

Benjamin Carroll Eddins was the entrepreneur behind WFMH AM-FM radio. The FM's 100,000 watts became a favorite in Alabama, parts of Georgia, Mississippi, and Tennessee. During World War II, in the Army Air Corps Signal section, he checked out high altitude bombing radar on the first B-29s that bombed Japan. Eddins committed his stations to county fair broadcasts; was honored by the Quarterback Club for broadcasting Cullman Bearcat Football 41 years, and sponsored Kiwanis Radio Day. He brought cable television to Cullman and oversaw Sunday broadcasts of First United Methodist Church, where he and Mrs. Eddins were members. The Carroll Eddins Humanitarian Award was established to honor him. Eddins came to Cullman in 1938 as Alabama's youngest highway patrolman. He married Elsa Kempson. When Sen. John Hollis Bankhead's body was transferred back to Jasper, Eddins was to ride a motorcycle, assigned to guard Pres. Franklin D. Roosevelt, attending the funeral. (Both images courtesy Mary Evelyn Jones.)

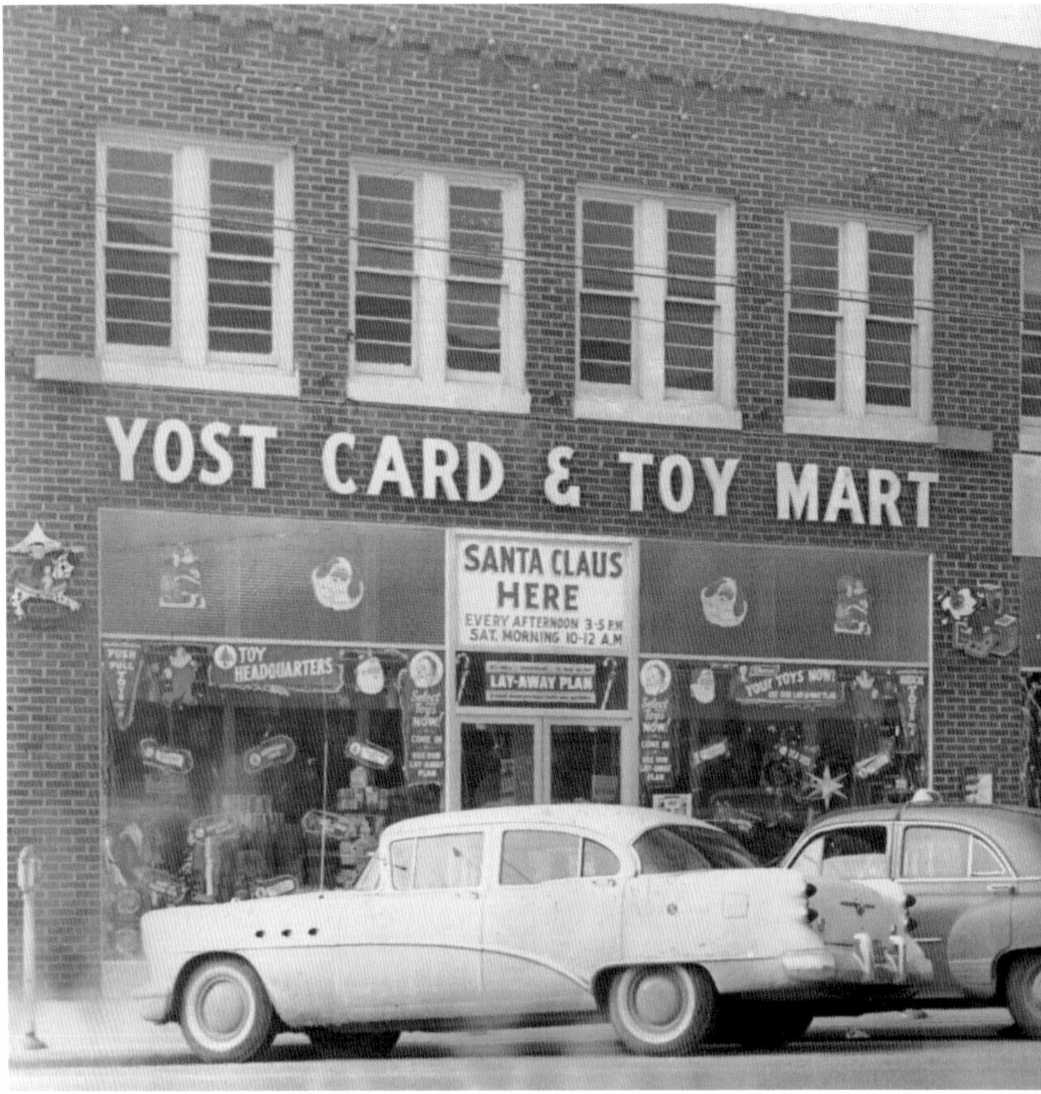

Raymond Yost

Raymond Yost did not live in Cullman until he was an adult, but once he arrived he was all-in. Born in 1907, in Leith, Ohio, Yost moved with his family to Talladega in 1916. His father, Frank, bought part of a 5-10-25-cent store with a relative and went into business. When Yost graduated high school, he attended Howard College (now Samford University) and graduated in 1929 with a degree in accounting. Yost had worked in his father's store while in high school, and after a short time working as an accountant his father sent him to Boaz to run another store. After two years in Boaz, Yost saw little hope for earning a living from that store, so he moved it to Cullman in 1933. It was a huge success and became an institution. He sold the store in 1955 to the V.J. Elmore chain, but he also operated Yost Gift Shop from 1940 to 1965 and Yost Card and Toy Mart from 1955 to 1965.

In addition to his businesses, Yost was a cheerleader for his adopted hometown. He was heavily involved in the Kiwanis Club, serving as its president in 1943. He served in every other elected position

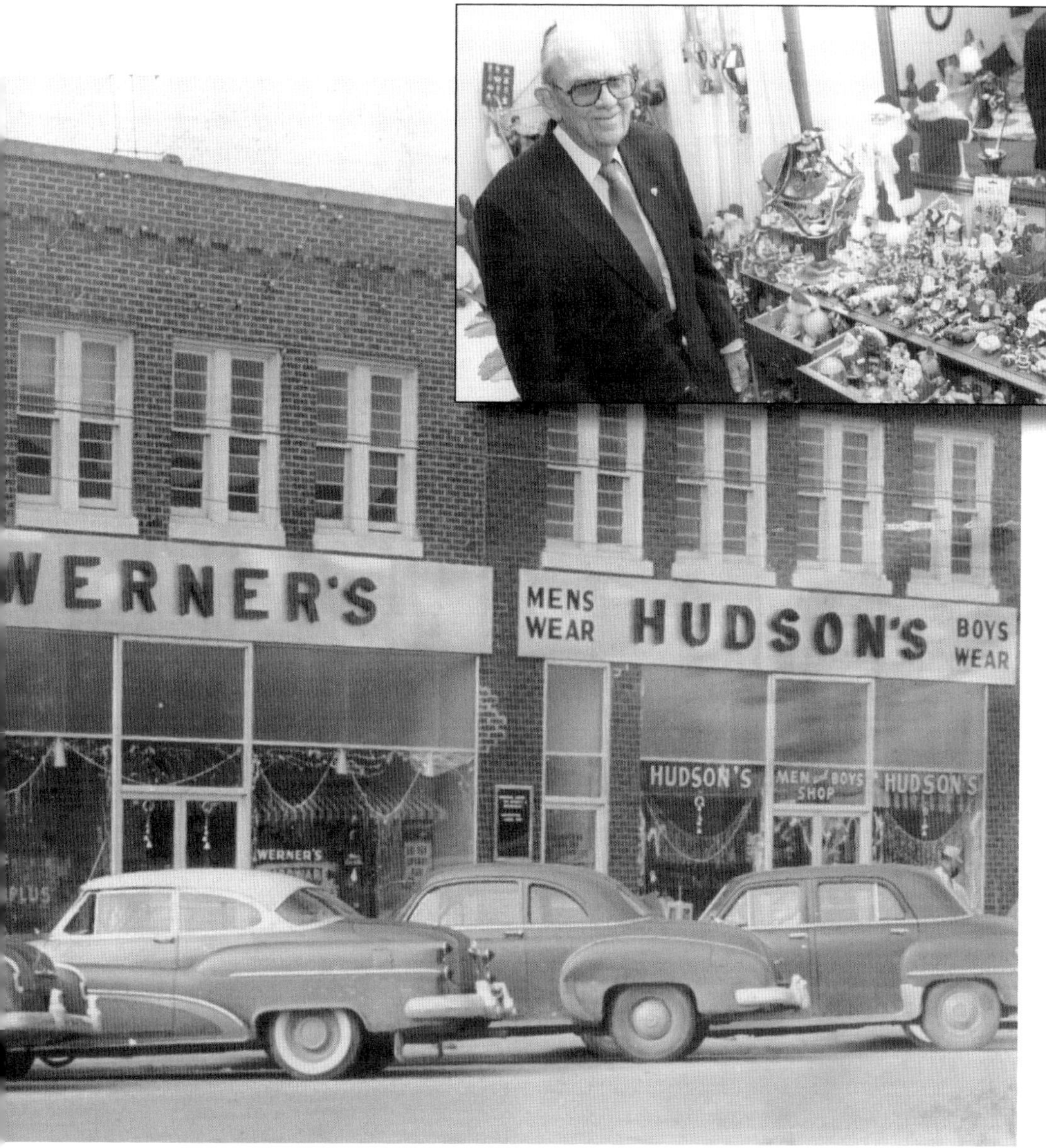

the club had and, in 1999, had been secretary for 19 years. As president of Kiwanis, he helped form the Cullman Area Chamber of Commerce and served as its first president. Yost was heavily involved in the community in other ways. He was chairman of the committee that built the Colonel Cullmann monument and has served as a leader in the Cullman County Historical Society, the Commission on Aging, the Community Concert Association, the German Club, the Larkwood Club, and Cullman Oktoberfest. He was Oktoberfest burgermeister in 1987. Yost was a meticulous keeper of information, compiling more than 100 scrapbooks of Cullman history, which he donated to the Cullman Museum. He also kept scrapbooks of his family and the Kiwanis Club, and his house was filled with his various collections, including state plates and Santa Clauses. Yost was named the *Cullman Times*' Distinguished Citizen of the Year in 1999 and was one of the newspaper's top 100 people of the 20th century. He was married to his wife, Gladys, from 1935 until her death in 1995, and died on the date of their wedding anniversary, March 9, 2002, at age 94. (Both images courtesy Barbara Yost.)

Chester Freeman

Chester Freeman spent his life bringing happiness to others. Born in the Brushy Pond Mountain area of Cold Springs on June 3, 1922, Freeman served as a spy in World War II in the South Pacific. He spent much time behind enemy lines gathering intelligence and was wounded twice during his service. While overseas, he corresponded with a young woman back home named Hilda Wood. When he returned home from the war, he married Hilda, and the couple raised two children. Freeman was well known as a candy distributor in Cullman, a job he held for 28 years.

He also was known for his extensive civic work, including his decades as a member of the Lions Club and as a member of the Parks and Recreation Board. He also was involved in the Cullman County Industrial Development Board and the Chamber of Commerce and was Chairman of the Advisory Board at Wallace State Community College for 32 years. Freeman was also behind bringing a park to Cullman for handicapped citizens. But his life of adventure started even before his induction into the Army. He helped solve the mystery of "Crybaby Holler" when he and a friend followed the spooky sounds of a crying baby, discovering the sound was actually made by two trees that had grown together. When strong winds blew, the trees rubbed together to create the sound. In the late 1930s and early 1940s, he would hitchhike to Nashville to see the Grand Ole Opry. Cleo Davis, who was from this area, was a singer for Bill Monroe and the Bluegass Boys. Knowing Davis allowed Freeman to get into Ryman Auditorium through the musicians' entrance. Freeman died February 9, 2013, at age 90 and was described as one of the most active volunteers in the area. According to an article on Freeman in the *Cullman Times*, John Hunt, director of the city's parks system, once said of Freeman, "Anything good that happens in Cullman, Chester is a part of it." (Courtesy Lions Club.)

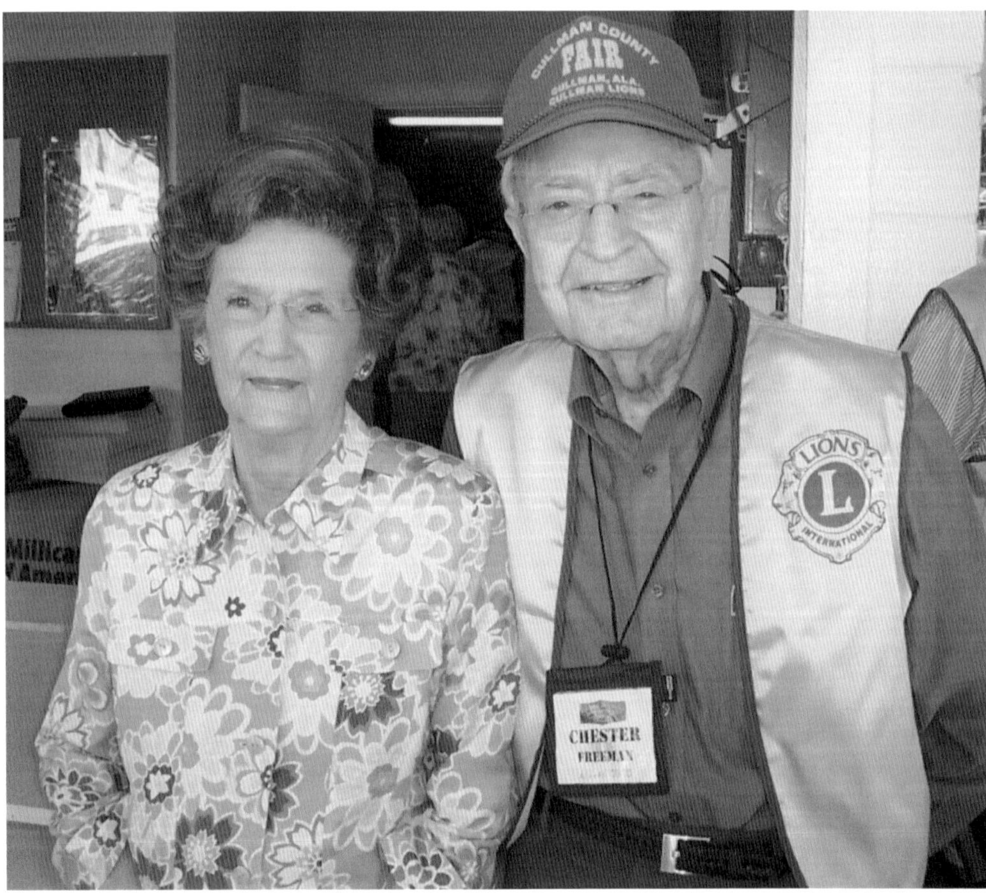

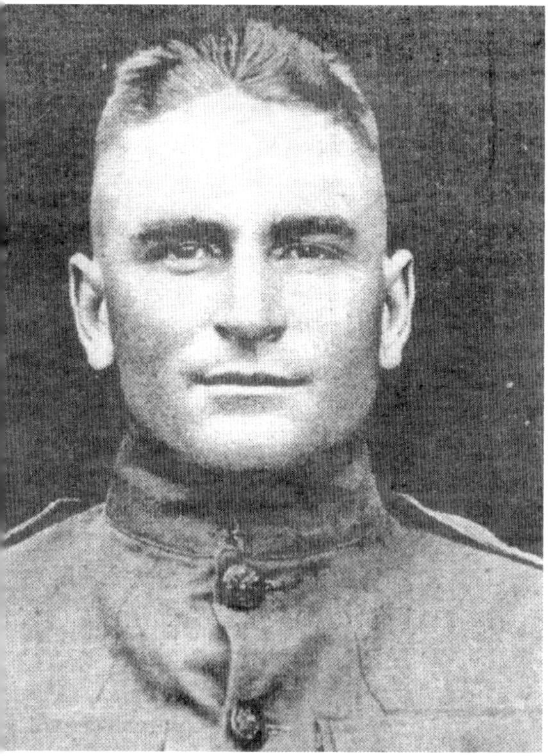

Virgil Fowler Sr.
Though there were a few scattered troops across Cullman County earlier, by the 1940s the Tennessee Valley Council of the Boy Scouts of America decided Cullman County should be more organized. It turned to Cullman's Virgil Fowler Sr., a World War I veteran, to help with that process. Fowler served as Cullman District Chairman from 1943 to 1947. Because of his constant efforts, more than 30 troops and Cub Scout packs were available to boys throughout the county. (Both images courtesy Cullman County Museum.)

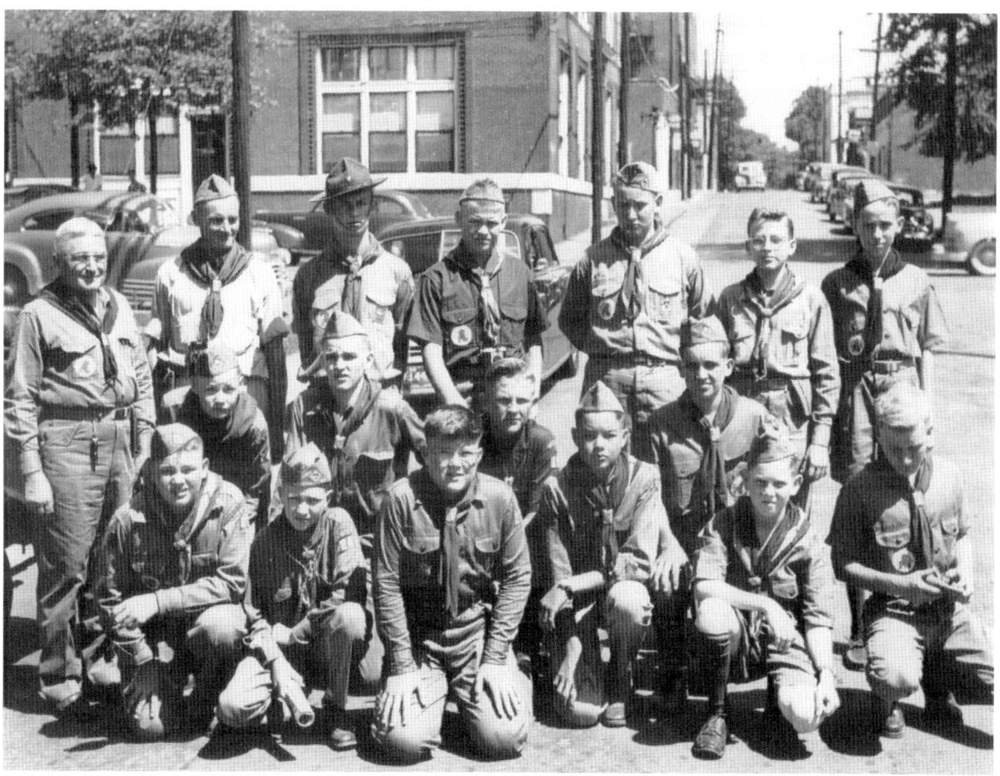

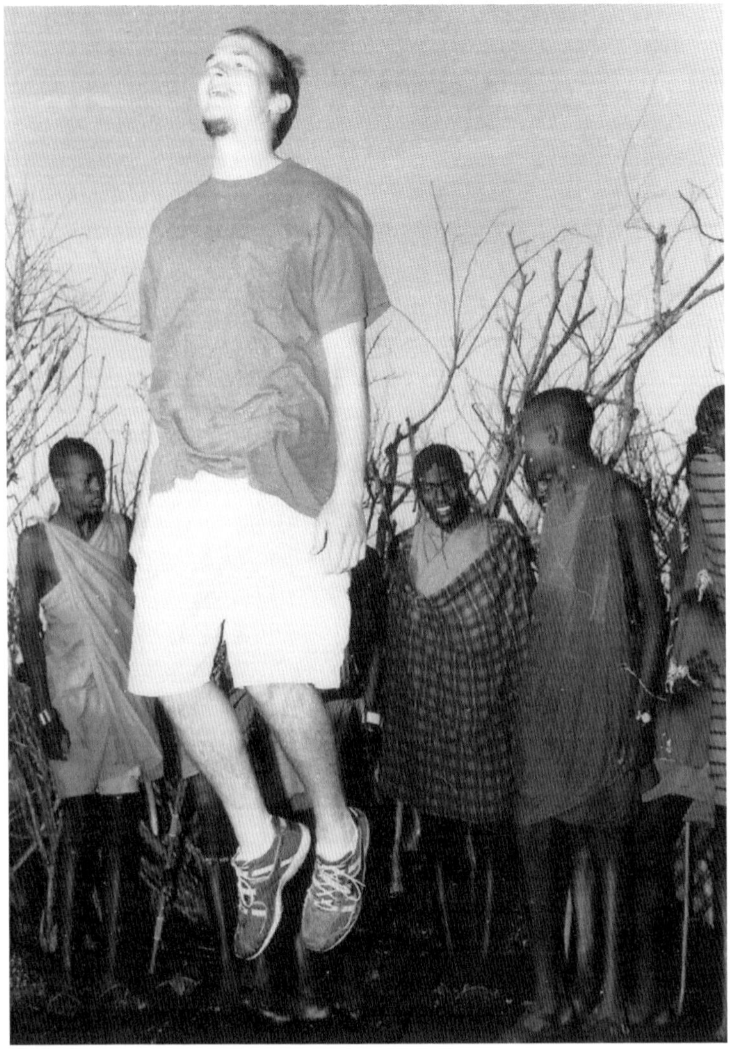

Whit Warren

Whit Warren had an impact on individual lives, not only in the United States, but also in Kenya, Africa. It is there one will find Whit's Place at the Mirindi Children's Home of Grace Orphanage, a multipurpose building constructed for the orphanage. The 1,716-square-foot building serves as a dining hall for the orphanage. It is here that Wade, his brother, planted a tree in memory of his youngest brother, Whit. The orphanage is sponsored by Kenya Relief, an organization founded in 2004 by Steve James. His daughter Brittney sponsored a child from Kenya. When she unexpectedly died in 2001, her father wanted to meet the child, Newton. Arriving in Kenya, the nurse anesthetist, also from Cullman, wanted to help by donating old medical equipment. Whit was not only a missionary to Kenya, but he was a musician, known locally for his voice. He took those talents to Kenya, Uganda, Canada, and Mexico on missionary trips. When the orphanage was named Whit's Place, the Women's Guild at St. John's Evangelical Protestant Church wanted to take on the special project of funding it. Along with the Women's Guild, Kenya Relief, and Steve James, the project was funded. On the day of dedication as the missionary group approached the orphanage, the people of Kenya planned a special surprise. Whit's music began to be heard over the loudspeakers in honor of the impact on the people and for the work he did in that area. (Courtesy Wes Warren.)

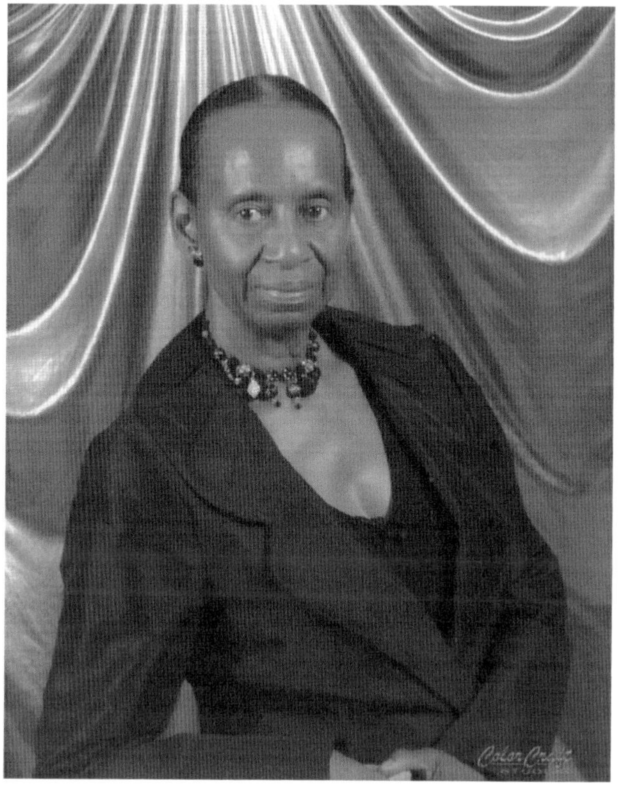

Earlene Johnson
When she speaks, the gentle, Southern tone in her voice reveals no hint of determined character and dedication to community or successful political career. Earlene Johnson has carved out a record of accomplishments in her community, Colony, and Cullman County. Her career in education spans 28 years, six dedicated to teaching in the Colony school. When it was consolidated into the Hanceville system, she was offered a job with the City of Decatur, but was asked to stay in Cullman County. She remained with the county's central education facility as librarian supervisor and media specialist for 23 years. Retiring in 1992, Earlene pictured herself sitting on the front porch, but that was not to happen. She was approached by Colony residents to run for mayor. She prayed for guidance and, when the campaign began, went door-to-door in the community of about 250 residents. Earlene Johnson was elected mayor in 1996, the first woman in Colony's 137-year history to serve in that position. She served three terms, discovering her responsibilities as community leader meant overseeing board actions, the library, tree commission, streets, drainage, community center, and education complex activities. During her terms, the pursuit of grants led to sidewalk construction, a walking trail, and lights for the ball field, renovating the community center and a water park. Although many of the mayoral responsibilities were not "spelled out," Earlene did whatever was necessary, from cleaning floors in the community's facilities to climbing in her pickup truck and picking up litter. She wanted a clean community. Action for a grant to construct an education complex was initiated in a previous mayor's term, and with a group of residents she pursued that goal. To obtain the grant, Colony was required to supply all furnishings. Understanding the community did not have the funds, she led a group of Colony residents to approach City of Cullman businesses for their help. Every item they needed to furnish the education complex was obtained. Even though she no longer serves in the political realm she is active with church work, singing in the choir, teaching Sunday School on Fifth Sundays, participates in a children's ministry, and serves on the Community Action Board and Aging Advisory Council for the North Alabama Regional Council of Governments. (Courtesy Earlene Johnson.)

Speegle Pioneers

Dewey Speegle, pictured, settled Ryan's Creek. Once Mississippi, it became Brushy Creek. His son Daniel Speegle and Col. Johann Cullmann, also in real estate, were involved in land disputes, ending in a violent hawk-bill knife slashing, leaving Cullmann scarred. Daniel's son David married Winifred Cranford, who became a celebrated healer and midwife. (Courtesy Herman Stringer.)

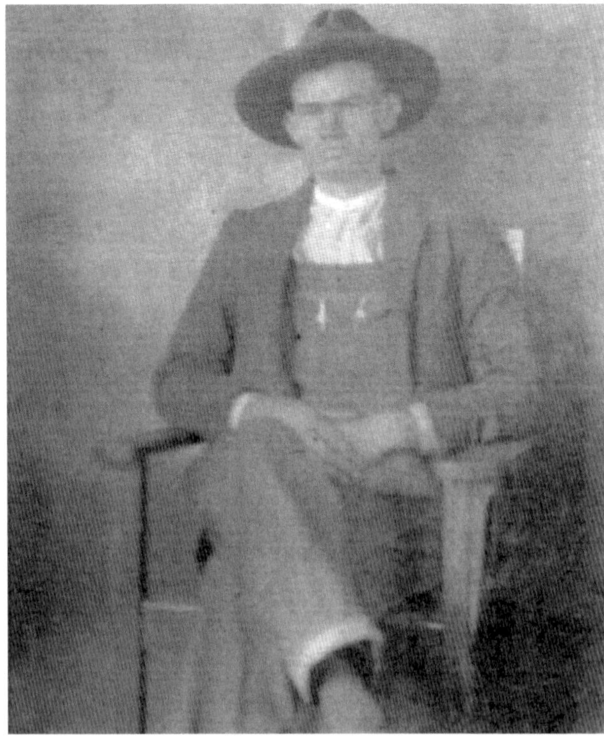

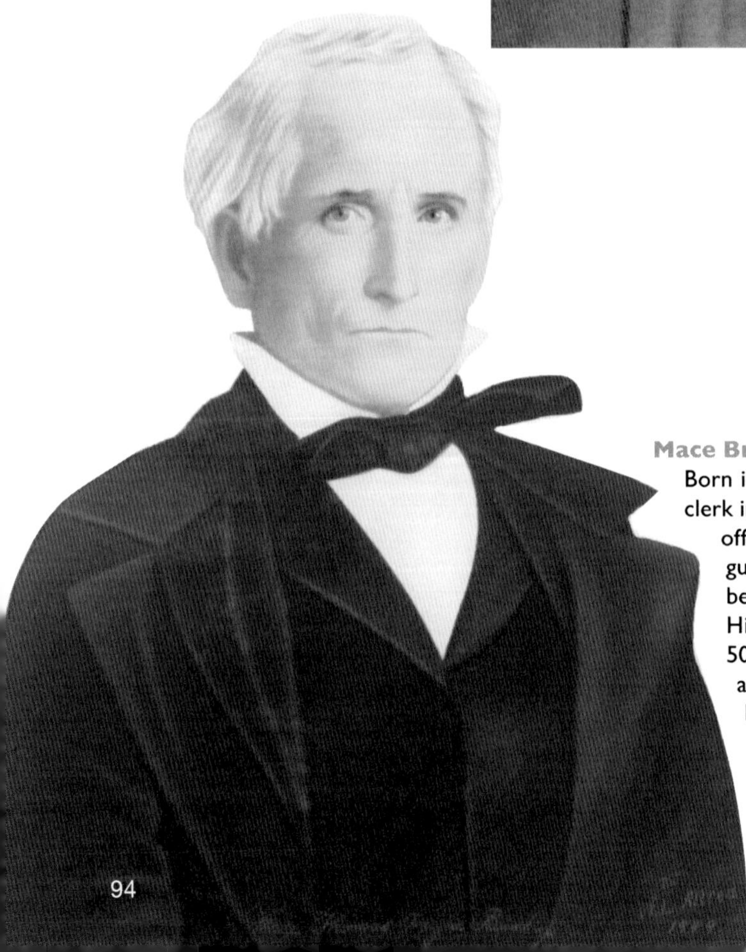

Mace Brindley

Born in 1801, Mace Brindley became chief clerk in the Blount County probate judge's office at age 18. In 1832, with an Indian guide, Brindley traveled to land that became known as Brindley Mountain. His family settled the area over 50 years before Colonel Cullmann arrived. Brindley was elected to both state legislative houses and was state tax collector. (Courtesy Cullman Museum.)

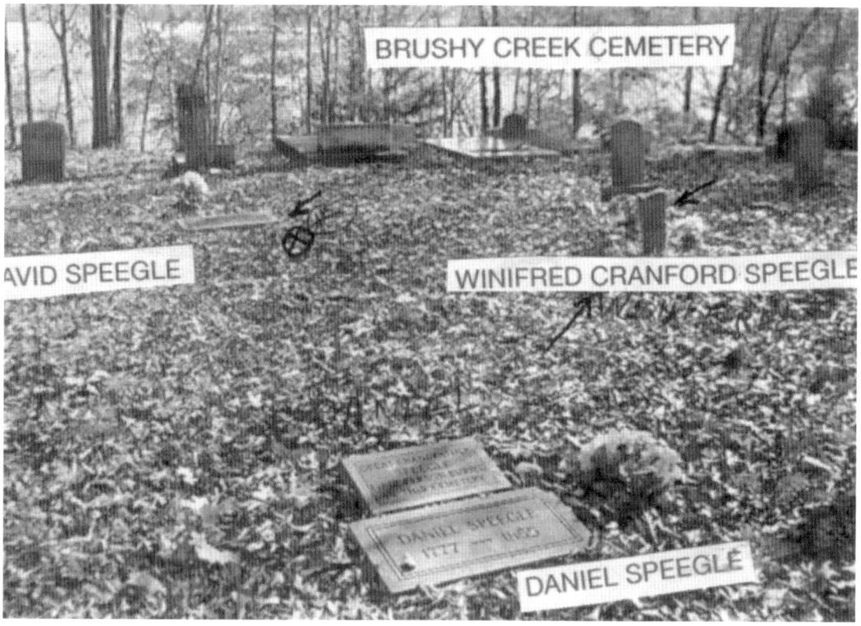

Winifred Cranford Stringer Speegle

Winifred Cranford journeyed into forests and faced wild animals to tend the sick and perform midwife duties. Traveling south from Morgan County, her path became known as "Speegle's Blaze." She was a noted angel of mercy, healing and caring for family and neighbors and could be found traveling back roads, day or night, on horseback. She married David Speegle and moved to Brushy Creek in 1830 and bore 19 children. At Brushy Creek Cemetery are gravesites of Daniel, David, and Winifred Speegle. An avid preserver of history in Cullman County, Herman Stringer, US Marine Corps (retired), is the great-great nephew of Winifred Speegle. He has traveled the South 35 years, following trails of family genealogy, historical events, and the Civil War, digging out and documenting his findings. (Both images courtesy Herman Stringer.)

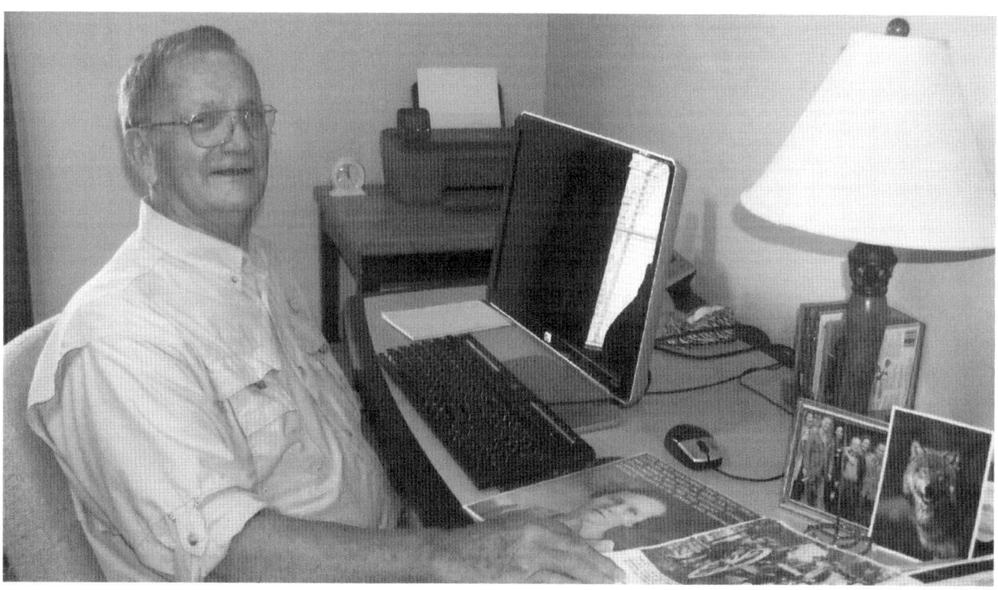

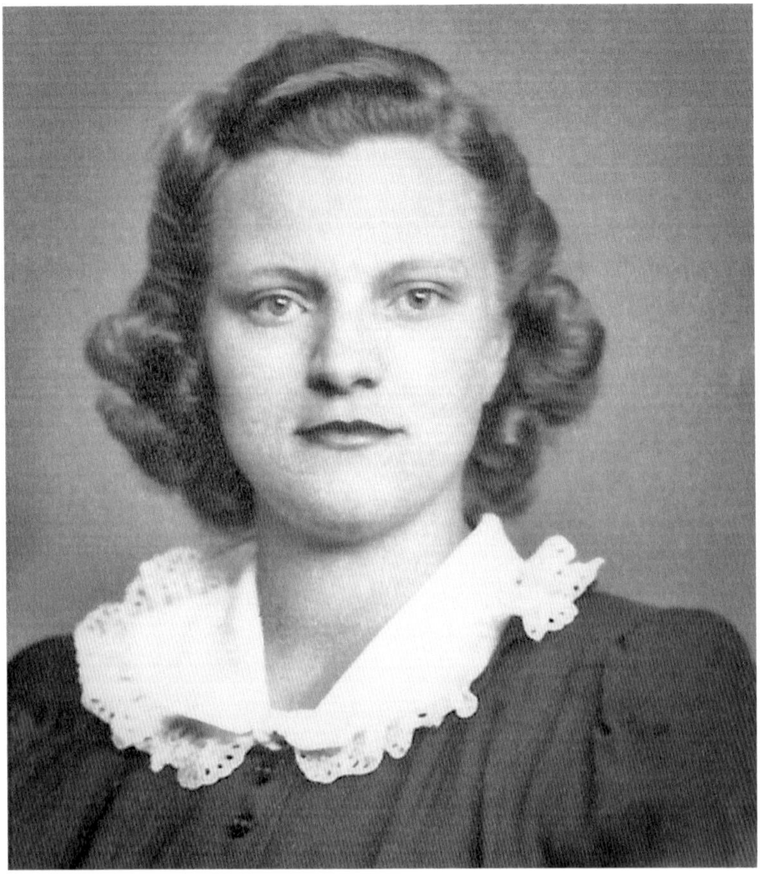

Catherine Clark Voss

In 1936, Cullman's State National Bank was small and struggling with two employees, Mr. Rene Clark, manager, and his daughter, Mrs. Catherine Clark Voss. To be open all day, they took separate lunch hours. Between 11 o'clock and noon on December 10, 1936, while Mr. Clark was out to lunch, a young man entered the bank, checked to see if Catherine was alone, and asked for money. She became very bold and told the young man she would not help him and he would have to get the money himself. He went behind the counter to the teller cage and took the cash, about $1,200. All the while, she was telling him how wrong he was, and that God would punish him for his deeds. When he made for the change drawer and other small bank receipts, she pushed him away and said he had enough money. He and Catherine scuffled, and her glasses were knocked to the floor. During the fray, the robber lost his gun. Both glasses and gun were quickly recovered. He aimed the gun at Catherine and told her to get in the vault and lie down or he would kill her. She refused to move. He threatened again, and again she refused. She was shot. The bullet went into her shoulder, struck the bone and was diverted upward, out of the back of the shoulder and into the ceiling. The force of the shot threw her to the floor and knocked her unconscious momentarily. As the man ran from the bank, Catherine began screaming. Men across the street heard her, got guns from G.W. Johnson's Hardware Store, and gave chase. Other men grabbed rakes and hoes from a barrel in front of the hardware store and also got into the chase. They caught the robber about three blocks away. He hid the money in a garage behind Katie Azar's house. It was all recovered. Dr. C.E. Herrin, local eye, ear, nose, and throat doctor, tried to get a group of men to take the robber out and hang him then and there. Catherine spent a week in the hospital and about a month later received the gold medal of valor from National Surety Corporation for her courage. (Courtesy Fr. Marcus Voss.)

Pastor Bob Kurtz: Golf's Ironman

Hard work and dedication, plus a passion for golf, equals over a quarter of a million dollars raised for abused children's agencies in Cullman County. For Bob Kurtz, it sums up 56 golf tournament wins, six world records, two listings in the *Guinness Book of World Records* and a listing in *Ripley's Believe it or Not*. The *Ripley's* listing was for 1,850 holes played in one week, and heat index temperatures at 105 degrees when he was 70 years old. Sports journalists call him "Man of Steel." This title was earned by playing 500 consecutive holes in 39 hours of golf in the Ironman Marathon at Chesley Oaks Golf Club in Fairview in 2009. Fairview mayor Randall Shedd described the awesome sight, "watching him play at night with glow balls." In one week, June 4–11, 2011, he played 1,850 holes, earning him a place in *Guinness Book* as the "Ironman" and then set another Guinness World Record (Most Times Scoring One's Age or Lower in One Day) August 1, 2012. He scored 71, his age or lower seven times that day. Bob Kurtz is the retired senior pastor of St. John's Evangelical Protestant Church. His stamina personifies an active lifestyle. Ninety percent of the funds raised for his MTC, ministry to children, goes to aid abused children. In his marathon of 1,850 holes, the year the tornado devastated a huge section of Cullman County, funds went to help Cullman Caring for Kids, Day Star Harbor House, and $20,000 was given to the city and agencies to help residents. His physical stamina personifies an active lifestyle for this retired minister's life. He has always had a love for sports and especially golf. He was the football announcer for the Denver Broncos and Minnesota Vikings, National Football League teams, along with the Air Force Academy. Prior to that, he played high school basketball and ran track. He started earning titles during his high school years, including All Conference, All District, and All Tournament in basketball. (Courtesy Baker Productions.)

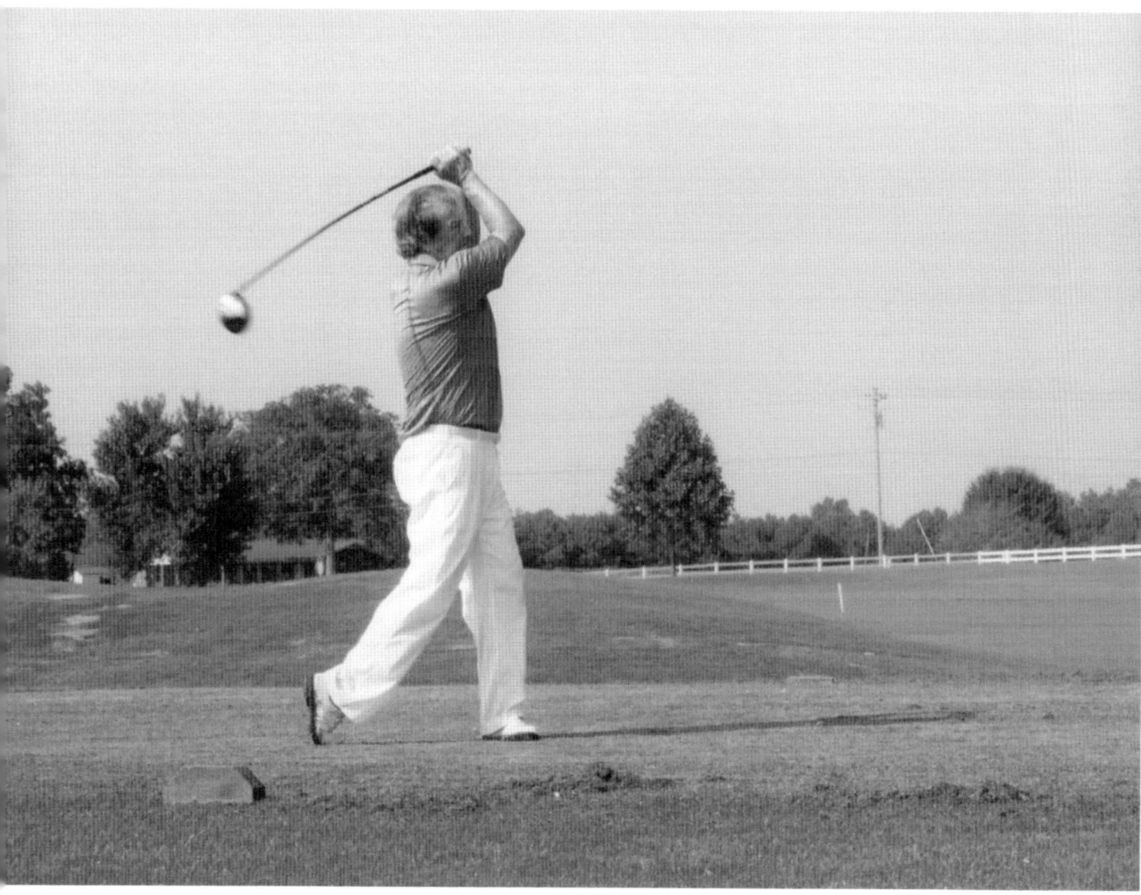

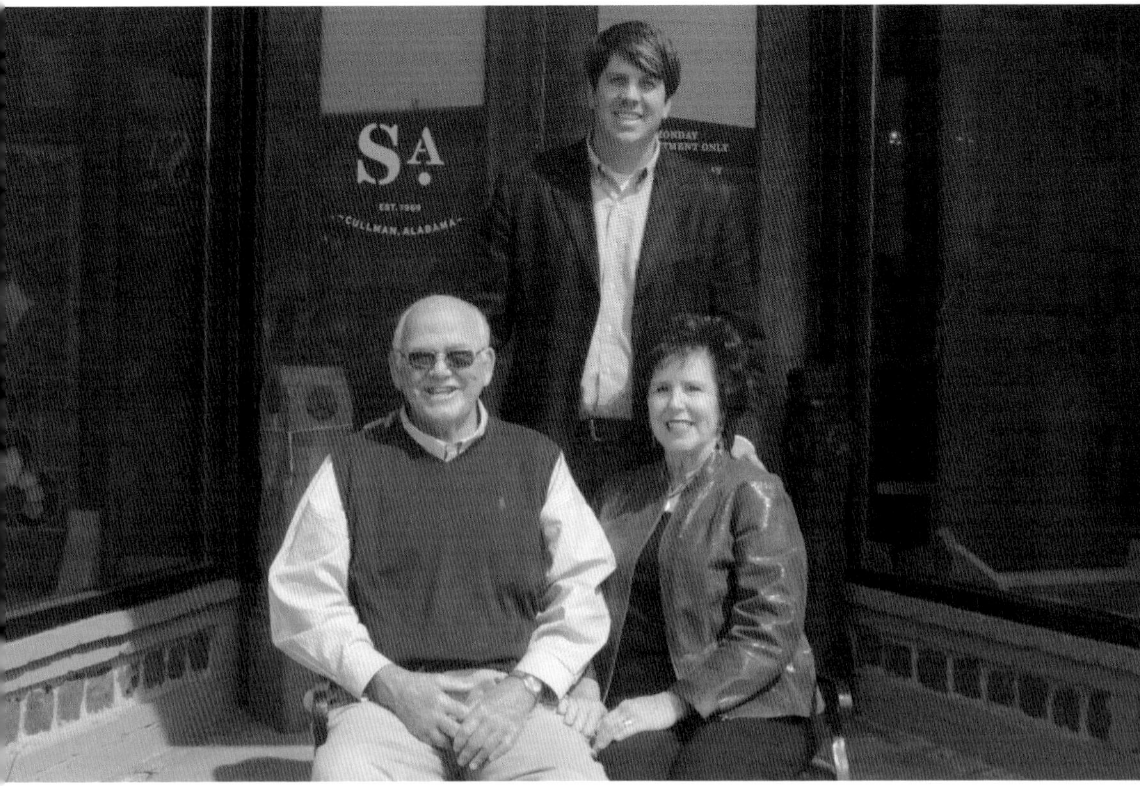

Gudger Family

The Gudger family has been preserving Cullman history since 1969. Dr. Garlan Gudger Sr. first got the bug when the old Cullman Hotel was being torn down and he bought a cast-iron bathtub for $30. Before he got it to his truck, a woman offered him $80 for it. Gudger quickly learned there was an interest in old architectural items, and he began salvaging items from houses under the tutelage of George Whisenant. Word got out about the items in Gudger's garage, and soon he was making a good side business in Saturday sales. Once his inventory outgrew the garage, he opened a store in Vinemont, which eventually moved to its current location in downtown Cullman. Southern Accents is now one of the premier sellers of architectural antiques in the country. Garlan Gudger Jr. took over the store in the mid-1990s and carries on the tradition today. Garlan Gudger Jr. carried his love of preservation into public service, running for Cullman City Council on a platform of preservation. Today, he serves as the body's president and was behind the effort to restore downtown buildings to their historic character after the April 27, 2011, tornado. Garlan Sr.'s wife, Dot Gudger, is past president of the Cullman County Historical Society. Under her leadership, the historical society's mural project has brought the past back to life on the sides of many of Cullman's historic buildings. Garlan and Dot Gudger's connection to Cullman history extends even to their house. They live in the former home of Elsa Hartung, niece of Cullman founder Col. Johann G. Cullmann, and many furnishings in the house have been added from the homes of other notable Cullman residents. Garlan Sr. first renovated the old Cullman Paint and Wallpaper store, now occupied by Fairview Florist, and the adjoining building now occupied by Southern Accents. He also donated the fountain and Christmas tree in Depot Park, the former site of King Pharr Canning. Garlan Jr. renovated two buildings on First Avenue Southeast where Berkley Bob's Coffee House and Michael's Florist are housed. He purchased a building housing a printing company and renovated it to be Carlton's Pizza. He then turned his attention to the oldest house in Cullman on its original location, catercorner from Christ Lutheran Church, completely restoring it to its original look. (Courtesy Greg Richter.)

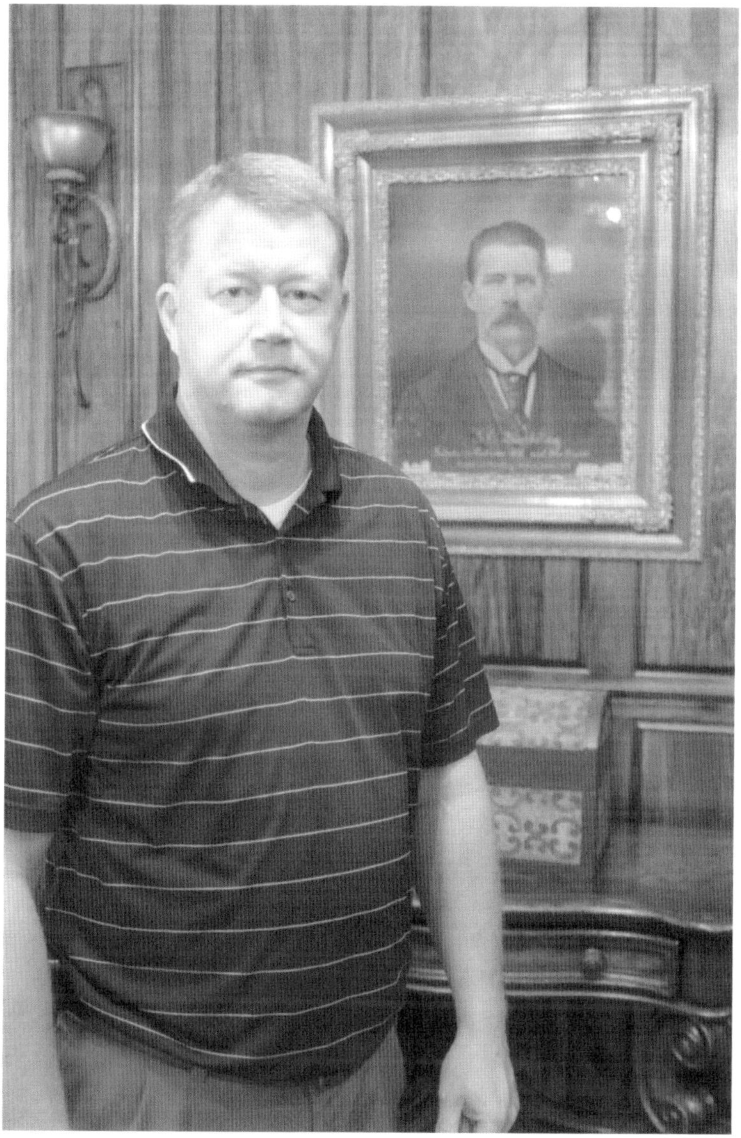

John Riley
John Riley grew up in an Upstate New York farmhouse without television. There was snow on the ground from October to April, so he had to find a way to fill the long winter hours. Previous residents had left lots of history books in the attic, and when a young John Riley found them his love of history was born. He brought that passion with him to Cullman a quarter of a century ago. "The place is oozing of history," Riley says of his adopted home. He's been here so long that people whose families have lived here for generations will ask him questions such as, "Where was the old Woodard Building?" He might not be a native, but Riley finds Cullman's history as interesting as it is to someone who has lived here since birth. "I'd compare it to picking up another book," he said, adding that just because it is not about his family does not mean it is not interesting. Riley, president of Cullman Savings Bank, has taken to preserving Cullman's history. He salvaged a picture of the bank's first president, G.O. Dinckelberg, from the basement and gave it prominent display and led an effort to have a monument placed at Dinckelberg's unmarked grave. (Courtesy Greg Richter.)

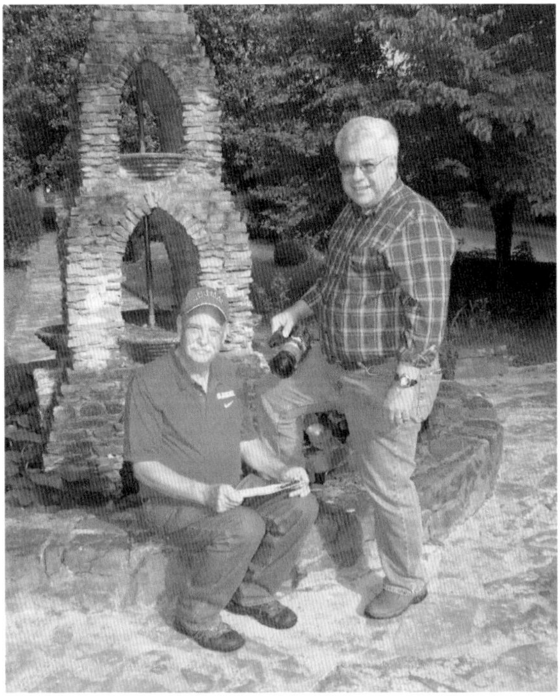

George Spear, Dan Fulenwider

The preservation of local and state history is paramount in the goals of Dan Fulenwider and George Spear. They have dedicated years to researching Cullman County's rich history. Fulenwider has traveled, on foot, the path Civil War Union Army colonel Abel Streight took during the ill-fated raid in 1863 from the Mississippi to Georgia state lines, trekking through backwoods and crossing streams, unearthing colorful stories about the chase Confederate general Nathan Bedford Forrest gave in pursuing Streight. His exploits are documented, providing a compelling reading as he authors a column in the local newspaper. Fulenwider, by comparing American maps, journals, diaries, and historical documents has located the historical routes of the Speegle Trace, Day Gap Road, Bylar Road, and Old Federal Road. He is responsible for ensuring proper signage on the historical routes. His historical knowledge has earned him recognition by fellow historians and tour groups, and he was awarded the prestigious Civil War Trust Chairman's Awards in recognition of his efforts to preserve endangered Civil War sites. Fulenwidner also enjoys searching out ancient Indian historical documents.

George Spear is a retired Marine with a passion for producing television documentaries on Cullman County communities, researching roots all the way down to the very first homestead claim and history of area schools. His productions include documentaries on the West Point community and Logan Junior High School. Sometimes local lore and word-of-mouth accounts passed down through generations differ from researched and documented histories. After viewing Spear's documentaries, some residents had to rethink their family's history. It has been discovered that, on occasion, ancestors fought for the Union and not the Confederacy, as they always believed and was narrated by keepers of the family history through generations. Recently, he and Fulenwider completed an hour-long documentary titled *The Story of Streight's Raid*, a film almost 10 years in the making. It has been embraced by the Cullman County Museum and other history-preserving institutions around North Alabama. Taking the occasion to revisit some of the documented locations of historical significance, they have been shocked the sites that were filmed are beginning and have disappeared due to neglect. However, they remain committed to saving and preserving the precious heritage. Dan Fulenwidner, sitting, and George Spear visit another historical setting in the City of Cullman, the sunken rock garden on the campus of the Southern Benedictine sisters. (Courtesy Kay Cagle.)

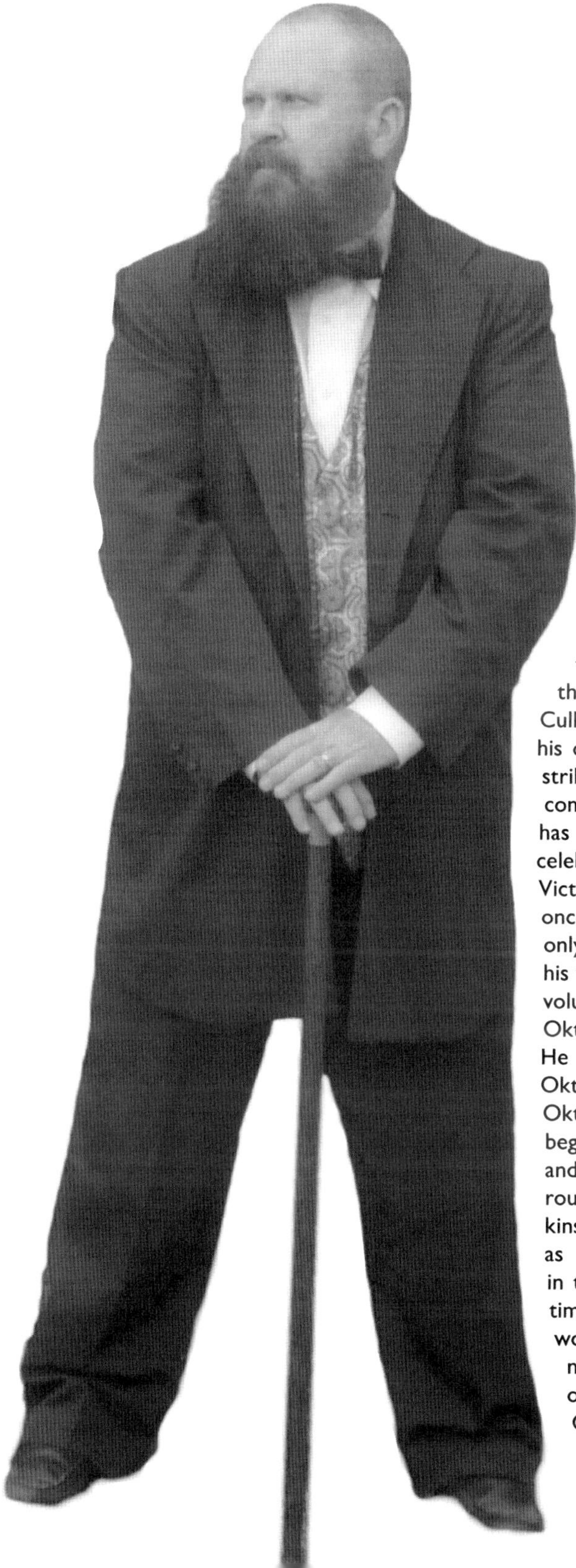

Larry Rowlette

Col. Johann Cullmann lives today in the person of Larry Rowlette, who portrays the Cullman founder at Oktoberfest and other events throughout the year. Rowlette was born in Nashville, but was living in Cullman in 1999 when Oktoberfest began looking for someone to portray Colonel Cullmann. Longtime Oktoberfest official Elaine Fuller and St. John's Evangelical Church Pastor Bob Kurtz attended a lecture in Decatur where city planning department director Rob Walker gave a talk as Commodore Stephen Decatur, for whom the city is named. This sparked the pair the search for someone to portray Colonel Cullmann. Kurtz had to look no further than his own congregation. Rowlette, who bore a striking resemblance to Colonel Cullmann, complete with beard, was happy to oblige. He has been the center of Cullman Oktoberfest celebrations ever since. Rowlette has several Victorian outfits and becomes the colonel once he has donned the costume. He answers only to "Colonel" when in costume—even to his wife, daughters, and friends. Rowlette has volunteered for more than a decade to emcee Oktoberfest and lead the crowd in dancing. He was named burgermeister of Cullman Oktoberfest in 2001. Not long after his first Oktoberfest as Colonel Cullmann, Rowlette began receiving calls to speak as the colonel, and his volunteer job quickly became a year-round portrayal. Rowlette says he feels a kinship with Colonel Cullmann. Both worked as engineers, both came to Alabama later in their lives, and both enjoy having a good time. By now, even friends, family, and co-workers call him "Colonel," even when he is not in costume, and the front license plate on his car reads, "Colonel." (Courtesy Greg Richter.)

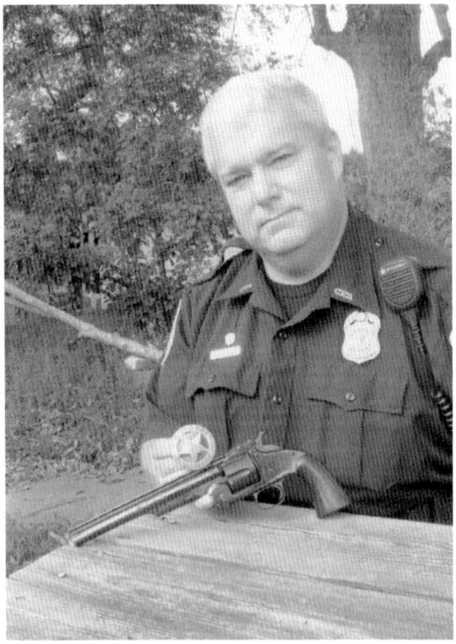

Rick Thiot

Cullman police officer Rick Thiot poses with a revolver and badge owned by Bill Schneider, city marshal from 1902–1906. When Thiot joined the Cullman Police Department in 1991, he noticed there were no historical pictures or documents on the walls, so he set out to discover the background of the force. He has preserved several stories by speaking to retired officers and the families of many of Cullman's law enforcement leaders. (Courtesy Greg Richter.)

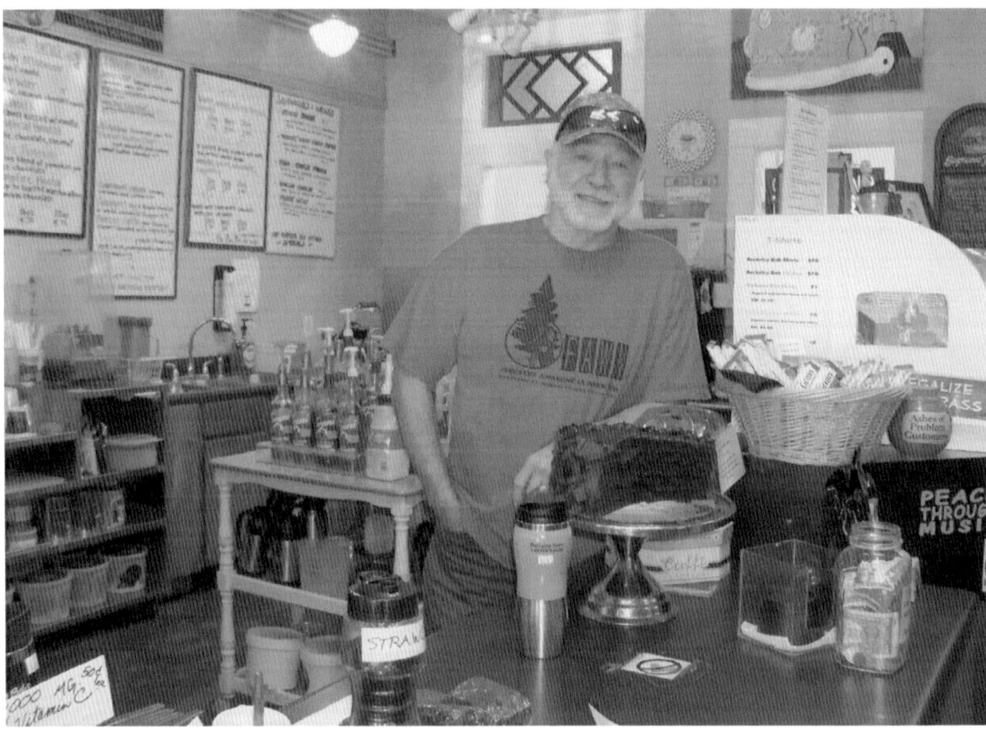

Berkley Bob

Step back and visit a 1960s coffee house, Berkeley Bob's. Bob and Geri Keefe opened the popular establishment in 2003 on the site of Colonel Cullmann's original home. A retired California forester, Bob wanted a place where musicians could break into the industry. He opened Berkeley Bob's, a place for good food and great coffee, where strangers congregate and become friends and the music plays on. (Courtesy Kay Cagle.)

CHAPTER SEVEN

Arts, Entertainment, and Athletes

It was reported in the local newspaper, "This little city is both literary and musical." As of the early 1900s, Cullman had bands, theaters, and one of the largest entertainment halls in the state. As the city and county grew, Cullman's German brass bands and opera houses were considered some of the very finest in the state. The Max Schmidt, John Sutterer, and F.L. Hauk bands were among the most popular bands for public entertainment. By 1910, Cullman was second only to Birmingham as a cultural center in North Alabama. Cullman's progress and desire for cultural events was diversified from the beginning and ranged from the staging of frequent celebrations for special occasions, or for no particular reason other than to bring out the brass bands and beer mugs.

Cullman County teems with a variety of talent and notable entertainers who are lifelong residents and natives of Cullman County. Providers of the culture and arts have grown as talents are exhibited in a variety of mediums. Artist Dot Graf produced pen-and-ink drawings to preserve the image of architectural homes and buildings and was famous for her Arty Yard Parties; artists adorned the sides of buildings with historical pictures of Cullman County. Art is displayed in the culinary talents of Chefs Frank Stitt III, Dyron Powell, and Cliff Holt, who all own popular restaurants in Birmingham, promoting the incorporation of farm fresh produce in food preparation.

There are the vocal talents: Roland Johnson, known for his musical prowess and served many times as mayor of Garden City; Candi Staton, backup singer for famous rock entertainers, a gospel singer in her own right, and an Emmy nominee; Eric Bennett, popular bass singer for the Triumphant Quartet; and the late Deborah Jo White, gospel and pop singer who all used their voices to entertain. The entertainment mediums widen as Fr. Patrick O'Neil's life became the subject of the 1939 movie *Mutiny in the Big House*. There are also the athletes who will be remembered for their accomplishments and abilities.

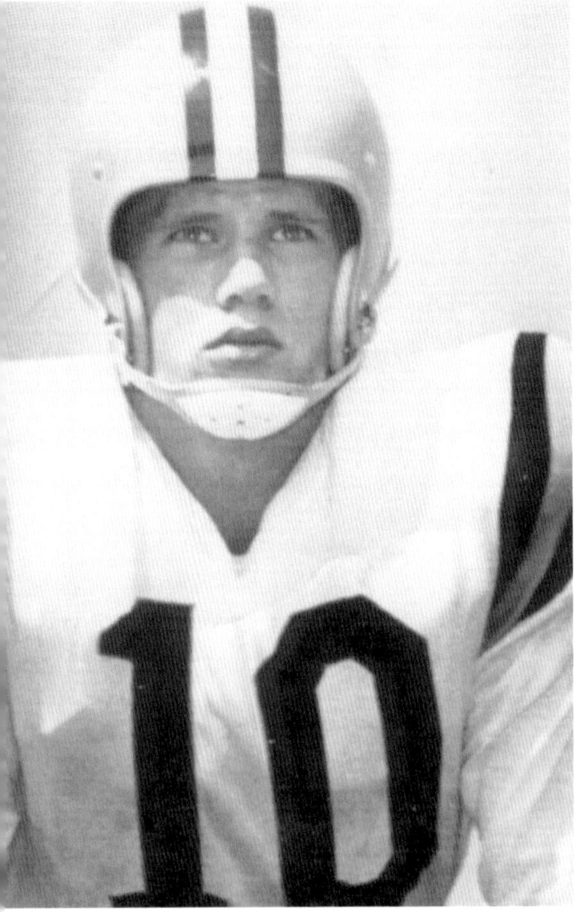

David Knight
David Knight is passionate about football. The retired attorney was chosen as the only quarterback for the 1959 All TVC 11-Man Team by the *Huntsville Times*, the coaches All TVC Team, Most Valuable Player of 1959 by the Cullman Quarterback Club for the Cullman High School Bearcats, and played on Auburn University's freshman team. He was inducted into the Cullman County Sports Hall of Fame in 2011. (Courtesy David Knight.)

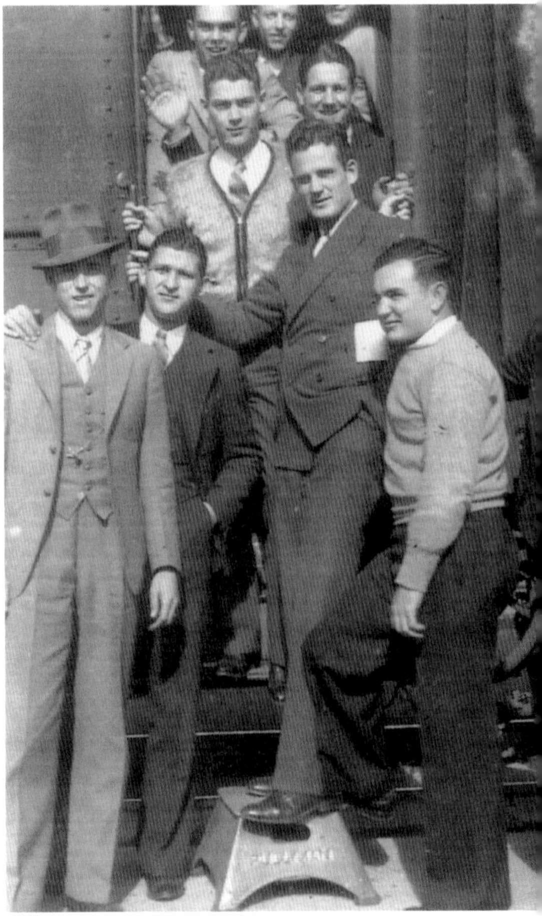

1935 Rose Bowl
Alabama beat Stanford 29-13 in the 1935 Rose Bowl. From the left, the second player is Roy White, freshman; the tall player in the center is Paul "Bear" Bryant, senior end; and directly behind him with only his head showing is "Tarzan" White, freshman. They were All American players. Roy and Tarzan are cousins from Hanceville. It took about five days to travel by train from Alabama to Pasadena. (Courtesy Tom Drake.)

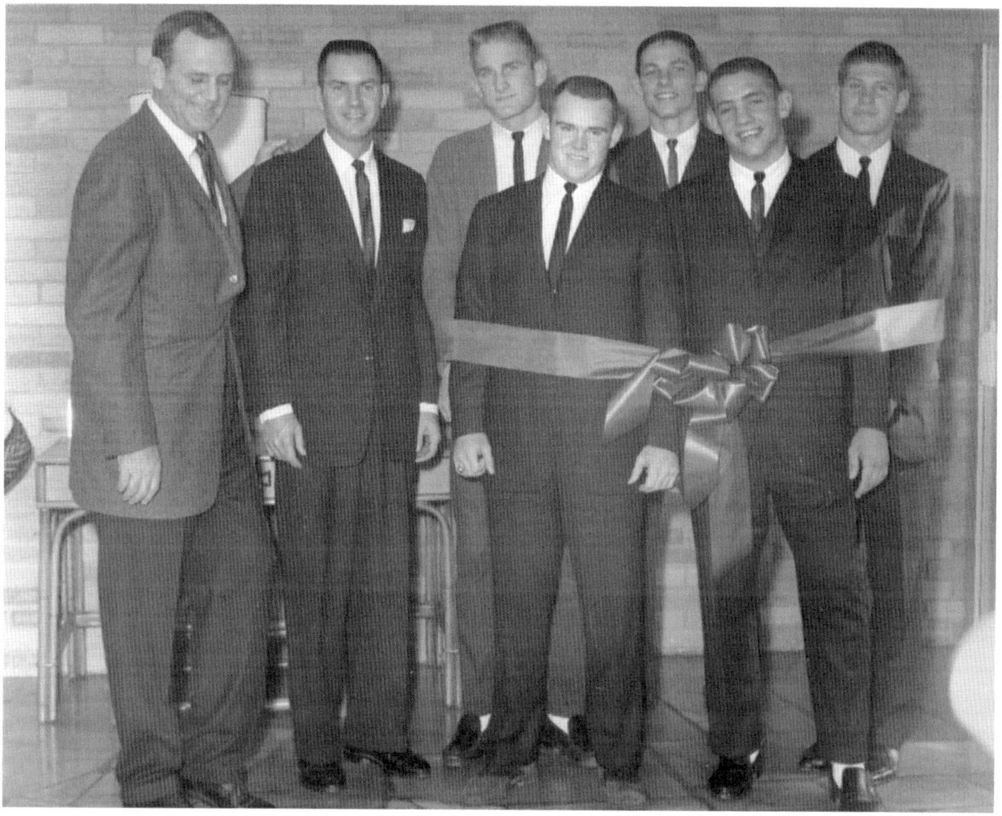

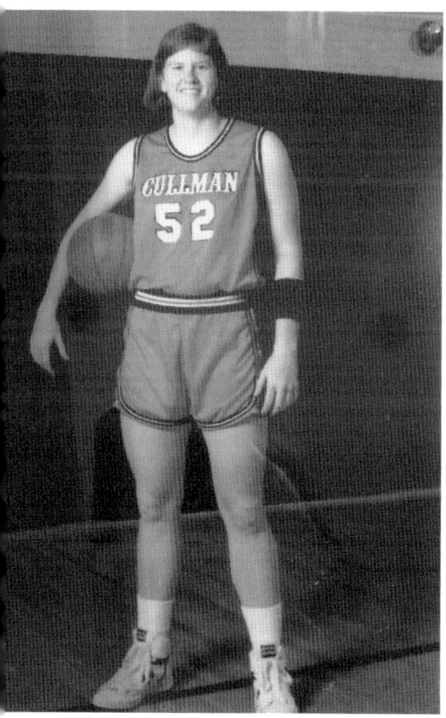

1962 Championship Team

Thousands packed the field for the 1962 state championship between Cullman and Decatur. Gene Stallings, assistant coach to "Bear" Bryant, was scouting five Cullman players. Several schools had approached them: Georgia Tech, Auburn, Tennessee, and Florida. The friends signed with Alabama. Pictured here from left to right are (first row) Barry Willoughby and Johnny Calver; (second row) Coach Bryant, Coach Oliver Woodard, Les Kelley, Wayne Trimble, and Wayne Chappell. (Courtesy Barry Willoughby.)

Dr. Ginger Holt

Her basketball talents made her an All State and All American athlete. A Cullman High School graduate, she ran track and was the youngest swim team member at three. She holds track and swim records at UAB Medical School and was named to the Cullman County Sports Hall of Fame. Today, Dr. Ginger Holt, daughter of Jean and Dodd Holt, is a practicing orthopedic oncologist in Nashville. (Courtesy Ginger Holt.)

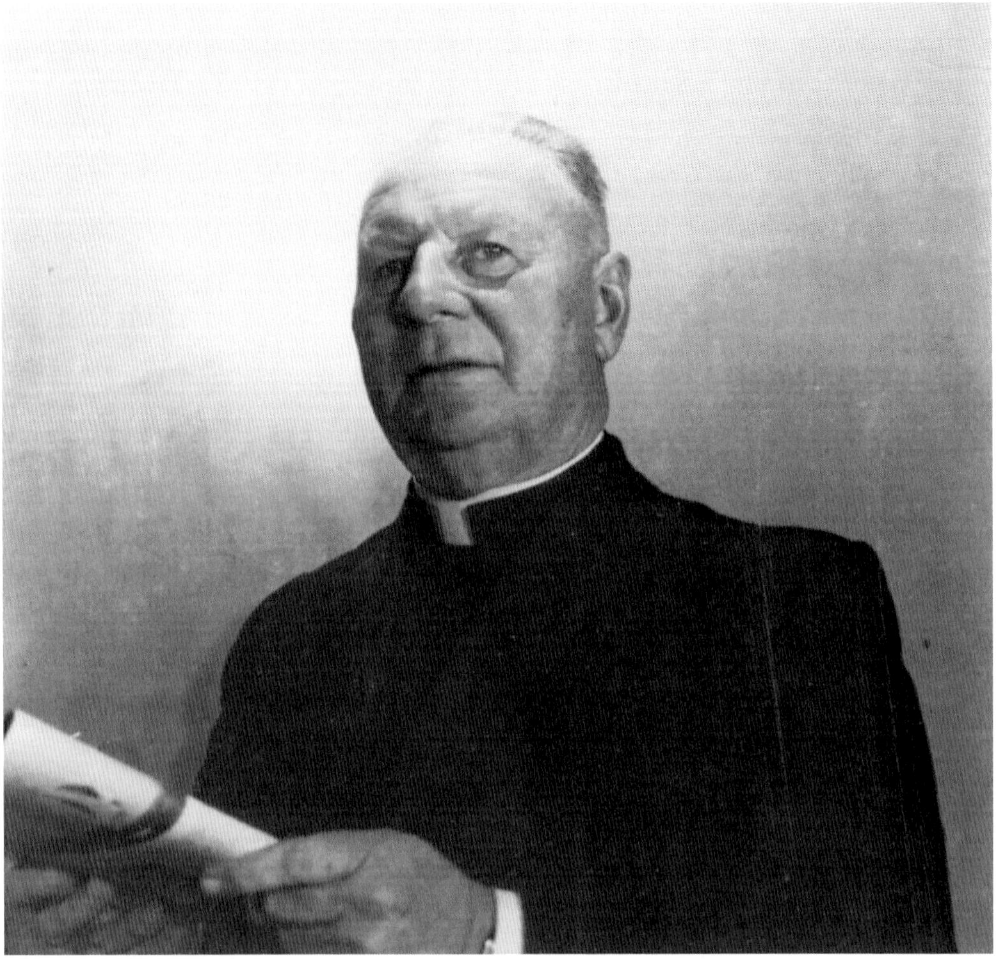

Rev. Fr. Patrick O'Neill

Rev. Fr. Patrick O'Neill was a priest at St. Bernard Abbey. Because of his role in quelling a prison riot in Colorado, at great personal risk, he received the Carnegie Medal for Bravery. He wrote the story, and it was used as the script for the 1939 movie *Mutiny in the Big House*. Local moviegoers were treated to the premier showing at the Cullman Theater in October 1939. The picture starred Charles Brickford and Barton McLane. The story plot was written about a heroic priest and inspired by the bravery of "Father Pat" for containing a prison break in Canon City Colorado in 1929.

At the 1939 showing, William R. Griffin, local theater owner, said the premier showing included congratulatory remarks from a representative of Monogram pictures, the company releasing the production. It was one of the most ambitious and successful works to be produced by Monogram pictures, according to the critical *Motion Picture Herald*. "This pulsating prison play included the character conflict between a crusading chaplain and a hardened convict for the future of a newly committed inmate. The film included a dedicatory message on work done by prison chaplains and in particular on the heroism of the Benedictine Cleric, Rev. Patrick O'Neil. Fr. Patrick came to St. Bernard in Cullman at the age of 16. He traveled to Rome to study and in 1915 was ordained priest in the Basilica of St. John Lateran. Caught up in World War I, he spent four years at Innsbruck, Seckau, and Freiborg in Switzerland. He returned to St. Bernard in Cullman in the fall of 1917 and began a career as professor of English, philosophy, and education. He was a singer and drama coach and well known throughout the South for his reading of Tennyson's epic, *Enoch Arden*. (Courtesy St. Bernard Abbey.)

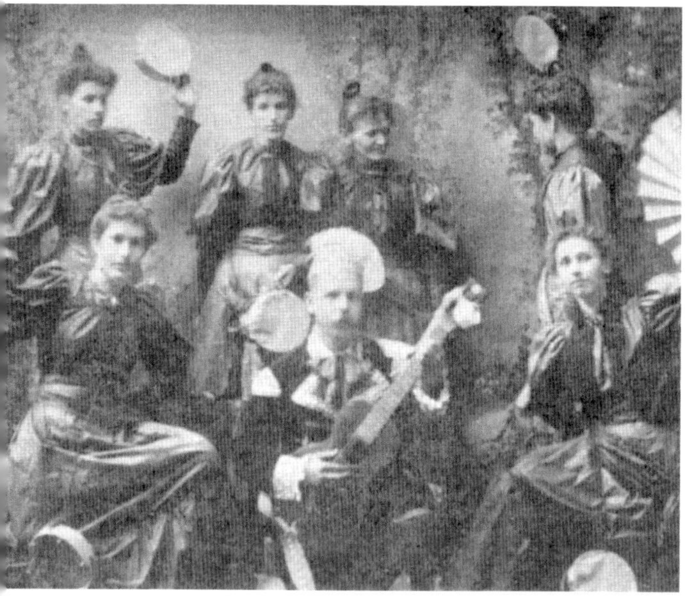

Kullman Hall Entertainment
Old World customs and love of music followed colonists to Cullman. By the late 1800s, the town gained a reputation of having the finest entertainment halls and German bands. John Sutterer strums a guitar at Kullman Hall surrounded by the Kullman Girls and Miss Gussie Eyer. Culture thrived as traveling stage companies flocked to Cullman to present their theatrical and musical productions. (Courtesy Cullman County Museum.)

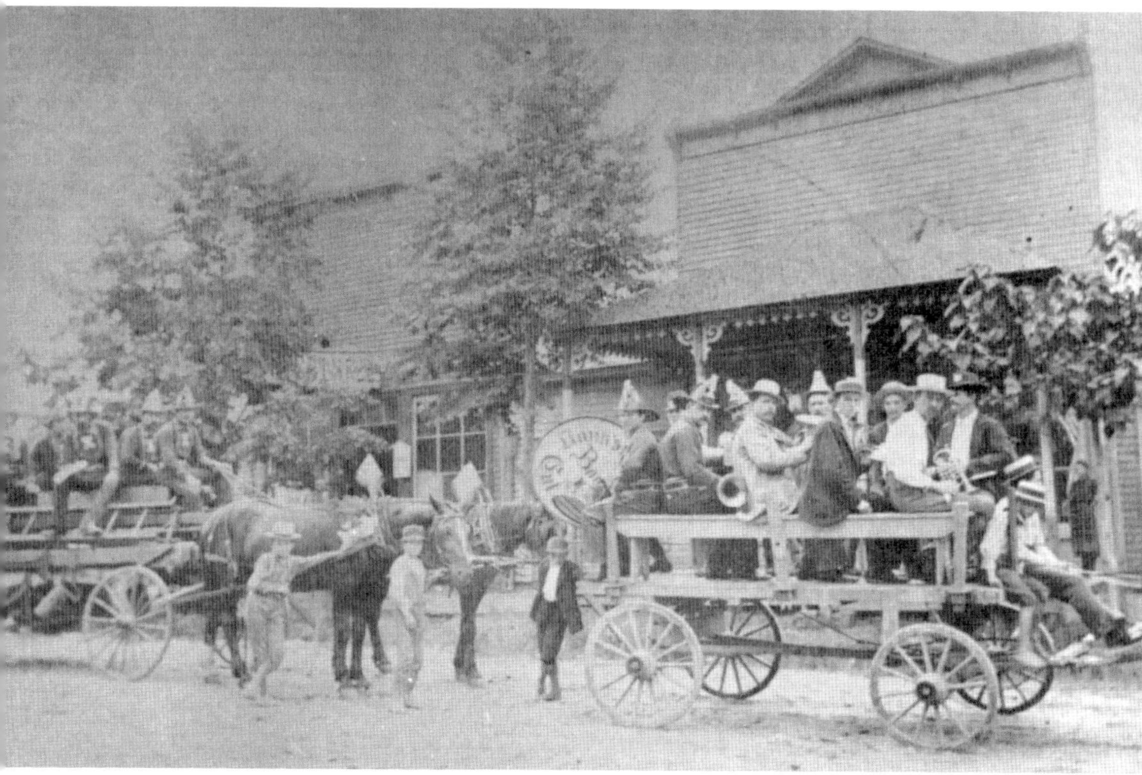

Hauk's Band
Immigrants brought their country's traditional music with them to their new homes. Citizens loved their music at family gatherings and parades during the early days. Leading this parade is Hauk's Band, known as Cullman Cornett Band, in front, followed by the fire department. The band was founded by F.L. Hauk. Ross Luyben, father of John Luyben, directed the band. (Courtesy Cullman County Museum.)

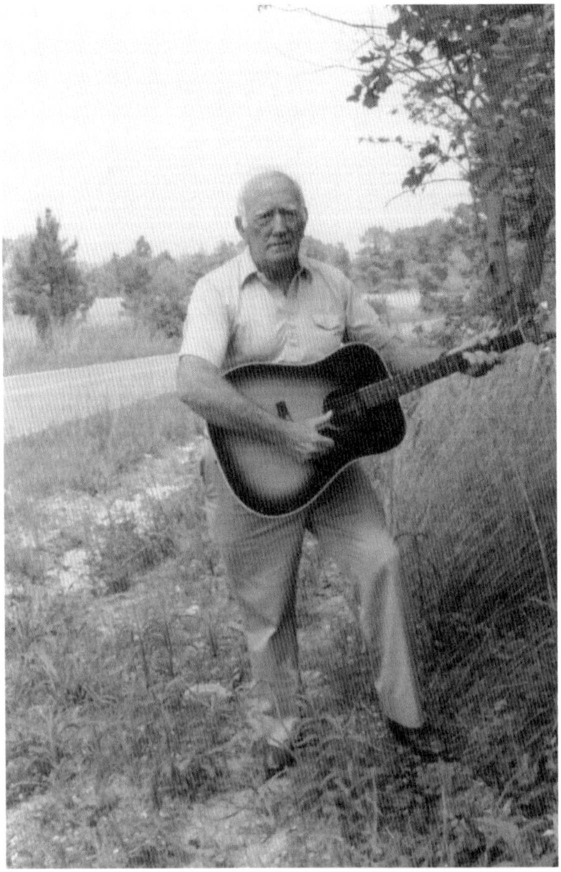

Roland "Racehorse" Johnson

Ten-term Garden City mayor, Birmingham Barons and Brooklyn Dodgers player, and North Alabama Country Music Association inductee are among Roland Johnson's accomplishments. The nickname "Racehorse" was earned for his running speed. Music jammed his life from the Strawberry Pickers Band to a Grand Ole Opry appearance and documented charted hits written with Earl Nunn; one was titled "I Traded her Love (for Deep Purple Wine)." He married Nelva Anderson. (Courtesy Johnson family.)

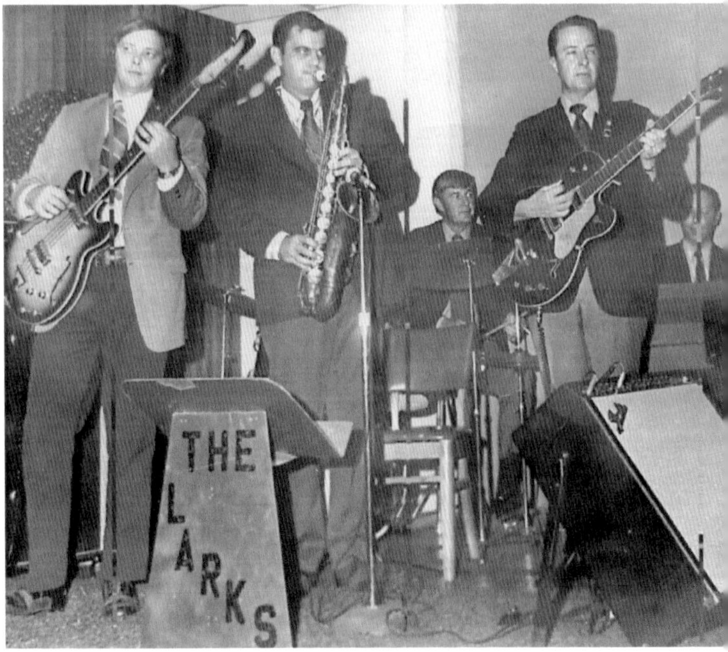

The Larks

Music was important through Cullman County history, and it was fun for businessmen and politicos who formed groups like The Larks. From left are the following: Bob Lowy (substituting for regular Charlie Eidson); a young Ray Buchman, Peoples Tires; Elmus Howlett, Texaco oil distributor; Fred Folsom, former Cullman County circuit court judge and senator; and Dwight Tucker, minor league, high school, and junior high school coach. (Courtesy Ray Buchmann.)

Candi Staton
Candi Staton has captivated a new generation of music lovers with her sweet, rough-twanged voice. From Hanceville, she sang in church at four, went pro at 12, and toured with Sam Cooke, C.L. Franklin, and Mahalia Jackson in the 1950s. Her voice is heard with Mick Jagger, Aretha Franklin, and in the music documentary, *Muscle Shoals*. She performs her biggest hits around the globe every year. (Courtesy Candi Staton.)

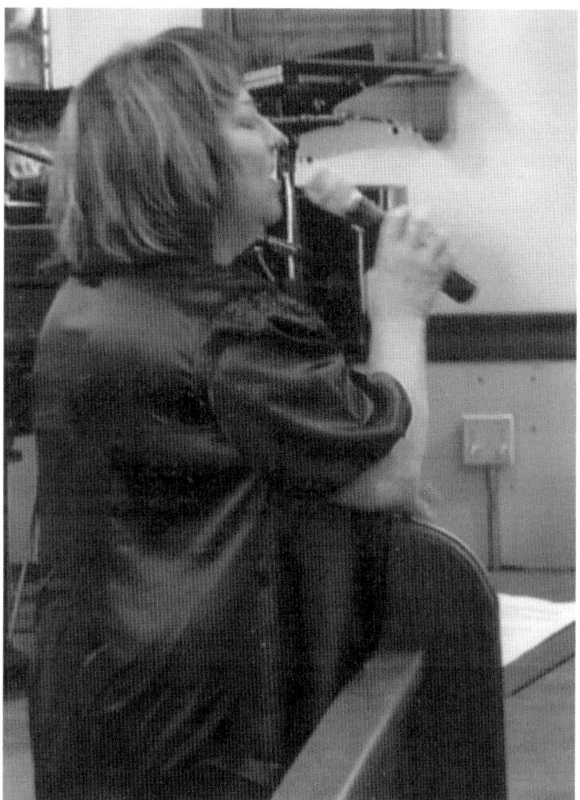

Deborah Jo Billingsley White
Deborah Jo Billingsley White was a member of the Lynyrd Skynyrd backup singers, the Honkettes. Born in Tennessee and raised in Mississippi, she moved to Cullman when her husband took a job here. Leaving the rock-and-roll lifestyle, she became a gospel singer in area churches. She remained friends with the surviving members of Skynyrd, who nicknamed her "Rev. Jo Jo." She died in 2010. (Courtesy Baker Photography.)

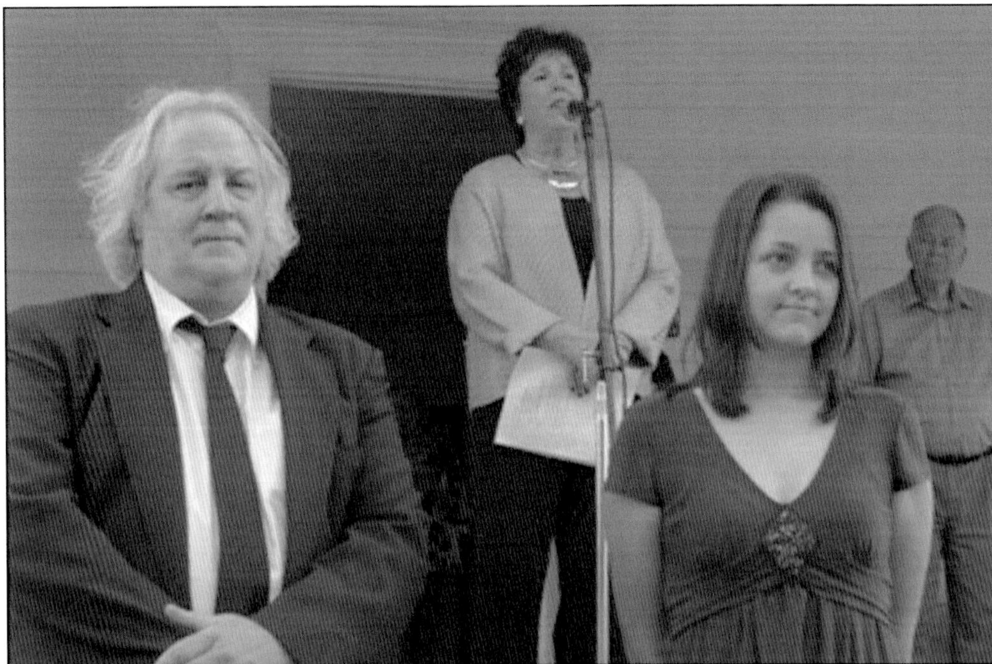

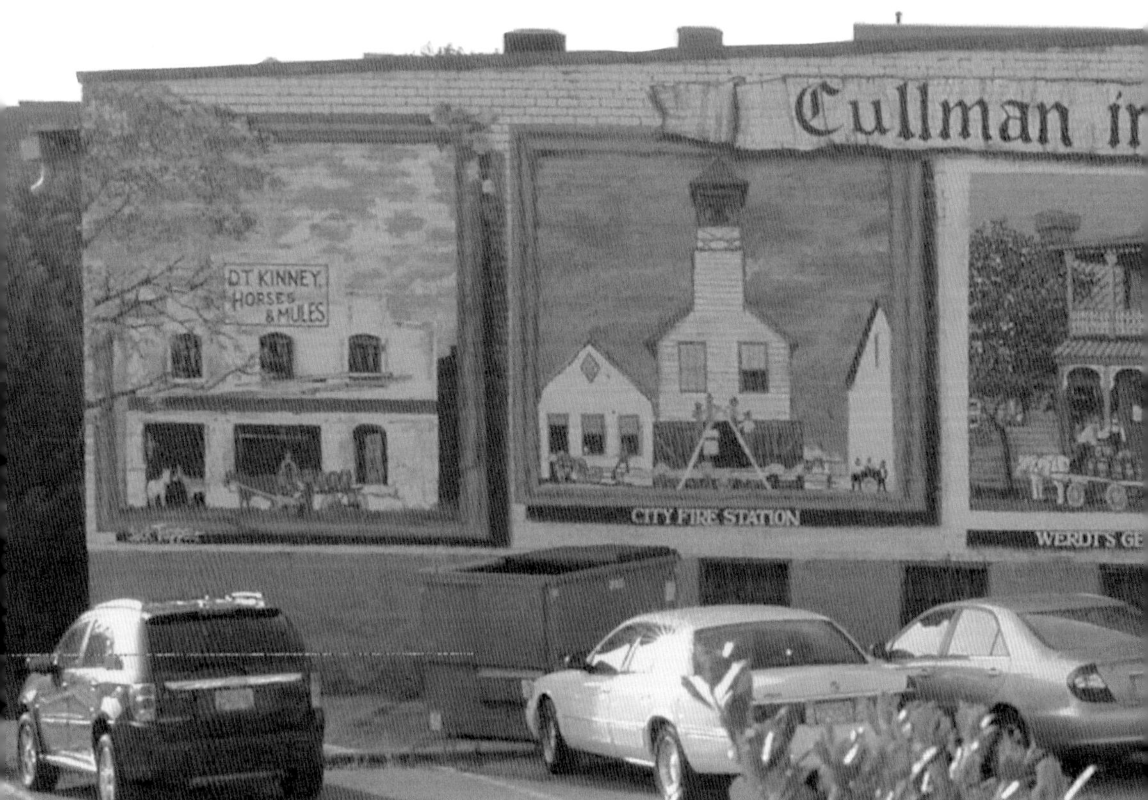
Cullman i
D.T. KINNEY
HORSES
& MULES
CITY FIRE STATION
WERDT'S GE

Mural Artists

It was a community-wide effort, spearheaded by the Cullman County Historical Society. The city and county donated $2,000 each for paint and other items for artists' drawings and paintings depicting historic scenes and buildings. Artists Bethany Kerr and Jack Tupper spent months on the project to bring the past to life through vivid paintings seen on historic buildings throughout the city and county. Tupper painted scenes of Cullman in the 1880s and the World War II vessel USS *Cullman* among others. Kerr painted the original Cullman High School, a Welcome to Cullman mural with a portrait of founder Col. Johann Cullmann and repainted the historic Cullman Banana Supply sign, which had faded over the years. Pictured are Tupper and Kerr receiving recognition for their efforts from Historical Society president Dot Gudger in background. (Both images courtesy Greg Richter.)

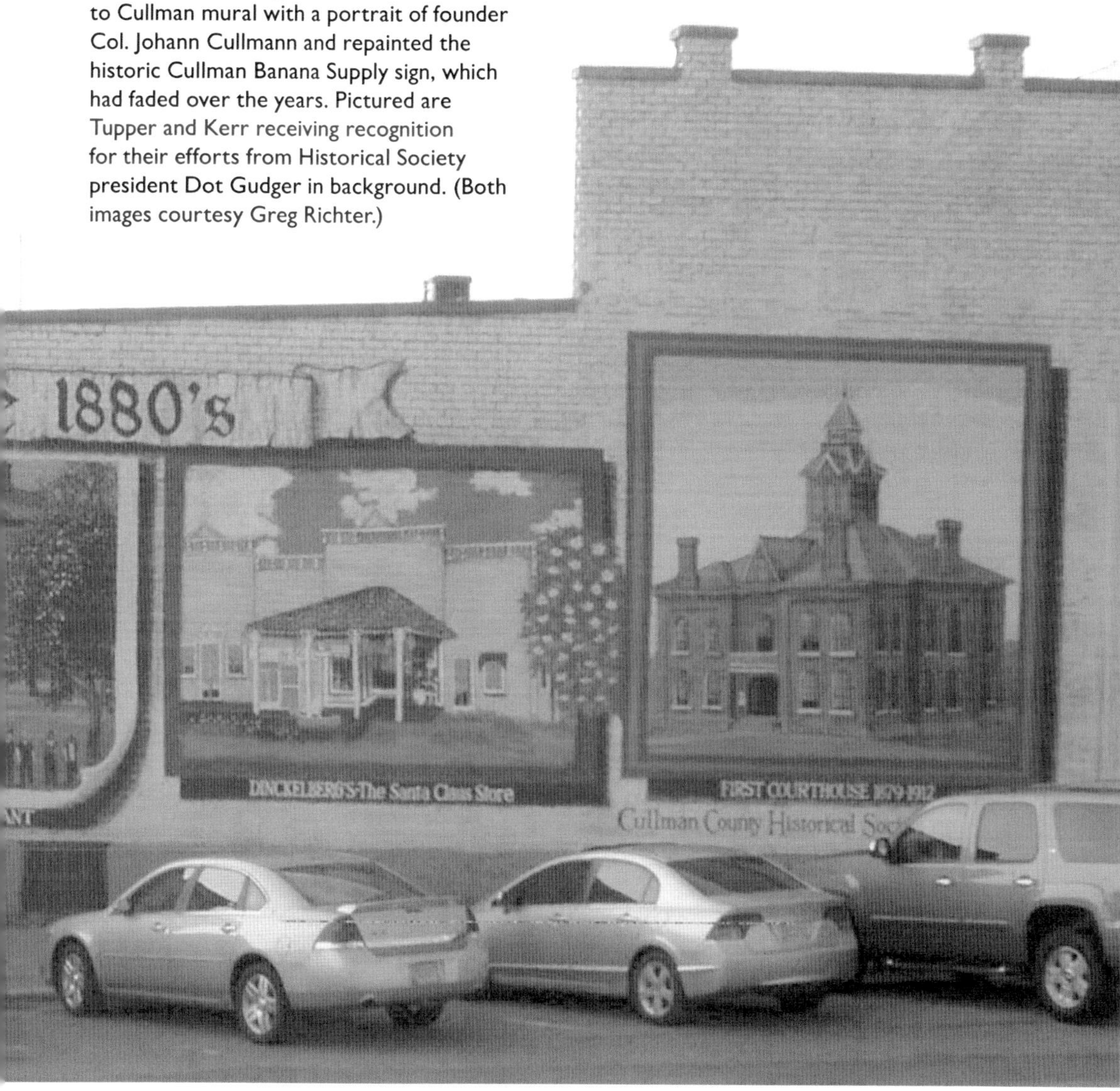

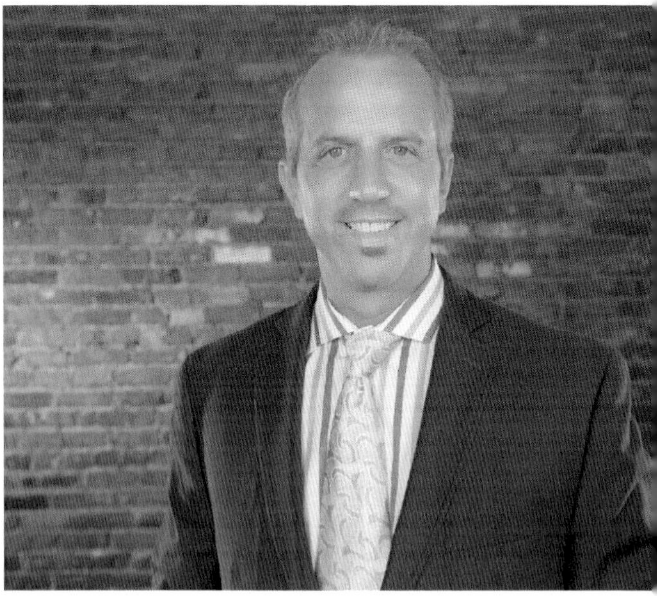

Eric Bennett
Growing up in Battle Ground, Eric Bennett knew the value of hard work, and the joy of singing showed him the value of music. He heard the Kingsmen and Cathedral Quartets and had the opportunity to pursue a dream. He sang at Dollywood, performing 12 seasons, nominated every year for *Singing News* fan award for Favorite Bass Singer and voted *Singing News* fan favorite 2009 through 2012. (Courtesy Eric Bennett.)

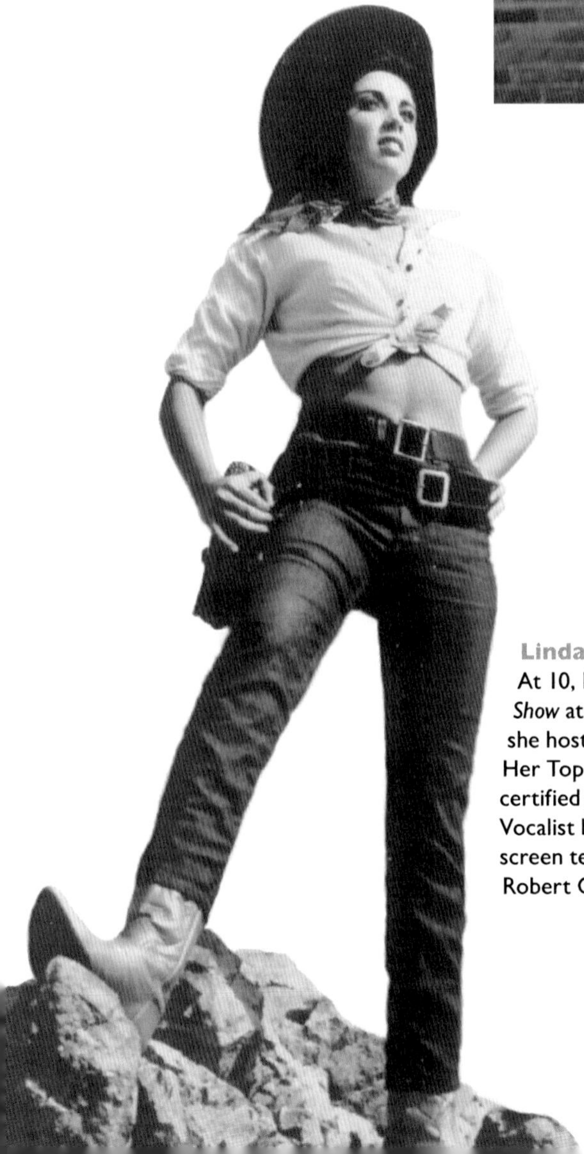

Linda Manning: Alabama's Diamond Girl
At 10, Linda Elaine Manning appeared on *The Cousin Cliff Show* at WAPI-Birmingham and sang "Paper Moon." At 18, she hosted *The Linda Manning Morning Show* in Cincinnati. Her Top 50–charting single "Shade Tree Mechanic" was certified gold. She was nominated Most Promising Female Vocalist by the American Academy of Country Music and screen tested for several movies, including a western with Robert Conrad. (Courtesy Candace Grissom.)

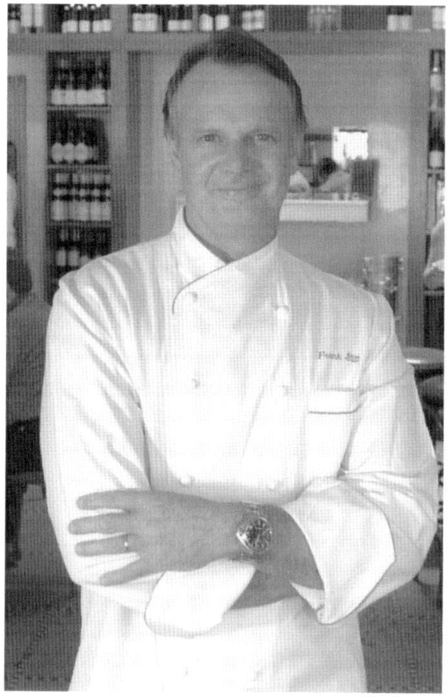

Chef Frank Stitt

Frank Stitt's fondness for humble southern ingredients comes from rural Alabama roots. He grew up in Cullman, a leading agriculture county, where there is a great deal of pride being a small family farmer. From an early age, he developed a spiritual connection to food from the land to farming. Another side came from his father, the county doctor. Young Frank was exposed to cosmopolitan cities and restaurants in New York and New Orleans. He also picked tender shoots of asparagus with his Grandmother White in her garden. Stitt's culinary journey began in San Francisco where he was a philosophy student. He noticed cookbooks took precedence over works by Plato and Kierkegaard. He honed kitchen skills in Bay Area restaurants, including the kitchen of Alice Waters, Chez Panisse. She introduced him to Richard Olney and he became his assistant for the Time Life Books *Good Cook* series. Following his travels through France and vineyard work in Provence and Burgundy, he returned to the South. His work today is steeped in extensive culinary experiences and a singular deeply rich and passionate approach to food. With his wife, Pardis, he founded the Slow Food chapter in Birmingham and is a standing board member of the Jones Valley Teaching Farm and Pepper Place Farmer's Market in Birmingham.

He uses area farmers' produce at his restaurants whenever possible. He was one of the first Alabama chefs and restaurateurs to champion sustainable agriculture, and his influence is noted in the community and beyond. The menu of his flagship restaurant, Highlands Bar and Grill, combines simple southern ingredients such as stone-ground grits and country ham with French sauces and braises. Highlands was a success, and he opened Bottega and Chez Fonfon in Birmingham. The cookbooks to his credit include *Frank Stitt's Southern Table, Recipes and Gracious Traditions from Highlands Bar and Grill, Southern Table, Bottega Favorita: A Southern Chef's Love Affair with Italian Food.* He was inducted into *Esquire* magazine's Restaurant Hall of Fame and to the James Beard Foundation's Who's Who of Food and Beverage in America. Chef Stitt has received the Lifetime Achievement Award from the Southern Foodways Alliance and was inducted into the Alabama Academy of Honor, the most distinguished award given to an Alabamian. He has appeared on the *Martha Stewart Show*, PBS's *Chefs A'Field*, ABC's *Nightline*, and CBS's *Early Show*. The Stitts have a working farm where they raise chickens, gather eggs, and grow produce to use in their restaurants. (Courtesy Frank Stitt.)

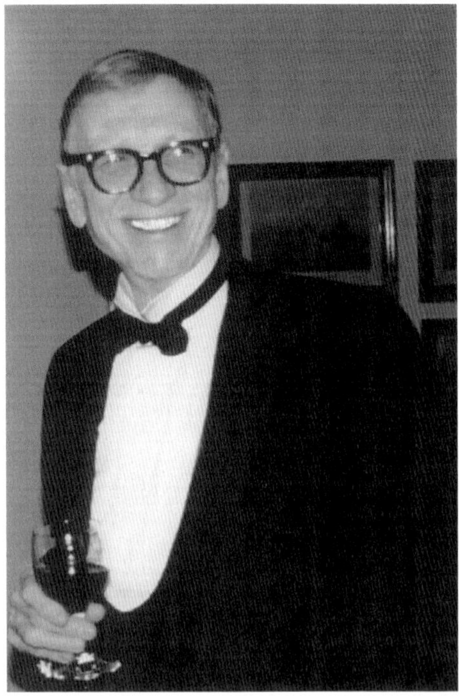

Charles John Kleibacker

Charles John Kleibacker, renowned fashion designer and master of the bias, was brought up in his family's ready-to-wear department store. Born November 20, 1921, he graduated from St. Bernard High School in 1939 and junior college in 1941, continuing his education at Notre Dame. He was a newspaper reporter before pursuing graduate studies in retailing at New York University. He worked as advertisement copywriter for De Pinna, a specialty store on Fifth Avenue. Working as a songwriter and on tour with Anna Sosenko, singer-entertainer Hildegarde's manager, Kleibacker was introduced to couture houses, including Dior in Paris. In 1954, he took a portfolio of his designs to Paris and landed a position as assistant designer with Antonio del Castillo and the head designer for Lanvin. He returned to New York as a freelance designer, then assistant designer at Nettie Rosenstein, Seventh Avenue New York fashion house.

Opening his own studio in 1960, he became known as "the master of the bias," his signature cut in women's clothing encompassing simplicity, fit, and comfort. The designs were critically acclaimed by the fashion media and attracted attention of *Women's Wear Daily*, *Vogue*, *Harper's Bazaar*, and *Town and Country*. His off-the-rack designs were featured at Bergdorf Goodman and Henri Bendel, while private clients included Mrs. Richard Nixon, Diahann Carroll, Rebekah Harkness, Mary Travers, Mrs. Nelson Rockefeller, and Mrs. Irving Berlin. In 1984, Kleibacker became visiting professor for the Department of Textiles and Clothing at Ohio State University. He obtained garments for the Ohio State Collection from notable fashion icons. Anchoring the collection was the gift of the avant-garde couture wardrobe of Isabel Eberstadt, noted fashion style maker of the 1960s. He became designer-in-residence at Ohio State and remained on staff until 1995. During that time, he oversaw the effort to preserve and house the collection in the newly constructed Geraldine Schottenstein Wing for the Historic Costume & Textile Collection. Kleibacker continued his curatorial activities after leaving OSU, working independently and since 2002 as adjunct curator of design for Columbus Museum of Art. He had an adjunct professorship at Kent State University's School of Fashion Design and Merchandising. He was invited to contribute his designs to the Museum at the Fashion Institute of Technology's *American Beauty: Aesthetics and Innovations in Fashion* exhibition, which opened in New York City in 2009. Kleibacker died in 2010. (Courtesy Columbus Museum of Art.)

Chef Dyron's Lowcountry

Dyron Powell's passion for food and cooking was cultivated at an early age, spending his childhood on the banks of Smith Lake and visiting his grandparent's farm in Houston, Alabama. His grandmother milked the cows, made her own buttermilk, and churned butter. Here, Dyron learned to enjoy the taste of raw milk. Summers were spent gardening and canning vegetables. It was these experiences that founded his passion and appreciation for the farm-to-table movement. His parents, owning a Dairy Queen, provided knowledge for the restaurant business he would eventually own, Dyron's Low Country. After marriage, and with their entrepreneurial skills, he and his wife, Sonya, started a company, but the opportunity to sell it knocked on their door. They bought a motor coach and hit the road, deciding on which cities to visit based on chefs and restaurants. When they returned from sojourning, they started culinary classes on the weekend at Culinard Institute in Birmingham.

Dyron confided to Sonya the desire to open his own restaurant. With her support, they began to pursue a dream. Their travels continued, exploring new cities, and when it was time to determine the core of their restaurant, their interest was immediately drawn to the Lowcountry cuisine found in South Carolina and Georgia. There, they found relaxed lifestyles combined with a one-of-a-kind culinary tastes—Southern food and fresh seafood. They appreciated an environment that represented the opportunity to experience a slower pace with great friends and great food. During the development of Dyron's Lowcountry, his goal was to create an atmosphere that was open to anyone, including children. When the couple arrived in Birmingham, they quickly discovered there were not many places they could take their children, Ethan and Emma, for whole, fresh food. The city offered fine dining locations with farm-to-table food, but not suitable for children. Dyron knew he could fill this void in Birmingham by offering fresh Lowcountry cuisine that families could also appreciate. Their dream became a reality as they opened Dyron's Lowcountry Restaurant in Mountain Brook to share their love for the culinary offerings of the region. It's a restaurant where people go to revisit memories and refresh their taste pallets and for individuals unfamiliar with the unique Lowcountry foods to discover and appreciate an authentic taste. (Courtesy Kay Cagle.)

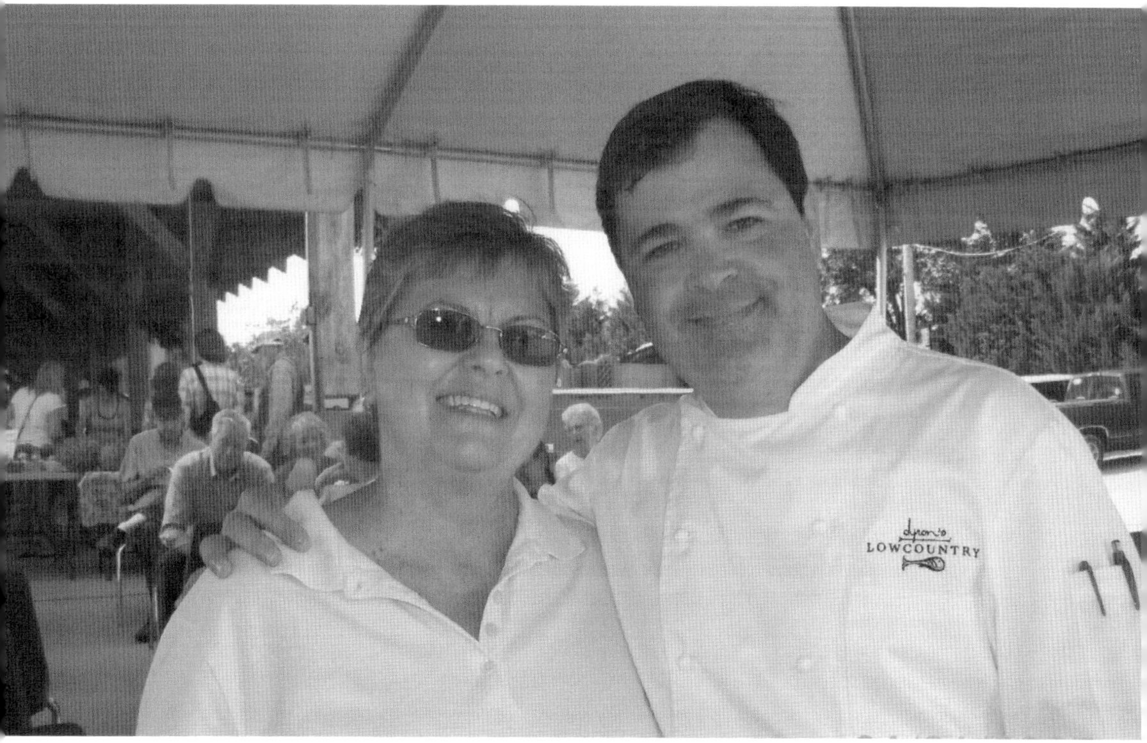

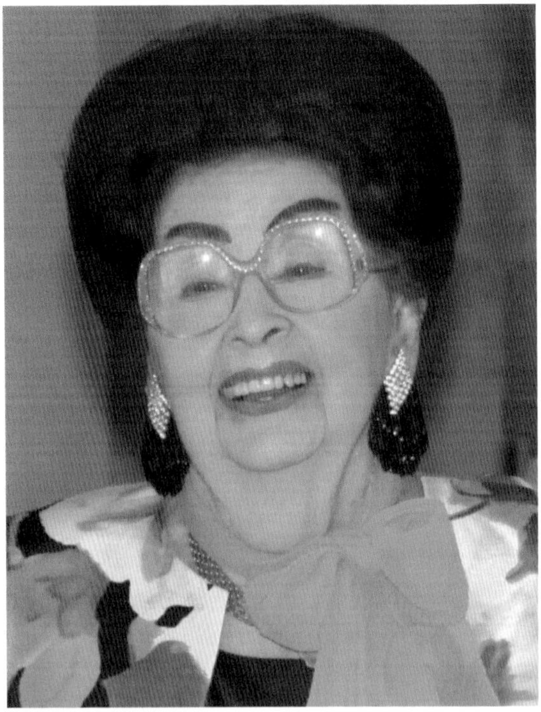

Evelyn Burrow
Mary Evelyn Hamilton became an entrepreneur in a time when that was unheard of for women. She collected porcelain and glassware and managed the Palomino Motel and Restaurant with her husband. Friends and guests gave them horse figurines. She ran an antiques business and set up a museum for her $9.53-million collection. In 2010, the museum was moved to the campus of Wallace State Community College. (Courtesy Burrow Museum.)

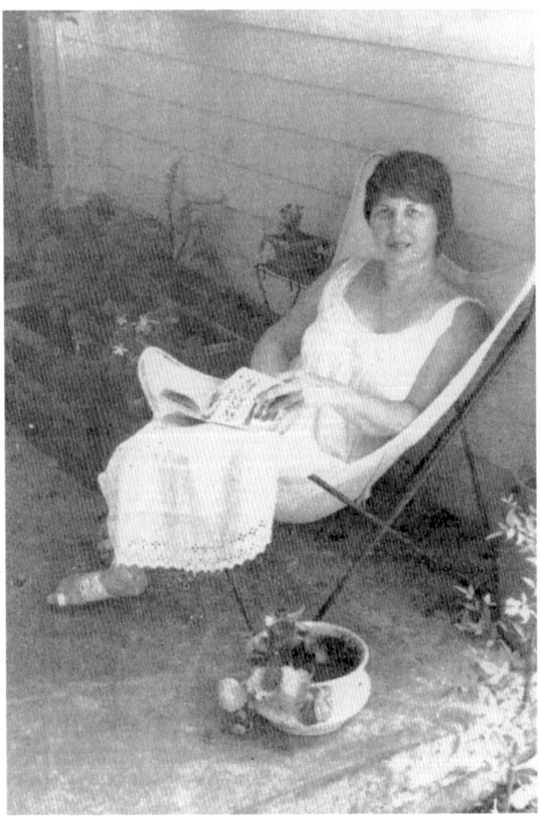

Dot Graf
Dorothy Jane Padgett Graf's artwork lives on after her death in 1985. She worked with the Cullman Historical Society to produce *If Walls Could Talk*, drawings of historical architecture and covered bridges. She also produced a *Color Cullman County* coloring book. Famous for her Arty Yardy Parties, Dot and her students, held an outdoor exhibit on the lawn at her home. (Courtesy Warren family.)

CHAPTER EIGHT

Tragedy and Growth

The German colony, which started with five families, grew. Retail outlets as well as medical and professional services expanded and spread into the county, promising greater growth on the horizon. The crude trails that first pierced the wilderness became well-worn dirt roads as individuals laid claims to land, built homes, raised families, and became a vital part of a progressive county.

Settlers went north, south, east, and west of the city to build homes and plow new ground, drawing from their individual strengths to raise families and the reaped bountiful crops from the good earth. Log cabins were eventually to become fine homes. Some communities surrounding the city were named for their founders, while others bore the names of former homelands. From the Mulberry River south to the Morgan County boundary north, Cullman County marched forward. Life unfolded from a melting pot of diversified backgrounds spanning two continents. And, where life exists, so do the human emotions of love and tragedy, a young minister who could not bear the loss of his beloved, the sheriff who served one day before he was killed, and a priest who was almost lynched for telling the truth. Progress was not blocked by any event, but continued on an upward path. Mayors were elected and businesses established.

In the western part of the county, Jones Chapel received its name after Turkey Tail Jones, 40 years after it was settled, and West Point was named by an outsider simply because it did not already have a name.

In the north, Vinemont was named after the fruit of the vine. In the east, Baileyton, Holly Pond, Fairview, and Simcoe became fledgling communities, then towns. To the south, fleeing from the Chicago fire, new families arrived, some still bearing scars from the burning inferno. Cold Springs was named after the sweet, cold water that flowed from the mountain, Garden City was truly a place where lush vegetation covered the landscape, and Hanceville claimed rights as being the second largest city in the county. There is Good Hope and Colony, settled by former slaves. Families came and continued to build homes and become part of Alabama's most north central county, Cullman.

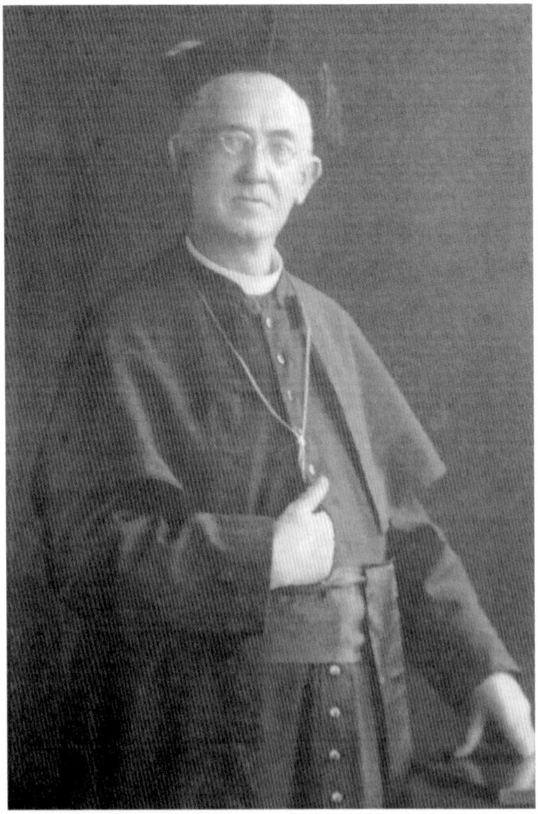

Fr. James Meurer

Fr. James Meurer, Sacred Heart Church's first priest, was threatened by unscrupulous land speculators who misrepresented the area to potential settlers in 1877. He wrote a letter that stopped the scheme. They vowed revenge. His congregation learned of the plan and attended Sunday Vespers armed to protect him. Parishioners forced the gang to retreat. Father Meurer stayed in Cullman for 10 years. (Courtesy Sandy Arndt.)

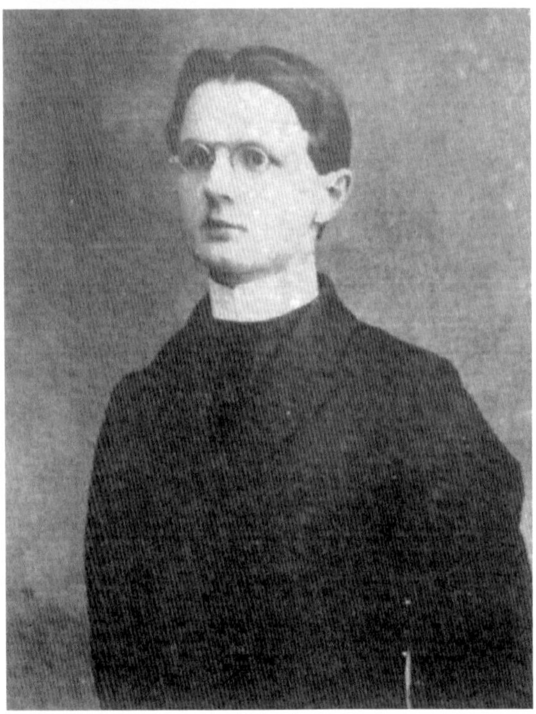

Otto Lenk

Rev. Otto Lenk, pastor of St. John's Church in 1901, was engaged to church member Minnie Hartung. A few days after their engagement party, Minnie fell ill with typhoid fever. She died on July 20, the eve of their wedding. Depressed over Minnie's death, Lenk shot himself three months later, dying the next day. They are buried together in Cullman Cemetery. (Courtesy St. John's Church.)

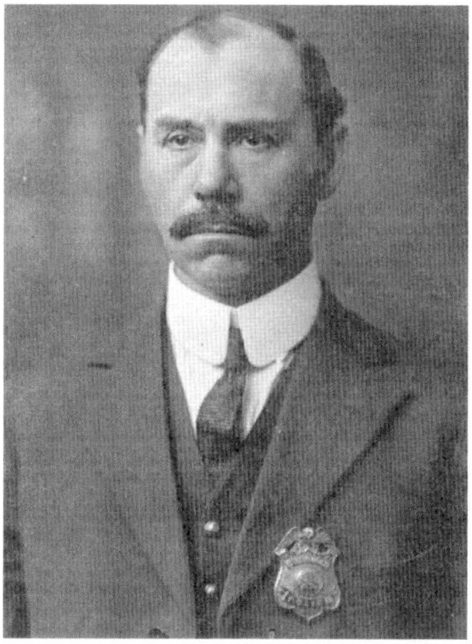

John Sparks

John Sparks is the only law enforcement officer in Cullman County shot and killed in the line of duty. Appointed Cullman police chief in 1915, he was elected sheriff in 1919. On July 20, 1919, Sparks led a raid of Leigeber Store. Leigeber employee John Mack was confronted by Sparks in a hallway. They shot each other. Mack died on spot. Sparks walked about a half block before collapsing. (Courtesy Rick Thiot.)

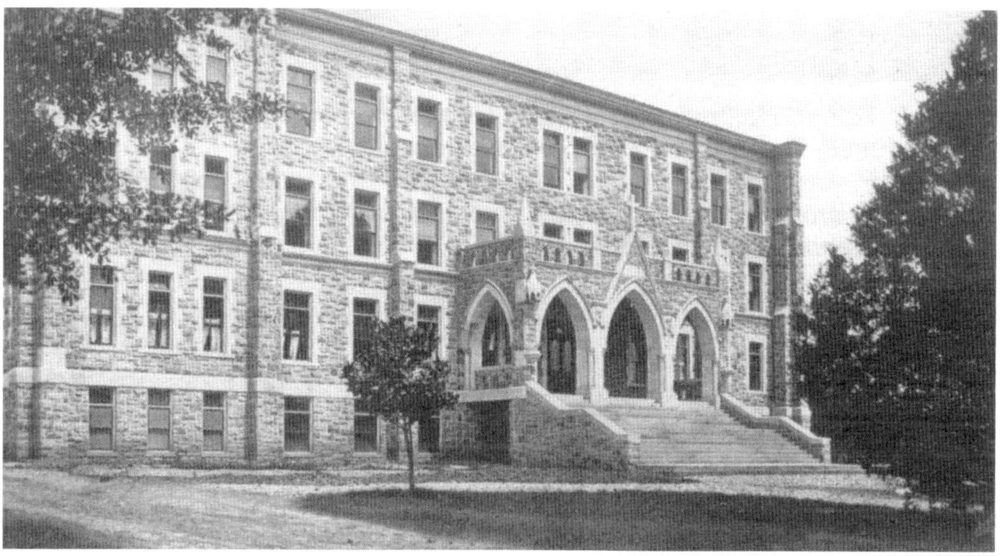

Brother Herman

Brother Herman's permanent residence is the administration building. He lounges on the third floor of the building. Father Luke said his first run-in with Brother Herman was many years ago during the college's Easter vacation. The late Father Lambert and Father Luke walked out of the dining hall. There was a hooded monk they had never seen before. Father Luke spoke, but there was no response. No one had mentioned a visitor. If the monk was a visitor, he would have been in the monk's dining hall eating. Brother Herman walked down the hallway. Father Luke and Father Lambert followed, but were not too close. Father Lambert continued down the stairs and walked out. There was no one. Father Luke walked out the side window, and there was no one there. Brother Herman was gracious enough to give the authors a minute of his time one night to answer a few questions. He said he was delighted to have students back, and the administration building was really spooky when he was there alone, but also said that now they at least turn on a bit of heat during the winter. He said he does not understand why people are scared of him. Some information was taken from a writing in 1955 by Melanie McCord in the St. Bernard student paper. (Courtesy St. Bernard.)

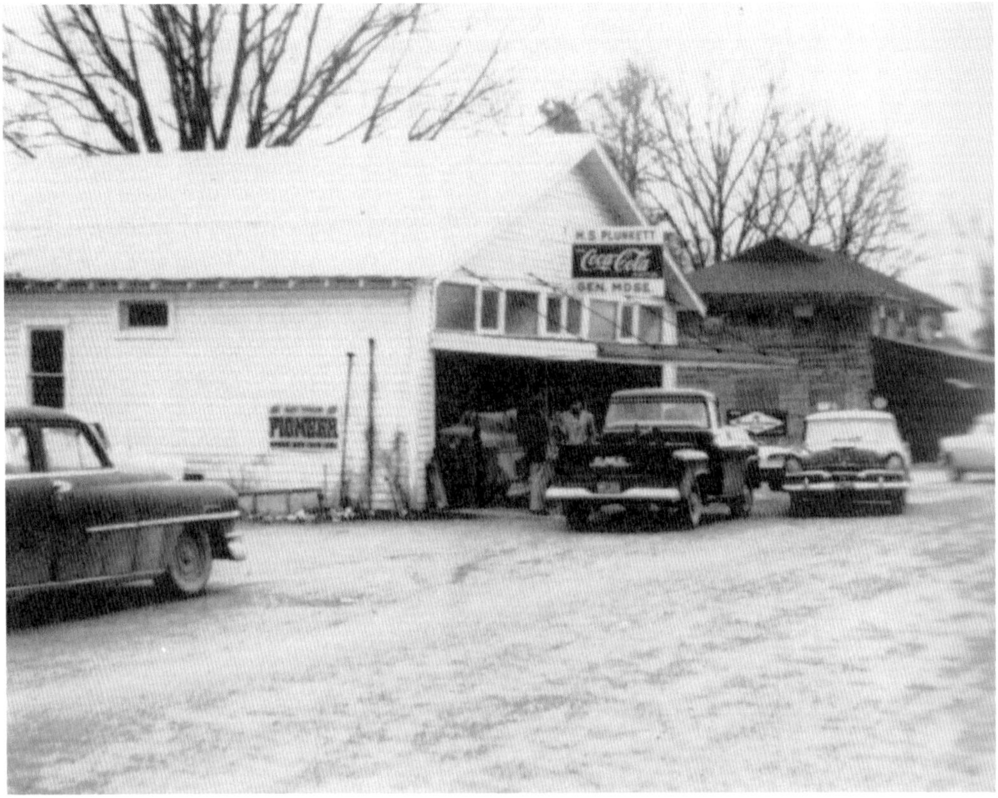

West Point
Iconic country general stores of early 1900s Americana, owned by prestigious businessmen, the Morgans, Plunketts, and Willinghams still exist in West Point. Known only as the crossroads, Jim Lamb got a job at Bud Jordan's cotton gin. Relatives asked where he worked. Jordan suggested he say, "west of the railroad." That did not satisfy Lamb. Herbert Jordan suggested he say a point west of Cullman. Lamb said they should call it West Point. (Courtesy George Spear.)

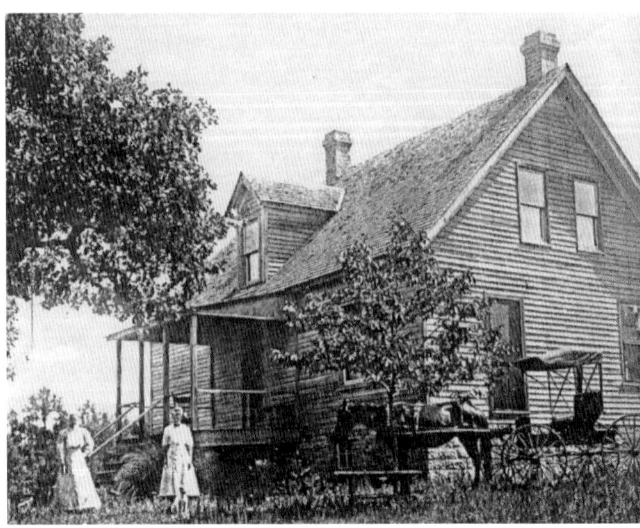

Vinemont
The name Holmes Gap was changed to Pinnacle when surveyors determined it the highest point between Cincinnati and New Orleans. Today, it is South Vinemont. The soil, conducive to fruit crops, resulted in founding the Alabama Vineyard Winery, then vegetable processing plant, and a villa for a healing mineral springs. Pictured are Mrs. Will Dickinson and her daughter Gertrude at their early-1900s home. (Courtesy Jane Teeter.)

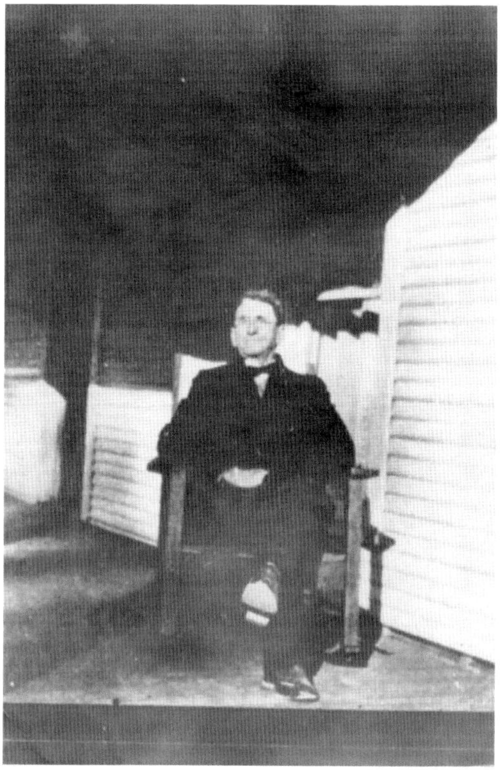

Jones Chapel

Jones Chapel, settled in 1812, had no name for 40 years. Turkey Tail Jones, early storeowner, had a hobby of making fans from turkey feathers. The community carries his name. Grandson F.W. Jones distinguished himself as the seventh son of the seventh son with seven names, serving as minister to the oldest church in the community, Jones Chapel Methodist Church. (Courtesy Evelyn Wilson.)

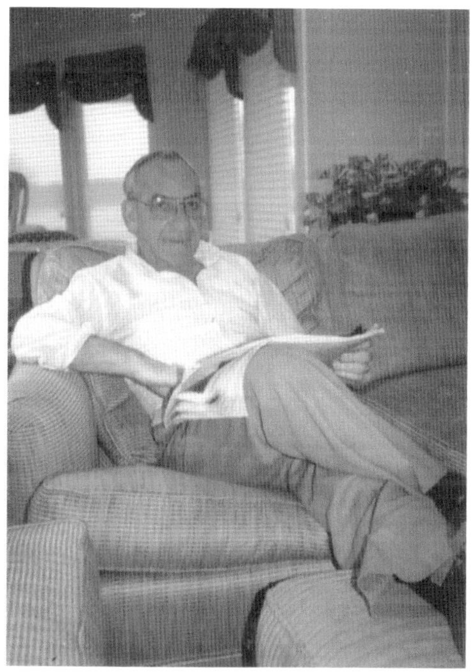

Baileyton

The community was named Baileyton in 1881. Growth included construction of a post office, cotton gin, Episcopal church, hardware stores, a school, a medical facility, and a blacksmith shop. Brothers Cecil D. "C-Buck", pictured, and Ralph M. Walker established a general merchandise store in the mid 1940s. From a two-man operation, it has grown to over 100 employees and is still owned by the Walker family. (Courtesy Walker family.)

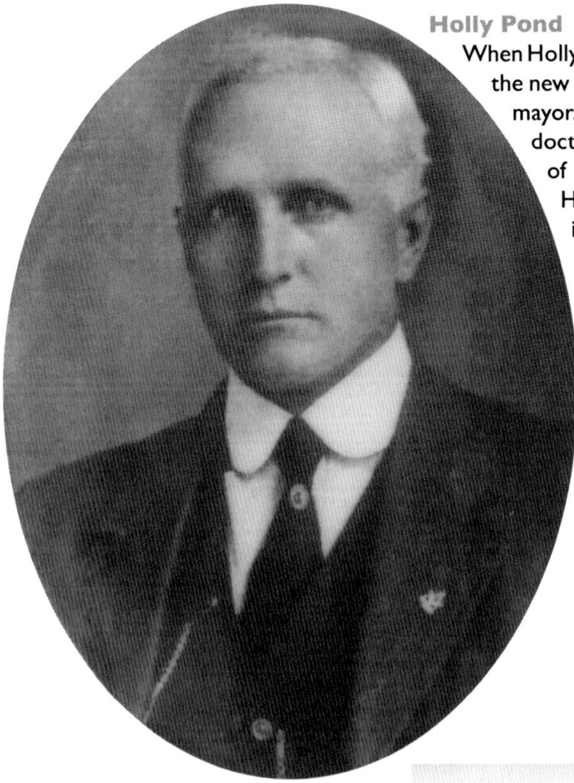

Holly Pond

When Holly Pond was incorporated in 1912, residents of the new town elected Dr. Hence Watts as their first mayor. Watts was not only a second-generation doctor, he also was essential to the formation of Holly Pond's first telephone exchange. He purchased the switchboard and had it installed in the home of Myrilzia Haynes. Watts's goal for the phone line was to allow him to reach patients more quickly. (Courtesy Holly Pond Historical Society.)

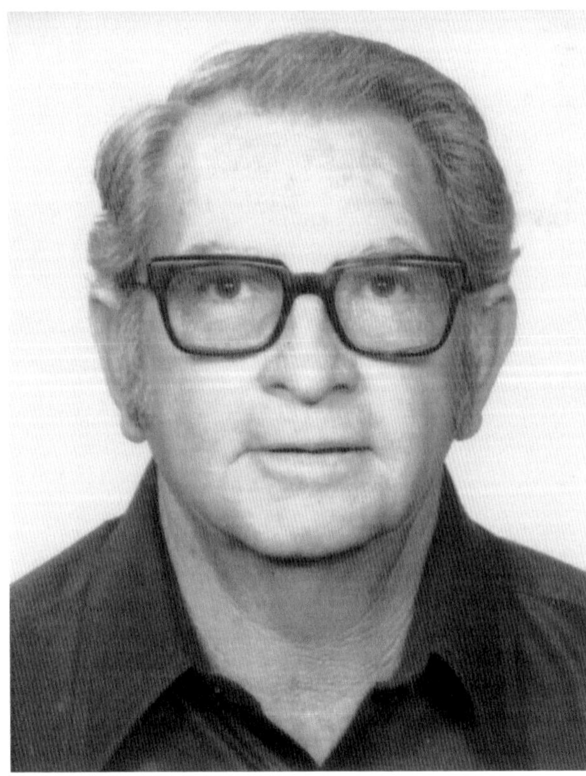

Fairview

Panoramic views drew settlers from Morgan County. before the Civil War— the Latams, Kings, Lawrences, Kellers, and Donaldsons arrived around 1850. Also arriving were the Gardner, Pucket, Oaks, Ritledge, Johnson, and Cosby families. Earnie Kraft, pictured, served as the first mayor. A Mr. Lane had been elected to the position, but being a government employee he could not serve. The position was filled by Kraft. (Courtesy Town of Fairview.)

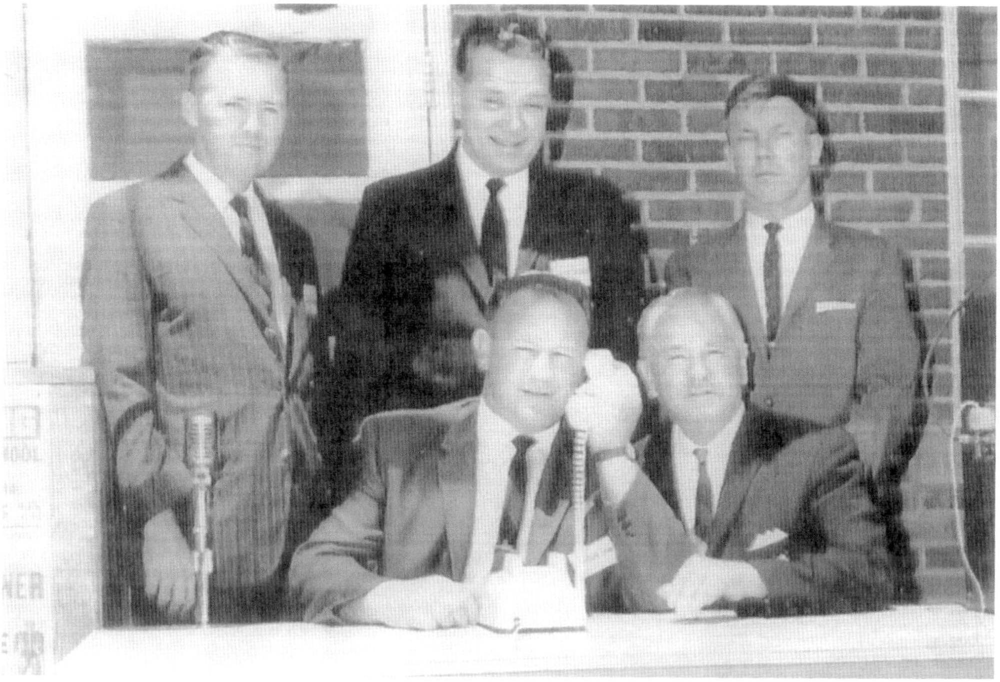

Cold Springs

Pure water gurgling from the mountainside is rumored to be the source of its name, Cold Springs, and it was settled around 1890 by the Byrd, McCoy, Willoughby, Florence, Stricklin, Parker, Huffman, Cage, McClendon, and Kelly families. Making the first call when Cold Springs received phone service are Rep. Tom Drake, Sen. Harlan G. "Mutt" Allen, Wayne Stisher, and South Central Bell and school principal Mr. Williams. (Courtesy Tom Drake.)

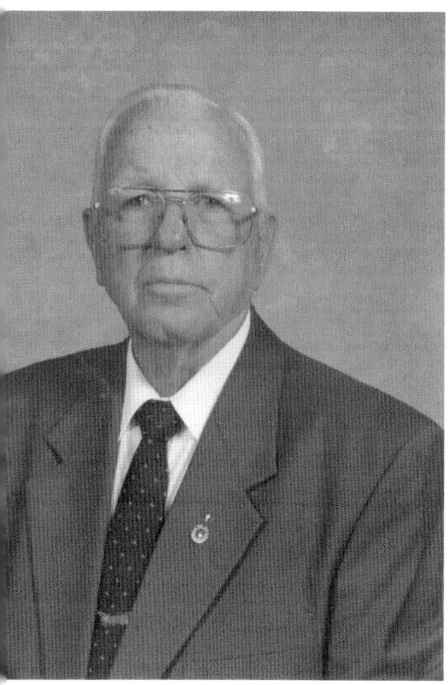

Good Hope

Farmers migrated inland and homesteaded five miles south of Cullman. These settlers were the Livingston, McMinns, Owens, Millers, Grimmets, Hoenigs, Cordeses, and Hinkle families. The area was named Good Hope in 1842. An 1899 Confederate veterans convention drew 1,500 people. Fifty-three Confederate veterans answered roll call. Pictured is Good Hope's second elected mayor, Herman Reid, still active in community events, projects, and veteran's activities. (Courtesy Town of Good Hope.)

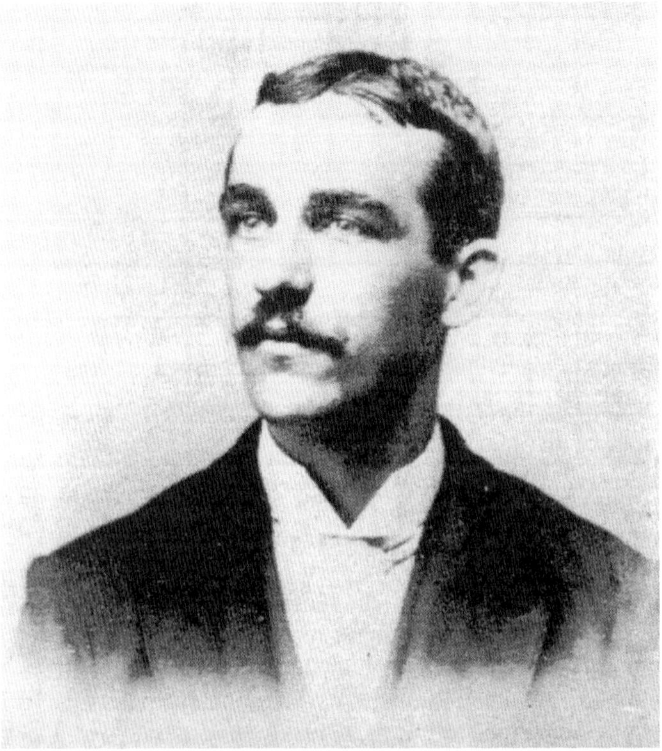

Garden City
Col. Johann G. Cullmann advertised the garden spot of the world. Founded as Garden City, William Koch cut the first tree in 1877. Settlers, some bearing scars from the 1871 Chicago fire, trekked to the area. Among the first families were the Kirchners, Hagarmanns, Kirks, Stenders, Kretzschmars, Donelsons, Ludwigs, Halsmans, Carstensens, Fursts, Scheiles, and Schhagels. Otto Scheile (pictured), was elected mayor in 1911. (Courtesy Town of Garden City.)

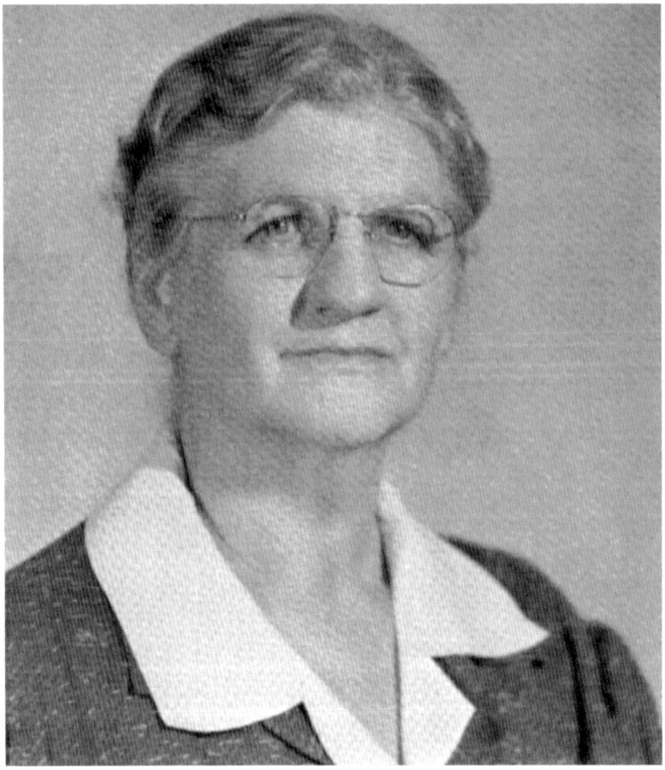

Hanceville
Hanceville is Cullman County's second largest community. Founded in 1879 by families fleeing from the 1871 Chicago fire; among them were the Self, Allred, Williams, Kinney, Martin, and Holland families. Remembered as making a difference, Emmie Smith (pictured) was a beloved fifth grade teacher at Hanceville Elementary School. She was known throughout Cullman County as a teacher who made every adult and child feel special. (Courtesy Hanceville Library.)

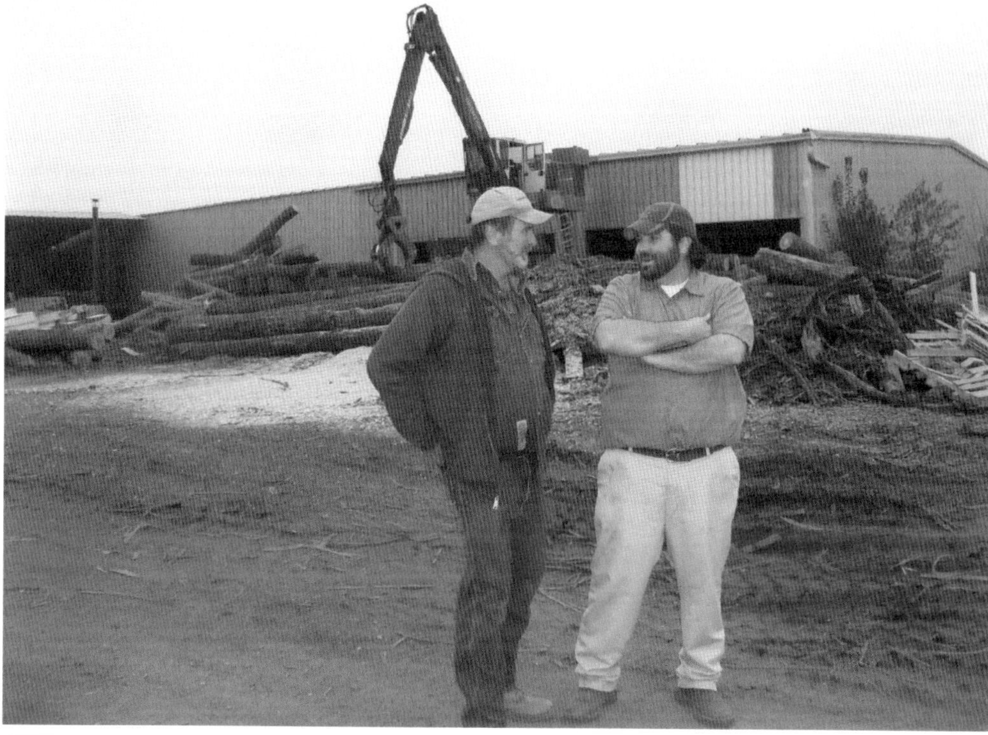

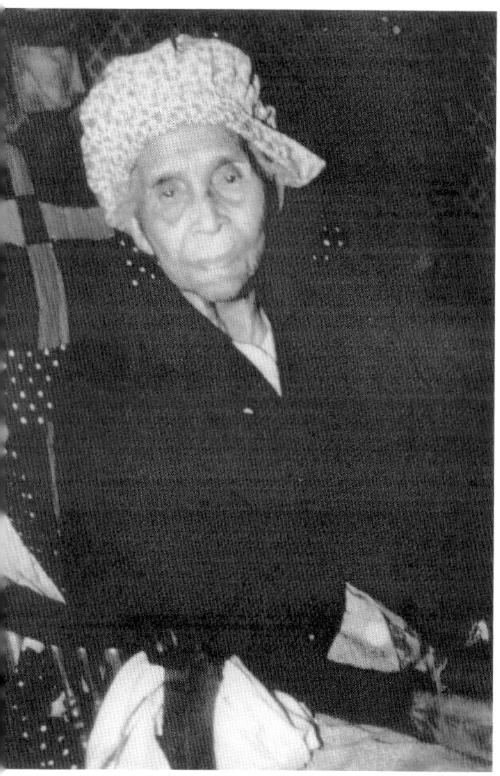

Simcoe

It was 50 years before Simcoe was named, settled by the Brindleys, Oaks, Glasscocks, Loveladys, and Watkinses. It was named after a Canadian lake by then-postmaster Starling Austin and is now the home of Simcoe Wood Products, owned by father and son Bill and Ty Pruett. The sawmill business covers 24 acres and employs 75 people. It ranks in the state's top 30 percent for related businesses. (Courtesy Kay Cagle.)

Colony

Colony was settled by freed slaves following Reconstruction. Land claims were made in Huntsville by George Wilson, John Johnson, Major Reid, and Enoch Montgomery, some traveling in wagons while some walked. Kizzie Montomery Leeth, daughter of Enoch Montgomery, a midwife and early Colony resident, traveled in a mule-driven wagon or walked over rocky paths to deliver a baby. Colony's population today is approximately 350. (Courtesy Earlene Johnson.)

INDEX

INDEX